Literature and Human Equality

Rethinking Theory

Literature and Human Equality

Stewart Justman

Northwestern University Press
Evanston, Illinois

Northwestern University Press
www.nupress.northwestern.edu

Printed in the United States of America

1 0 9 8 7 6 5 4 3 2 1

ISBN 0-8101-2323–1 (cloth)
ISBN 0-8101-2325–8 (paper)

Library of Congress Cataloging-in-Publication Data

Justman, Stewart.
Literature and human equality / Stewart Justman.
p. cm. — (Rethinking theory)
Includes bibliographical references and index.
ISBN 0-8101-2323-1 (cloth : alk. paper) — ISBN 0-8101-2325-8 (pbk. : alk. paper)
1. Equality in literature. 2. Knowledge, Theory of, in literature. 3. Fiction—History and criticism. I. Title. II. Series.
PN3352.E68J87 2006
809′.93353—dc22

2005036778

♾ The paper used in this publication meets the minimum requirements of the American National Standard for Information Sciences—Permanence of Paper for Printed Library Materials, ANSI Z39.48-1992.

Contents

LITERATURE AND HUMAN EQUALITY

Introduction

The elevation of unknown persons to positions of literary prominence inspired new ways of constructing and telling a tale.

When Odysseus and his men drive a red-hot beam into the eye of the Cyclops, the burning eye hisses like hot metal thrust into cold water in the blacksmith's forge:

> As when a man who works as a blacksmith plunges a screaming
> great ax blade or plane into cold water, treating it
> for temper, since this is the way steel is made strong, even
> so Cyclops' eye sizzled about the beam of the olive. (9.391–94)

This simile is remarkable not only because Odysseus himself authors it (hero merging with poet momentarily) but in its transfer of imagery from a familiar setting to one about as far as imaginable from the everyday world. However, both parties to this resemblance—the blacksmith on the one hand, Odysseus and his men on the other—remain exactly who they are. The blacksmith is not ennobled or made heroic by association with Odysseus. His work does not prepare him to deal with one-eyed cannibals. He will never meet such a creature, but even if he did he would have to think his way out of danger, like Odysseus, rather than simply falling back on the habits of his craft. Nor, of course, does the simile imply that Odysseus trained as a blacksmith or that he somehow lowers himself by resorting to a mechanical skill. He is responsible for the simile in the first place and does not construct it at the expense of his own honor.

Although most of the extended similes in the *Iliad* refer to the natural world and not the human arts, in one instance Homer pictures a woodcutter preparing his supper:

> But at that time when the woodcutter makes ready his supper
> in the wooded glens of the mountains, when his arms and hands have
> grown weary
> from cutting down the tall trees, and his heart has had enough of it,
> and longing for food and for sweet wine takes hold of his senses;
> at that time the Danaans by their manhood broke the battalions.
> (11.86–90)

Even more emphatically than in the case of the blacksmith, we can say that this simile does not ennoble the woodcutter, for all he does is prepare his meal, while the Greek warriors mount an offensive. The woodsman knows nothing of the heroes on the plains of Troy, who for their part think nothing of the woodsman. Blacksmith and woodsman both perform necessary work, both fill a place in the order of things, and both live outside the realm of the heroic.

As Shakespeare's Richard II loses his power, the action of the play pauses, amazingly, for a conversation between a gardener and his assistant. Speaking in verse, both perceive disorder in the state and portray that disorder in horticultural terms. According to the gardener, if only Richard had cut his favorites down to size, they might have survived and he retained the throne:

> O, what a pity is it
> That he had not so trimm'd and dress'd his land
> As we this garden! [We] at time of year
> Do wound the bark, the skin of our fruit-trees,
> Lest being over-proud in sap and blood,
> With too much riches it confound itself;
> Had he done so to great and growing men,
> They might have liv'd to bear and he to taste
> Their fruits of duty. Superfluous branches
> We lop away, that bearing boughs may live;
> Had he done so, himself had borne the crown . . . (3.4.55–65)

The activity of the gardener lies much closer conceptually to that of the king cultivating his friends than the woodcutter to the warrior. Clearly it would be possible to work out a theory of statecraft as gardening, with much planting, pruning, weeding, and with the well-ordered commonwealth likened to a flourishing orchard. But as complimentary to the gardener and his labor as such an analogy would be, its author would unquestionably be a man of learning and not a gardener. That a gardener should make such an impossibly conceptual speech about statecraft in *Richard II* is in itself a symptom of a seriously disordered commonwealth, one where the most ordinary persons feel free to pass judgment on a king. For illustrative purposes, statecraft resembles gardening; but this does not mean that the gardener holds a position of honor.

Finally, consider an extended simile in *War and Peace* illustrating the fatuity of schemes to capture Napoleon in his westward flight:

> All the profound plans about cutting off and capturing Napoleon and his army were like the plan of a market-gardener who, when driving out of his garden a cow that had trampled down the beds he had planted, should run to the

> gate and hit the cow on the head. The only thing to be said in excuse of that gardener would be that he was very angry. But not even that could be said for those who drew up this project, for it was not they who had suffered from the trampled beds. (1146)

Writing as always in ordinary language, Tolstoy makes it clear that no gardener would be as stupid as the dreamers who sought to hasten the destruction of an army already quickly destroying itself. The gardener is still excluded from the realm of the heroic, but that is to his advantage, the heroic being in Tolstoy's view a fallacy. The gardener knows to close the gate, and as Tolstoy reads history, it is that kind of sense that saw Russia through its own epic, its struggle with the French. As though Tolstoy had ironized the terms and tenor of a Homeric simile, those in the background of events are the actual protagonists of history, while those who imagine themselves heroes prove history's fools. One of those in the shadows of history, Platon Karataev, went out one day to cut wood—and as a result found himself a soldier.

Let this sequence suggest something of the revaluation of the commoner in the course of literary history.

Surveying the course of European fiction over the centuries, Northrop Frye observes a steady decline in "the hero's power of action." In next to last place comes the hero "of most comedy and of realistic fiction," not superior to others as in the worlds of myth, romance, epic, and tragedy, but simply "one of us." "We respond to a sense of his common humanity."[1] From another point of view, the same set of developments might present itself as a story not of declining power but of rising possibility. As Erich Auerbach tells the tale in his study *Mimesis: The Representation of Reality in Western Literature,* modern realism, having broken with classical doctrines of decorum, treats the hero like us with a level of seriousness that would have been impossible in ancient times. The present study, rather than tracing the literary ascent of commoners step-by-step (beginning perhaps with Greek New Comedy), deals mainly with four works of nineteenth-century fiction that seem to reinvent literary categories and practices in telling of ordinary persons unknown to history. In markedly different ways, all bear out Auerbach's account of the rising seriousness of everyday life in the eyes of literature. In each case, too, the literary portrayal of unknowns dictates that the reader be denied superior or privileged knowledge, humbled, reminded of what it is to be uncertain and to err.

The famous opening chapter of *Mimesis* concerns itself in part with the strange absence of suspense in the *Odyssey.* When the action of the tale pauses at a moment of high tension, as with the leisurely digression on Odysseus's scar in book 19, the effect isn't to raise suspense by keeping us in uncertainty, as might be the case in a modern novel. "For the element of suspense is very slight in the Homeric poems; nothing in their entire style is calculated to keep the reader or hearer breathless.

The digressions are not meant to keep the reader in suspense, but rather to relax the tension. And this frequently occurs."[2] The *Odyssey* does not build to the revelation of the unknown. After all, with Athena at the hero's side and his victory over the suitors ordained in the heavens (5.22–24), the outcome of the tale is given in advance. Even in the case of his adventure with Polyphemus, where the gods play no part and he is on his own, the very fact that Odysseus narrates this trial to the Phaeacians means he survived it. Indeed, Odysseus listens with rapt interest to the story of his own exploits at Troy as sung by the bard of the Phaeacian court, though he cannot be in any doubt or suspense regarding their outcome. Had the *Odyssey* been meant as a tale of suspense, surely the hero would have shown or at least felt some uncertainty, some anxiety about Tiresias's mysteriously conditional prophecy that he just might manage to return to Ithaca if certain things happen. Odysseus never does. (If the critical question is whether Odysseus "can contain [his] own desire, and contain [his] companions'" [11.105] when they arrive at the island of Thrinakia, Odysseus's power of self-command is not really in doubt and he is not going to worry himself over whether his less heroic crew can summon up the resolve not to touch the sacred cattle.) Suspense is the game played by Penelope with the suitors—leading them on with ambiguous indications but withholding the awaited result; it is not Homer's game. Their minds so disordered that each seems to imagine himself the one favored out of 108, the suitors are seized with tense uncertainty and a kind of parched anticipation. The audience presumed by the *Odyssey* itself is not of disordered mind. It does not live, like the suitors, "in expectation" (21.156). The *Odyssey* does not leave things in darkness that they might be brought to light with greater effect, nor does it place the hero in a condition of uncertainty the reader or audience is meant to share.

In the same essay, Auerbach remarks on Homer's all but exclusive focus on the nobility in the *Odyssey*. The house servant Eurycleia and the swineherd Eumaeus are "the only [characters] whom Homer brings to life who do not belong to the ruling class. Thus we become conscious of the fact that in the Homeric poems life is enacted only among the ruling class—others appear only in the role of servants to that class."[3] If the swineherd Eumaeus is raised up out of the background of the action into the light of prominence, if the poet himself addresses him with a familiarity amounting to endearment, this is not only because his exemplary loyalty to Odysseus sets him apart from those who exploit the great man's absence, but also, it may be, because he is himself of noble birth, the son of a king (15.413). Indeed, he too owns a slave (14.449–50). But if Homer refers to Eumaeus as the "noble swineherd" of "noble Odysseus" (14.3,4), this does not establish any kind of parity between the two. The nobility of Eumaeus lies in his acceptance of his lot—for never does he seek to recover his lost position (in contrast to the treacherous nurse who stole him in an attempt to return to "the high-roofed house" of her parents [15.432])—and in his fidelity to his master even without assurance that the man is alive. Every test set by the disguised Odysseus he passes superbly, as though his superiority, his nobility, were manifesting itself in the form of service. So too, no matter how interesting the story of Eumaeus's life may be, the poet does not tell it. It is left to the swineherd himself to do so to his disguised master. The tale exists literally in relation to Odysseus. Not for millennia would it be possible for commoners to be the heroes of literary works, interesting in their own right.

But perhaps the absence of suspense and the concentration on the nobility in the *Odyssey* come to the same thing. Whether Odysseus's crew will be able to keep their hands off the sacred cattle is an issue of life and death, but Odysseus suffers no agonies of worry or anticipation over what his all-too-human companions may do at the last moment, while the poem itself forecloses suspense by dismissing them as fools in its opening lines. (On the island of Thrinakia, Odysseus seems not to suffer from the hunger that drives his men beyond the limits of their endurance, just as they and not he feast on the sacred cattle.) That the suitors are in suspense over Penelope's choice, as if they could bear to wait no longer, simply confirms their ignobility in our eyes. As for the noble, like Odysseus, it is because they are godlike that the Olympians take an interest in their affairs; and it is because the Olympians take this interest that the outcome of human dramas is imposed from above and not simply worked out in the course of events themselves.[4] An *Odyssey* whose outcome was a matter of uncertainty and thus a source of suspense would be an *Odyssey* without gods. Equally inconceivable would be an *Odyssey* where the gods take a passionate interest in the affairs of swineherds and housemaids. Eumaeus became a swineherd, and Eurycleia a housemaid, as a result of purely economic transactions worked out by the parties themselves. Like the kidnapper of Eumaeus who herself had been sold by pirates for "a fair price" (15.429), Eurycleia is purchased for twenty oxen and Eumaeus purchased, also by Laertes, "with his own possessions" (15.483). The freedom of the buyer and seller to do business as they see fit corresponds to the non-freedom of the object of the sale. Just as the gods do not concern themselves with mortals' mere economic exchanges, so, it seems, they take no interest in slaves.

Now it is revealing that in the most renowned work of the only novelist who can credibly be compared with Homer (and so compared himself) the conditions of Homeric mimesis are effectively subverted. Pouring ridicule on the fallacy that views history as a stage with the few at its center, *War and Peace* relentlessly ironizes the heroic. Though the servant class is relegated to the background in *War and Peace* much as in the *Odyssey*, Tolstoy leaves no doubt that those unknown to the historians have more to do with the making of history itself than the courtiers, generals, and salon women who figure more prominently in the chronicles of human affairs. (That Anna Pavlovna Scherer places Pierre on the "lowest grade" of the social hierarchy in her drawing room [9] is a point in his favor.) As to the few, their sense that life is enacted and history decided among them constitutes their supreme delusion. So too, while the outcome of the French invasion of Russia is unalterably given and thus known to us in advance, like the fall of Troy, the domesticity with which *War and Peace* ends, if it can be said to end, is so arresting that it has the power to surprise even the reader returning to the tale a second or third time.

By setting *War and Peace* in the proximate past and, furthermore, treating that past as present, Tolstoy rules out the heroizing effect of historical distance—the illusion that those of the past were greater than ourselves, precisely by virtue of being long gone. Homer's phrase "such as men are now" marks the difference between the post-heroic world of the present and the age of the Trojan War, when Zeus conceived the destruction of the heroic race but had only begun to carry out his plan.[5] For its original audiences the *Iliad* must have had great poignancy, both suggesting how it is that the heroic came to an end and allowing "men such as men are now" a vision of history denied the greater ones of the past. Our contemporaries might be called our equals in time. Each of the modern works at the center of this study interprets with high originality the novel's charter as an investigation of ordinary lives, and each concerns people not only of the same order as the reader but close to the reader in time. *Great Expectations* seems to be set in the unheroic period between Napoleon and Victoria ("at that time" is Pip's way of placing the tale), so that by the time Pip becomes an adult he catches up with the present moment. So insistently modern is "The Death of Ivan Ilych" that it not only brings up the legal reforms of the 1860s—as does *The Brothers Karamazov,* also on our list—but has the hero die in 1882, a mere four years before the work's publication. Incidentally, "The Death of Ivan Ilych" ironizes the ennoblement of the dead by making the hero appear dignified in death but not in life.

Our authors carry the de-heroization of their heroes still further by qualifying their centrality or depriving them of it altogether. Almost as if his devaluation of the heroic called for a similar boldness toward the literary institution of the hero, Tolstoy in *War and Peace* divides the tale among several protagonists. (The title of *Anna Karenina* might be read as an act of misdirection, distracting us from the importance of less sensational figures. This work too shuttles back and forth between various centers of interest.) Similarly divided is Dostoevsky's drama of suspense, *The Brothers Karamazov.* The novel is tragic, with comic splashes; but the fact that Dmitri is singled out for trial and conviction, that he magnetizes all eyes to himself, that he attracts gossip and commentary irresistibly and holds center stage in the public imagination of the Karamazov case—this in itself makes for parody of a feature of some high tragedies, a Ptolemaic focus on a single hero. Hamlet alone, the observed of all observers, is charged with putting Denmark right (that kingdom itself occupying in the play's geography a vaguely central position in relation to England, Wittenberg, France, Norway, and Poland). It happens that Dmitri is but one player in the complex drama of his father's murder, a fact lost on a public unable, for all its fascination with the case, to grasp the many-centered nature of the Karamazov family. What makes *The Brothers Karamazov* a "Galilean" novel[6] is not only its way of placing different "languages" in contention, but its deliberate lack of a single hero marking its indisputable center, which is also to say its leveling of a literary institution. Pip occupies the very center of *Great Expectations,* but in the ironic sense that the designs of others converge on him in a way neither he nor even they (nor we) understand.[7] If only from his practice in *Little Dorrit,* where the hero—not Amy Dorrit but Arthur Clennam—is camouflaged, we know that Dickens was interested in the deheroization of the hero. So strong is the camouflage effect in *War and Peace* that some of the novel's original reviewers could not at first tell who the main characters were.[8] But so do *Great Expectations* and *The Brothers Karamazov* place the reader in the position of not knowing things of the first importance; and in each case, as will be seen, the way this task is handled measures the author's art.

The swineherd Eumaeus was born the son of a king. In Dostoevsky a nobleman reduced to poverty might be consumed with impotent resentment and crazed imaginings. In Dickens one of lowly position might imagine himself a nobleman; such is the case with William Dorrit. In neither event would the person be at one with his social position, like the Homeric swineherd. The world of inequality implied in the similes of the blacksmith, the woodcutter, and the gardener is one of fixed and defined social positions. In some of the works of central concern here such definitions seem to have been purposely suspended—the protagonist of *Great Expectations,* for example, never becoming a blacksmith. Exactly what stable position is occupied by an ex-lieutenant (Dmitri Karamazov), an occasional journalist (Ivan Karamazov), a novice who leaves the monastery (Alyosha), to say nothing of a cook who also happens to be his employer's son (Smerdyakov)? By razing social definitions, Dostoevsky clears a way for uncertainties that could never conceivably enter into such a work as the *Odyssey,* where a king can play a beggar without really impairing his status as a king. (Near the end of *Anna Karenina* Levin comes to the realization that beggars and kings live by "one and the same thing," as though the difference between them were incidental [800].) Writing at a time when, as Tolstoy said, "everyone is at least dimly aware of the equal rights of all people,"[9] each of the modern masters in these pages probes deeply into the uncertain, as well as considering carefully the position of the unnoticed and the unknown.[10] That Tolstoy and Dostoevsky are themselves mighty opposites except, perhaps, for their belief in equality and their love of Dickens—such opposites that Tolstoy could not bring himself to finish *The Brothers Karamazov,* while Dostoevsky envisioned his rival as an artist of the aristocracy, the chronicler of a stable world fast disappearing and in any case remote from the interests of humanity—suggests that the revaluation of the heroic goes even deeper than their differences of vision and technique.[11]

Our triumvirate offer three responses to the crisis of faith in their age, expressed by George Eliot in the statement that God is inconceivable, Immortality unbelievable, but Duty "peremptory and absolute."[12] Dickens reminds us of Duty in language with King James resonance but little definite religious content. Tolstoy eventually all but resolved God into Duty. Dostoevsky weaves the question of the Duty's independence of God and Immortality into the dialogue and the plot of his last and greatest novel.[13] But notice that the belief in human equality resembles belief in God and Immortality in that it transcends and contradicts the evidence of the eyes. I believe master and servant, or king and beggar, equal in spite of the manifest and seemingly insuperable differences of their positions; I deem them equal by means of a secular act of faith. In, say, *Great Expectations,* the issue of human equality is as charged as it is, in part because it has something of the character of questions of faith per se. (And the Christian faith itself, of course, underwrites a belief in the equality of souls.) Faith arises from humility. The novels of Dickens, Tolstoy, and Dostoevsky discussed here impress upon us the humility of ignorance.

According to the great literary critic M. M. Bakhtin, the protagonist of a novel "cannot become once and for all a clerk, a landowner, a merchant, a fiancé, a jealous lover, a father and so forth": a principle of indeterminacy observed in one way or another by each of the masters just cited.[14] (So it is, for example, that Pierre is introduced to us in *War and Peace* as not yet having entered either the military or civil service.) Additionally, though, each raises Bakhtin's principle to a higher level in fashioning a work that overflows conventional *literary* definitions. *Great Expectations* is tragic, comic, dramatic, "autobiographical"; wisely, we simply call it Dickensian, as if that were a genre in itself. In addition to complicating tragedy with comedy, *The Brothers Karamazov* comes about as close as narrative can to the non-narrative form of drama. *War and Peace* resembles no other novel and defies the genre itself. "The Death of Ivan Ilych" is a tragedy whose hero lacks every traditional requirement of tragic stature. In each case, and regardless of his actual political views, the author disputes accepted literary conventions as if they were some hereditary distinction being swept away by the force of a revolution. All three novelists would know just what Dr. Johnson meant when he wrote in 1750 that the heroes of modern fiction are "leveled with the rest of the world," except that they would also sense forces in the word "leveled" perhaps undreamed of by Johnson.[15] In these worlds the sort of equality or fraternity that springs up between Huck and Jim, or Ishmael and Queequeg, is not to be had (though on the other hand these runaways couldn't have had it on land either). Equality figures in the works examined here less as an achieved social fact than as the inspiration of literary experiment. Certainly the revaluation of the institution of the hero goes along with a revision of the most fundamental practices of narrative.

My impression is that the elevation of commoners into positions of importance not only changed the appearance of literature, but indeed made possible new ways of constructing a tale. It is said that the heroes and heroines of the Greek prose romances, "although they must have the conventional sanction of belonging to some myth or legend . . . are practically unknown to the world at large, even by name. They can therefore be written about with the utmost freedom, very nearly as much freedom indeed as would be the case if the characters had been invented outright as in the average modern novel."[16] In the anything but average works discussed in these pages, freedom is exercised to the point that the tales break with the founding conventions of the novel itself as a more or less predictable series of surprises. Bound by the same limitations as the characters they are reading of, readers experience new forms of uncertainty, as though the portrayal of persons unknown to history called for unknown outcomes as well. Even the fact of being unknown acquires a new significance. In Bakhtin's view, it is the belief that a human being cannot be summarily known or defined that underwrites the indeterminacy of Dostoevsky's great novels. *The Brothers Karamazov* is a mystery novel. In the *Odyssey* there are no mysteries. The shade of Agamemnon asks Odysseus what has become of his son Orestes, and Odysseus answers that he does not know, but the reader emphatically does know, having learned as early as book 1, and from no less a source than Athena, of the glory won by Orestes "among all mankind" (1.299) for killing the killer of his father. In the Polyphemus episode Odysseus pretends to be Nobody. Pip of *Great Expectations* really is a nobody, and in direct contrast to Odysseus's encounter with the Cyclops, which was prophesied before it ever occurred, the tale of Pip's experience can be told only in retrospect. However, at no point in that tale do we know more than Pip himself did, so that his experiences of surprise are ours as well. And far from being a product of comic machinery as in, say, Fielding's *Joseph Andrews*, the most dramatic surprise of *Great Expectations* is not comic and is not imposed from without but arises from the depth of human motivation. When, in the third chapter of the novel, the hunted convict we later know as Magwitch replies, "Thankee, my boy," to a kind comment by Pip, we cannot possibly imagine just how much life-effort he will pour into thanking Pip and how literally he will regard Pip as "my boy." (In *Joseph Andrews*, both the hero and Parson Adams have the same sort of nominal connection with legendary forebears—Joseph and Abraham—as a principal in Greek romance. Pip does not.) Time and again Alyosha Karamazov, the nominal hero of *The Brothers Karamazov*, comes face-to-face with his lack of knowledge—"But what do I know of that?" he asks himself at one point, characteristically (196)—but readers know no more, however superior they may think themselves to this naif. That a tale about complete unknowns should be read with surprise might itself seem a given, but in the case of the novels of special interest to this study this principle authorizes a new theory and practice of fiction. Immediately after the shade of Achilles famously remarks to Odysseus that he would rather be a thrall on earth than king of the dead, he requests information about his son. The misery of death is also a miserable lack of knowledge. In *The Brothers Karamazov* or *Great Expectations* everyone, high or low, including the reader, is bound by the limitations of knowledge.

By contrast, it is only by departing from his own practice that Shakespeare makes the audience of *The Winter's Tale* share Leontes' ignorance that his wife is alive. "The concealment of vital elements of the story is foreign to the conventions of the Elizabethan-Jacobean stage generally."[17] The early history plays of Shakespeare depend especially on the policy of revelation. In 3 *Henry VI*, it has been said, "characters act and speak in ignorance of what we and the others already know. . . . The whole ironic spirit of the play is supremely concentrated and symbolized in the scene (II.v) where the nameless father kills his son, and the son his father. . . . The son makes the final all-embracing comment, 'I knew not what I did.'"[18] Not until he uncovers the dead man's face does the son know what he did, but a stage direction identifies him as "a Son that hath kill'd his Father" the moment he appears in the text. Analogously, the combatants in the civil war do not understand their roles in the great drama of crime and redemption they are bringing to fulfillment, while the audience, knowing the reign of Elizabeth to be that fulfillment, do understand. This sort of knowledge over the heads of the characters is denied to readers of *Great Expectations* or *The Brothers Karamazov*—denied not only for the sake of suspense but because ignorance belongs to what we have in common, the human condition—while even readers of *War and Peace*, who of course know in advance the fate of Napoleon's invasion of Russia, find themselves in the presence of the unforeseeable, the unknown and the unknowable. It is Tolstoy's Napoleon, the nominal hero of another historical drama, who imagines himself in possession of complete knowledge.

"I know everything! . . . I know everything," declares Napoleon in *War and Peace* to an envoy of Emperor Alexander (664). It is the definitive expression of his delusion of grandeur. All three novelists make sure that readers know they do not know everything. All humble our pretenses of knowledge by constructing their tales in ways that baffle prediction and amaze understanding. Who has read *War and Peace* without this experience? Who could have foretold that an Ivan Ilych would ever awaken to the horror and error of his own life? Is it not revealing that critics who point out the workings of foreshadowing in *The Brothers Karamazov* can see these signs so clearly only in retrospect? (No doubt foreshadowings of part 2 of *The Brothers Karamazov*, the volume Dostoevsky didn't live to write, are inscribed in part 1. Part 2 not having been written, no one quite knows what they are.) Such critics are something like the historians Tolstoy argues with in *War and Peace* who imagine themselves in possession of superior knowledge. For our purposes, Tolstoy's polemic against the historians' delusion of omniscience in *War and Peace* represents a special case of a campaign waged against the pride of imaginary knowledge.[19] If Dostoevsky was a bitter critic of the intelligentsia, that group is distinguished precisely by a theoretical superiority of knowledge.

A certain doubt of the grounds of knowledge may be built into modern realism. In tracing the origins of that literary revolution to Descartes and Locke, Ian Watt names two great doubters.[20] In the chapter of the *Essay Concerning Human Understanding* entitled "Of the Extent of Human Knowledge," Locke characteristically deems our knowledge "so narrow [that] it will perhaps give us some light into the present state of our minds if we look a little into the dark side, and consider the *causes of our ignorance.*"[21] The novel might be considered the literary form of limited knowledge—the fullest expression of the form's constitution being the great fictional experiments of the nineteenth century, the age when the social question, that is, the question of human equality, broke upon the world.

"What do I know of that?" asks Alyosha. But in some circumstances less knowledge may be better than more. When Vronsky, in *Anna Karenina,* takes up painting, he ponders what style to use—ponders because

> he understood all kinds and could be inspired by one or another; but he could not imagine that one could be utterly ignorant of all the kinds of painting and be inspired directly by what was in one's soul, unconcerned whether what one painted belonged to any particular school. (465–66)

The true artist knows nothing of the conventions of religious, historical, realistic, or genre painting, not because he affects ignorance in imitation of Socrates but because true art will level the hierarchy of styles like some force of equality doing away with artificial distinctions. A Tolstoyan novel is religious, historical, and realistic all at once. Both *Great Expectations* and *The Brothers Karamazov* put tragedy, a poetic form of high nobility and ancient lineage, into prose, and mix it with comedy. Far from belonging to a school and imitating its conventions, Dickens and Dostoevsky constitute, each of them, a sort of inimitable genre of one. Certainly they know of their rivals and predecessors, but their greatest works display something like the indifference to artificial distinctions attributed by Tolstoy to the artist who simply knows and cares nothing about them.

Tolstoy the sage, who knew one big thing, repudiated almost everything he had written. The modern novel is less interested in such absolute knowledge than in the question of who knows what, and furthermore how we know what we know. Says Bob Loveday to his brother in Hardy's *The Trumpet-Major,*

> "Would I had never found out this about [Matilda Johnson]! John, why did you interfere? You had no right to overhaul my affairs like this. Why didn't you tell me fairly all you knew? . . . I tell you she was good enough for me, and as long as I knew nothing about what you say of her history, what difference would it have made to me?"

When John expresses surprise at his brother's continued loyalty to Matilda Johnson, Bob comments, "That's because you didn't know your man." Later in the novel, concerning another lover, Bob says, "I suppose Anne never caught a capful of wind from that quarter?" to which John replies, "She knows all about it."[22] "You know I am a guilty woman?" says Gwendolen Grandcourt to Daniel Deronda following the drowning of her husband. He replies, "I know nothing," and neither does the reader.[23] In Henry James's remarkable drama of discovery, *What Maisie Knew*, forms of the word "know" run through the tale like a subtle music, at times virtually dissolved into the flow of speech.

> "You'll never know what I've been through about you [says Maisie's mother]—never, never, never. I spare you everything, as I always have; though I daresay you know things that, if I did (I mean if I knew them), would make me—well, no matter! You're old enough at any rate to know there are a lot of things I don't say that I easily might."[24]

"All I really know is that he was a fine fisherman," says the author of his brother in *A River Runs Through It*, a memoir close enough in spirit to a novel to make an issue of limited knowledge.[25] Or consider this exchange in Iris Murdoch's *The Sea, the Sea*:

> "How can you—you don't know what you've done—how could you push in, spy on us like that—it was nothing to do with you—how could you intrude into secret things which you couldn't possibly understand—it's the wickedest vilest most hurtful thing anybody's ever done to me—"
>
> "Hartley, darling, you know I only did it to help, I mean because I had to know, I had to be sure, to be certain—"
>
> "As if you could *know* anything."[26]

The tale holds us in prolonged uncertainty, in "expectation." In these worlds knowledge is a problem. "The novel," writes Bakhtin, "speculates in what is unknown."[27]

Asked by a priest how he can doubt the existence of the Creator, Levin in *Anna Karenina* answers characteristically, "I don't know" (441). (By one account, Tolstoy's own last words were "I do not understand what it is I have to do.") Only when he poses a question to which no answer can be given—"Why, why dost Thou torment me so terribly?" (160)—does the awakening of Ivan Ilych begin. Smerdyakov was very likely the natural son of old Karamazov, Dmitri reminds his interrogators. "Do you know that?" (476). Ivan Karamazov knows and does not know of the impending murder of his father. As he sinks into a delirium that destroys the last traces of his pride, Pip loses knowledge as well. "I knew that [illness] was coming on me now, and I knew very little else" (57.468). Earlier in the novel, addressed by Pip's convict, Joe Gargery replies, "We don't know what you have done, but we wouldn't have you starved to death for it" (5.39). "We don't know" might serve as the motto of *Great Expectations*, with "we" including the reader. Much like characters in modern novels, readers of modern novels are subject to ignorance and error. The fox knows many things, the hedgehog knows one big thing, and the reader knows some things and not others.[28]

In the suitor drama Odysseus plays a beggar, one beneath notice and without so much as a name. In keeping with their own interest in the unknown and the nameless, the masterworks investigated in this study feature despised or disregarded persons who rise to importance like some unnoticed detail of great significance in a mystery. *The Brothers Karamazov* is a mystery of sorts, with the murder committed by a background character considered by others beneath regard and incapable of the act itself. Unknown persons yield unknown outcomes: if Smerdyakov's origins were known—if he could be identified for certain either as the son of Fyodor Pavlovitch or not his son—he would no longer be in the position of one viewed by the brothers as no relation at all but proclaimed by his own name the son of their father. And the tension of this position helps drive the drama of *The Brothers Karamazov*. Although Telemachus isn't sure who he is (because "Nobody really knows his own father" [1.216]), Athena refers to Odysseus as his father and assures him that "The gods have not made yours a birth that will go nameless / hereafter" (1.222–23). In *The Brothers Karamazov* the matter of Smerdyakov's birth is never resolved, and the narrative itself is correspondingly "unfinalized," once again in direct contrast to the *Odyssey*.

Had Fyodor Pavlovitch not invented a kind of mock name for him, Smerdyakov would in fact have been nameless. Tolstoy too illumines the nameless. Under the influence of Platon Karataev, the kind of person invisible to the historians, Pierre in *War and Peace* learns that the life going on before his eyes—the very thing he once thought beneath notice (1180–81)—is a great and unfathomable mystery. In the opening section of "The Death of Ivan Ilych," the important figure of Gerasim, the butler's assistant, blends into the background exactly like the wonders of the ordinary eventually revealed to Pierre, and also exactly like a clue in a story of detection. The hero's fatal slip on a stepladder is camouflaged perfectly as the non-event it originally seemed to be, the moment itself ironically illustrating the Tolstoyan principle that "even the most ordinary action of the most ordinary person" is potentially significant.[29] Each of these works, and *Great Expectations* as well, is a tale of discovery in a sense going far beyond the revelation of Odysseus's identity—already known to the reader—to one character after another. All belong in some sense to the age of detective fiction. Not long after their appearance, Freud, a detective of another order, would begin to construct his theory of the unconscious. But it can be argued that fiction had already brought to light a kind of social unconsciousness, as when each of the legitimate brothers in Dostoevsky's novel, even the earnest Alyosha, even Ivan the daring freethinker, acts as if he had never heard that their father's cook is probably also their father's son.

In the famous closing words of George Eliot's *Middlemarch*,

> [Dorothea's] full nature, like that river of which Cyrus broke the strength, spent itself in channels which had no great name on the earth. But the effect of her being on those around her was incalculably diffusive: for the growing good of the world is partly dependent on unhistoric acts; and that things are not so ill with you and me as they might have been, is half owing to the number who lived faithfully a hidden life, and rest in unvisited tombs.[30]

Each in accordance with his own original vision, Dickens, Tolstoy, and Dostoevsky also subscribe to an ethos of the unheroic. Describing Joe Gargery as "a sort of Hercules in strength, and also in weakness" (2.6), the hero-narrator of *Great Expectations* places this character—the moral rock of his world—squarely in the tradition of the comic or unheroic Hercules, a figure identified by Bakhtin as "an enormous influence on all of world literature."[31] Pip himself, having discarded the dream of becoming a somebody, acknowledges those who live faithfully a hidden life. "It is not possible to know how far the influence of any amiable honest-hearted duty-going man flies out into the world," says Pip (14.108). As a mystery, the entire work plays on the phrase "it is not possible to know." Just before her eulogy to the unknown of the world, George Eliot remarks that under modern conditions tragedy can no longer preserve its ancient shape. Like *Great Expectations* in its fashion, "The Death of Ivan Ilych" bears out this principle, its protagonist a man of no apparent distinction or significance who nevertheless undergoes tragic suffering. Reading "The Death of Ivan Ilych," we seem to be in the presence of the same fury that would later drive Tolstoy to dismiss, in the name of equality, almost everything known to the world as art, except that in this case the result of his iconoclasm is itself a work of tragic art. The saintly sage Father Zosima of *The Brothers Karamazov* teaches in his own language not only the equality of humankind and the limits of our knowledge but the diffusive effect of good ("all is like an ocean," he says [319]), while the actions of the novel's principals enmesh in a way that implicates them all, as though that effect were realized in reverse among them. Moreover, because the revaluation of the heroic dictates a rethinking of the form of fiction itself, each of these works opens up a new way of writing a tale.

As if in his own ironic interpretation of the phrase "a hidden life," Tolstoy in "The Death of Ivan Ilych" portrays one whose life was hidden from himself. As the dying Ivan Ilych looks back over his life, he comes to the realization that

> his scarcely perceptible attempts to struggle against what was considered good by the most highly placed people, those scarcely noticeable impulses which he had immediately suppressed, might have been the real thing, and all the rest false. (164)

As in detective fiction—a form that would soon reach the height of its fame in the Sherlock Holmes stories—the scarcely perceptible becomes a clue of the utmost significance. (Moreover, from time to time in "The Death of Ivan Ilych" unknown persons appear, like the unidentified woman in black and the two young men, "apparently nephews," who appear at the hero's memorial [125]. Mysteriously inconsequential details like these are of the essence in Tolstoy's art.) As noted, *The Brothers Karamazov* really is a detective novel in some sense, except that the identity of the murderer is revealed well before the end and the solution of the mystery does not exhaust, does not begin to exhaust, the novel's interest. Ivan Karamazov's agony begins in earnest only at that point. Both of these works (and possibly *Great Expectations* as well) could be read as detective fiction with a higher purpose, or infused with the memory of the original drama of investigation and discovery, *Oedipus*. In searching into "hidden life," they powerfully generate the very effect ruled out in a tale like the *Odyssey* where the end is given from the beginning: surprise. As if their authors appreciated in full the implications of choosing heroes unknown to the world, the tales themselves become investigations of the unknown.

A feature of romance is the discovery of identity, often through tokens, in dramas of recognition—a pattern originating in the Ithaca books of the *Odyssey*, punctuated as they are by recognition scenes centering on the hero's pin, scar, bow, and bed. In several of the works before us, the mystery of identity revealed is raised to another level as we ourselves make the gradual discovery of the hero's *literary* ancestry. For those with the necessary hermetic knowledge, the image of Odysseus, the complete man, shines through the figure of Joyce's Bloom. The works I refer to possess a certain translucency for the common reader. Behind Dickens's story of a young man haunted by one who uses him for purposes of revenge (a young man, too, suffering from a "confused division of mind" [18.147]) lies that of Hamlet—the prince's most famous attribute, his irresolution, becoming in Pip a lack of self-determination. There is a lot of Hamlet in the brothers Karamazov as well, but another great figure—Don Quixote—reappears in the errant hero who proclaims a disreputable local the queen of his soul. The mania that seems to possess Dmitri throughout *The Brothers Karamazov* is not the medical condition some within its pages suppose; it is more like Don Quixote's obsession with chivalry, which leaves the rest of his brain unclouded.[32] (Delivering Grushenka from the vileness of their small town would really be chivalric, if only the adventure didn't have to be financed with another woman's money.) Like Oedipus, and scarcely more cognizant of the scandal and horror of his life than Oedipus of his incestuous marriage, Ivan Ilych blindly follows a script and at last comes to perceive that it has proved his destruction. Of these three mythic figures, only Don Quixote isn't plainly tragic, yet to Dostoevsky his tale contained "the most bitter irony a man could express," as though it too were tragic after all.[33] Obscure persons—Pip, Dmitri Karamazov, and Ivan Ilych—are the equals of their great originals in the one sense that matters: their tales deserve no less to be told.

Compared to their tragic, or in the case of Don Quixote tragicomic, originals, our moderns are all subjected to humiliating limitations. Quixotic in the richest sense but trapped in a miserable town—for in his greatest work "the novelist of the city" chose a small world where people know, or think they know, everything about one another—Dmitri loses the freedom that is the indispensable condition of adventure. His most visionary delusion may be his dream of taking to the road with Grushenka. So too, the trap Ivan Ilych walks into, the script he follows to his own destruction, is not the work of Destiny as in *Oedipus* but—absurdly and even more terribly—of mortals indistinguishable from himself. Also absurdly, Pip is precluded from knowing that like Hamlet he is being called on to avenge the injuries of his "father," which is also to say that he is denied Hamlet's glory, consciousness. In each instance it is as though the tragic experience of being caught inescapably were somehow doubled, so that the moderns find themselves caught in circumstances too narrow to permit the complete unfolding of a tragic role itself in the classical sense. Their plight is at once hopeless, humiliating, terrible, and ludicrous—and their stories a reflection of their plight.

Odysseus, being godlike, not only performs exploits of cunning, courage, and endurance, but attracts the wrath of Poseidon, the second most powerful of the gods. As befits the ambiguity of one who has among the gods both a patron and a tormentor, Odysseus's name seems to denote both "troubles inflicted and troubles endured."[34] Some such ambiguity attaches to the heroic condition itself. Those who are glorious are also, and by virtue of being glorious, magnets for forces as dangerous as divine enmity. With commoners and unhistorical figures, it is of course otherwise. The moderns of special interest to this study are subject not to the malice of gods or the treachery of fate (though Dmitri Karamazov would like to believe he is) but to the ironies of circumstance. With Pip the coincidental object of two schemes and Dmitri Karamazov incriminated by purely circumstantial evidence, both *Great Expectations* and *The Brothers Karamazov* search into those ironies. Concerning the power of coincidence, Tolstoy writes in *War and Peace*:

> The deeper we delve in search of . . . causes the more of them we find; and each separate cause or whole series of causes appears to us equally valid in itself and equally false by its insignificance compared to the magnitude of events, and by its impotence—apart from the co-operation of all the other coincident causes—to occasion the event. (646)

In Tolstoy's judgment, an action takes on historical importance only as it joins up with countless other actions in a great confluence; the ultimate cause of a historical event bearing exactly the same character as the event's real authors, that of being unknown. In each of the masterworks these pages are centered on, a great mystery is accomplished in the lives of persons unknown, as though this were the location of history after all.

Not only this, but these works satirize the publicity that raises people out of the unknown and into the light of general notice. In *The Brothers Karamazov* such publicity takes the form of the journalism responsible for making the Karamazov case a topic of breathless gossip both local and national. Like apocryphal Don Quixotes, stories about Dmitri Karamazov's exploits race all around him, some in print, some oral, some fantastic, some only too accurate in their reproduction of his own lies. Tolstoy bitterly satirizes the machinery of fame in *War and Peace* and opens "The Death of Ivan Ilych" with a newspaper notice of the hero's death that practically advertises its own insincerity. In *Great Expectations*, Miss Havisham first learns of the lawyer Jaggers through the newspapers. The impostor Pumblechook puffs himself in the local press as "the Mentor of our young Telemachus," that is, Pip (28.233). When Pip's sister likens herself, fraudulently, to "a Negress Slave" (12.98), she draws her rhetoric from that of a publicity campaign. Magwitch similarly paints himself as Compeyson's "black slave" (42.353), yielding to the same furious resentment he struggles to master. The rhetoric of equality is as liable to misuse as any other. In Orwell's classic essay on "Politics and the English Language," the word "equality" appears in a catalog of "swindles and perversions."

Informing the fiction of Tolstoy and Dostoevsky, writes Auerbach, is the traditional Christian concept of the "dignity of every human individual regardless of social rank and position."[35] Regardless of all theoretical distinctions between Russian and "Western" realism, the same is surely true of Dickens. And in the hands of these artists the principle of the dignity of every soul, far from being an inert abstraction, actively shapes the telling of the tale and the definition of a hero.

The trajectory of literature takes it from the godlike heroes of Homer to the anonymous heroes of the novel—a form that preserves and transforms such originally Homeric conventions as disguise, recognition, and the reversal of fortune. And so persons who are not heroes in the sense of the performers of exploits become over the course of time heroes in the more modest sense of protagonists. Indeed, in the course of literary history the entire matter of "heroes" becomes a field for irony. Shakespeare's Julius Caesar makes his exit with half his play still to come. Henry IV is upstaged by others, including an obese braggart, in the play bearing his name. In *A Midsummer Night's Dream* the great Theseus seems to imagine himself at the center of things but in our eyes appears more like a figurehead of centrality in a world that revolves around no single person. If the novel arose from romances telling of private persons who are still vaguely legendary, Shakespeare has the legendary hero share the stage with an assortment of unknowns; in the course of the play nothing of interest happens to him, but much to them.

As noted, two of the novels under discussion in these pages seem completely decentered, with the role of protagonist dispersed among a number of figures. Like the *Iliad*, *War and Peace* depicts an event of such magnitude that it transcends any of its own participants, though the absence of a hero in this case also reflects the author's depreciation of heroism, that is, glory. So relentless, in fact, is Tolstoy's critique of glory that he assigns the credit for breaking the invading army to those Muscovites who had the sense to *desert* their city—desertion being the very opposite of an act of glory; that the protagonist of "The Death of Ivan Ilych" lacks the attributes of a tragic hero seems like a variant of the same principle and an expression of the same resolutely prosaic imagination. In *The Brothers Karamazov* the division of agency among three, or actually four, sons enables them to perform a murder none might have performed singly, and thus involves them in ordeals of responsibility that stretch them to the limits of their moral powers. (Then too, the murder of the father might never have occurred had the legitimate sons looked on Smerdyakov as a brother, that is, an equal.) Of the brothers one can say with certainty what Father Zosima says of humanity as a whole: each is responsible for all. In fact, in each of the masterworks awaiting us, no character is allowed the honor of centrality, at least not without ironic conditions attached. It is as though the equality so simple in principle—"All men are created equal"—found its literary realization in complex invention. The elevation of persons unknown to history to the literary status of hero enabled new ways of telling a tale. Indeed, unless a tale were told in a new way, it might subvert equality itself as a literary principle.

As with "Helios, who sees all things" (*Odyssey* 11.109), knowledge corresponds with the most far-reaching of the senses; and modernity associates it with what is rhetorically the highest of goods, freedom. Whether science will make us free, or (as the psychologists have it) insight into self, or (as the Marxists have it) insight into the logic and destination of history and the causes of false consciousness, knowledge is regarded as the source of progress and the master key of human happiness. Knowledge is also a source of pride. "Those twin objects, *human knowledge* and *human power,* do really meet in one," says Bacon. It is because they cannot bear to admit that they have no idea what is going on inside him that Ivan Ilych's doctors torture him with their lies, their tests, their treatments, and their shows of superiority, so much like the superiority he himself affected as a judge. A work of literature that placed the power of superior knowledge in the hands of the reader, especially if this power seems to come at the expense of the characters themselves, would not take equality very seriously. The masterworks at this study's focal point not only presume a reader subject to error, uncertainty, and surprise but by one means or another deprive the reader of superior knowledge. To take but one example: in *The Brothers Karamazov* we discover piece after piece of critically important information—the nature of the conflict between father and eldest son, Dmitri's history with Katerina, the whereabouts of Grushenka on the night of the crime, the details of Dmitri's money affairs, the facts of the murder itself—only as they are revealed to one or more of the characters themselves in the course of dialogue. It is Bakhtin's conviction that Dostoevsky made his heroes his equals, renouncing his own superiority as their creator. This isn't really demonstrable, but that *The Brothers Karamazov* denies the reader superior knowledge certainly is. The principle of equality underwrites a new way of telling a tale—the form called "polyphonic" by Bakhtin.

Heroes in Homer live and die for renown, but once they die they lose touch with life and sink into a pathetic ignorance. The dead Agamemnon has no idea of his son's fate and has not heard the story of "what glory was won by great Orestes / among all mankind, when he killed the murderer of his father" (1.298–99). All mankind knows, but Agamemnon does not know. And only when the soul of one of the suitors makes its appearance in Hades does Agamemnon learn of the return of Odysseus. Not-knowing is the condition of the dead. In the modern works examined in the coming pages, not-knowing is the human condition. Father Zosima in *The Brothers Karamazov* teaches that there is much in our common nature "that we cannot comprehend while on earth" and that much is "concealed from us"—all of us (320). Like death itself, ignorance is a great equalizer; and the work of drawing readers into uncertainty and wonder in order to bring them to a recognition of their common humanity calls forth our authors' highest powers. To read their work well is not "to understand it more thoroughly than all but the most perceptive first readers could or than anyone has since," as one critic of *Great Expectations* recently proposed to do,[36] nor to bring to the light of knowledge what the author himself could not know because he was unconscious of it, as another critic of *Great Expectations* claimed to do some decades ago,[37] but to give up the pretense of being above illusion or even above the text. The all-knowing reader of *Great Expectations* takes on a certain resemblance to the lawyer Jaggers, who views his companions at cards as "very obvious and poor riddles that he had found out long ago" (29.246). Among those card companions is Estella, whose father he does not know and who, to the last line of the novel's second ending, remains more or less opaque to the reader.

I might as well state here at the outset that this study is out of sympathy with those post-Freudian schools of interpretation which, even as they prosecute agendas that were not Freud's, continue to uncover repression and to view the text as a system of hidden meanings. But if the meanings are hidden, how do the critics know them? They know them because they possess the code's key, while those not in the critical priesthood, without the key, remain deceived. Many post-Freudian readings, as I have called them, claim to know not only what others do not but why others do not, and the better to separate themselves from the laity they offer strained readings in strained language. Such methods, I believe, are especially ill-suited to works of literature that strip away pretenses of knowledge, like those at the crux of this study.

Investigating the connection between unknown protagonists and unknown outcomes, and the bond between readers and characters equally subject to error and surprise, this study centers, then, on four great works of nineteenth-century fiction. First, however, by way of contrast I look into the unequal distribution of knowledge in the ancestor of the modern novel, the *Odyssey.* The more immediate precursor of the modern novel is the Greek prose romance, of which only a few survive. One of these, *Callirhoe,* taking a loosely equal interest in the hero and the heroine, claims the second chapter of this study. Also by way of contrast with the novelists of the nineteenth century, I discuss Shakespeare's manner of depicting and subverting social differences all at once, and at a time before it could be said that "everyone is at least dimly aware of the equal rights of all people." At that point attention turns to Dickens, Tolstoy, and Dostoevsky, some of whose greatest works speak and think of human equality in rich ways whether or not they espouse a politics of equality. That none of these authors adopts the formula, "Every man to count for one and no one to count for more than one," identified by Isaiah Berlin as the "irreducible minimum" of the ideal of equality, does not mean they are uninterested in equality: it means they do not view equality reductively.[38] In the spirit of non-reductive thinking, the last chapter is devoted to broad reflections on the literary representation of equality.

1

The Odyssey: *Inequality of Knowledge*

Knowledge in the Odyssey *is distributed unequally, like privilege, as the bestowal and concealment of information are acts of privilege.*

Only a few pages into *War and Peace,* at Anna Pavlovna Scherer's soirée, an elderly woman approaches Prince Vasili on behalf of her son. "What would it cost you to say a word to the Emperor, and then he would be transferred to the Guards at once?" (15). In this social world depicted as if through the lens of Rousseau's *Discourse on Inequality,* it seems that all depends on having friends in high places. In Athena Odysseus has an ally in the highest of places, and we might read the transaction in the drawing room as a travesty or reduction of Athena's appeal to Zeus on her favorite's behalf at the beginning of the *Odyssey* (a reduction on a par with the shrinkage of Helen to the beautiful and odious Hélène). In the one case a woman asks a prince to use his influence with the emperor, in the other Athena uses her own influence with her father, the mightiest of the gods. Had Athena not exploited the absence of Poseidon to make this appeal to Zeus, Odysseus would presumably have remained in a kind of living stasis on Ogygia. In the sense that Athena's appeal breaks the impasse and sets events in motion, the *Odyssey* thus hinges on the hero's passage from the status of one who, like any other mortal, has no divine protector or patron, to one who acquires these privileges. Later in the *Odyssey,* with the hero working in concert with Athena, the secret of his identity is his to keep to himself or to bestow on others, like a privilege in its own right.

By sheer power of antithesis, Tolstoy, a rival Homer, brings out the unusual distribution of knowledge in the Homeric world. It has been said that Tolstoy denies the characters, the reader, and even himself, the author of *War and Peace,* any "privileged vantage points."[1] In the charged world of literary study, the word "privileged" is often loaded with strong if vague political associations, and in this case we need to ask whether the elimination of special or privileged knowledge argues some actual belief in human equality. I believe it does. *War and Peace* demands to be read as a challenge to all the received structures of narrative, both historical and literary, and included in this is a challenge to the original poet of the West, who predates the distinction between historical and fictional narrative itself. In the Homeric world not only do higher vantage points exist, and not only are we let into them, but we are precluded from sharing the ignorance and delusion of mortals unaware of the gods' intentions. In contesting Homer, Tolstoy discards the picture of a universe where knowledge is distributed unequally, like privilege or power. The simple question of who knows what takes on real interest in the *Odyssey* not just because it is handled by the poet with technical skill but because the disposal of information in the poem reflects the very structure of the Homeric world.

That world is so ruled by inequality that the only ones truly "equal" may be slaves, and what they are equal to is a certain sum of money, their purchase price. Eurycleia was purchased long ago for twenty oxen. Eumaeus was kidnapped by a Phoenician woman who herself had been kidnapped and sold for "a fair price" (15.429). The suitors threaten to sell the beggar Odysseus for "a good price" (20.383). By contrast, possessions of the highest value in the *Odyssey* are beyond price, either because they were given as a gift (like Odysseus's bow or the mixing bowl fashioned by Hephaestus and bestowed on Telemachus by Menelaus) or because they are one of a kind (like Odysseus's pin or even his bed) and thus inexchangeable—outside the exchange economy that includes a traffic in slaves. Such possessions are not equal to anything. Equality in the *Odyssey* seems to be for the devalued. Those with value stand above some and below others (even Athena appears as a petitioner in one case, and even Eumaeus owns a slave [14.449–50]); and perhaps because it too is a thing of value, knowledge itself is unequally apportioned in the poem's world.

Not until the middle of the fifth book of the *Odyssey* does the hero make his appearance: a delay that places the reader in the position of knowing more, at this point, than Odysseus himself. Of the decision taken in the heavens to bring about his homecoming—a decision proclaimed by Zeus in book 1 and reaffirmed in book 5—Odysseus knows nothing. In his first speech in the *Odyssey* this inequality of knowledge produces a sharp effect of dramatic irony. When Calypso announces, with a certain unwillingness audible to the reader if not to Odysseus, that the time has come for him to return to Ithaca, Odysseus does not believe she is really letting him go. "Here is some other thing you devise, O goddess," he replies.

> "I will not go aboard any raft without your good will,
> not unless, goddess, you can bring yourself to swear me a great oath
> that this is not some painful trial you are planning against me."
> (5.173, 177–79)

Though some read this distrust as excessive (as if Odysseus were too devious for his own good), the fact is that Odysseus does not know that Calypso has just been ordered by Hermes, in the name of Zeus, to release him. Such is his mind that he suspects the truth all the same, without any real evidence for it other than Calypso's sudden and unlikely change of heart. Later, in his account to the Phaeacians, he remarks that he is uncertain whether Calypso let him go because she received "a message from Zeus or whether her own mind turned within her" (7.263): a characteristically Odyssean judgment, at once a superb leap of inference and a wary suspension of judgment itself. Calypso herself made no mention of any order for his release. She merely said, "Poor man, no longer mourn here beside me nor let your lifetime / fade away, since now I will send you on, with a good will" (5.160–61), instructed Odysseus to build a raft, and warmed him with the thought of seeing Ithaca again "if only the gods consent. It is they who hold wide heaven. / And they are more powerful than I to devise and accomplish" (5.169–70). In these last words we, but not Odysseus, can detect the note of one yielding with reluctance, and in spite of her own show of "good will," to superior power.

In a sense, indeed, Calypso stands to the higher gods as Odysseus himself does to her. Though, being an immortal, she recognizes Hermes as soon as he appears before her, she does not know the reason for his visit and according to the customs of courtesy must wait until her guest has dined in order to find out. Only then does she discover what we, the readers, already know: that Hermes comes from Zeus bearing the order for Odysseus's release. The order itself is delivered in an authoritative tone that leaves Calypso with no choice but compliance, whatever her bruised feelings. ("You are hard-hearted, you gods, and jealous beyond all creatures / beside, when you are resentful toward the goddesses for sleeping / openly with such men as each has made her true husband" [5.118–20].) She cannot disobey the will of Zeus; but she can take out her resentment of Zeus's power on the very object of her possessive love by withholding from him the knowledge that Zeus has, in fact, guaranteed his return to Ithaca and his mortal wife. (From the highly conditional prophecy of Tiresias—known to Odysseus but not, at this point, to the reader—Odysseus learns only that he may just possibly see Ithaca again.) It is almost as if Calypso cannot bring herself to name the power that has commanded her to deliver Odysseus to the sea. Even after notifying Odysseus that he is a free man—but not that Zeus issued the order—she tries to induce him to remain with her as an immortal, possibly reasoning that if he does so of his own will, she cannot be accused of detaining him and thus crossing the will of Zeus. He declines, some days later returning to the sea with a favoring wind and the goddess's blessing, but without knowing, or knowing for sure, that he has *Zeus's* blessing. So it is that when Poseidon in his rage churns up the sea, Odysseus mistakenly assumes that Zeus has sent the storm and that he himself is bound to perish:

> The knees of Odysseus gave way for fear, and the heart inside him,
> and deeply troubled he spoke to his own great-hearted spirit:
> "Ah me, unhappy, what in the long outcome will befall me?

I fear the goddess may have spoken the truth in all ways
when she said that on the sea and before I came to my country
I would go through hardships; now all this is being accomplished,
such clouds are these, with which Zeus is cramming the wide sky
and has staggered the sea . . .
My sheer destruction is certain." (5.297–305)

Odysseus is in error. Not Zeus but Poseidon staggered the sea (5.292), and not his destruction but his homecoming is certain, because Zeus himself has sworn it.

Asking the aid of the Muses as he embarks on the catalog of ships in the *Iliad*, Homer says, "Tell me now, you Muses, who have your homes on Olympos. / For you, who are goddesses, are there, and you know all things, / and we have heard only the rumour of it and know nothing" (2.484–87). Knowing nothing is linked, through the Muses, with knowing everything. In the *Odyssey* knowledge and ignorance seem correlated in the sense that if one knows, another is ignorant. Why should Athena encourage Telemachus, but not Penelope, with news of Odysseus in book 1—why unless it is the nature of privileged knowledge to be bestowed on one, like the favor it is, and withheld from another? Under the likeness of Mentes, Athena reveals to Telemachus that Odysseus "will not be long absent from the beloved land of his fathers" (1.203), but to Penelope, even in the comforting dream she sends in book 4, Athena will not disclose whether Odysseus lives or has died. Nestor does not know what has become of Odysseus but Menelaus does, having learned from the Old Man of the Sea that he is being held by Calypso. As Telemachus's quest for news of his father suggests, knowledge itself resembles a sought-for good in short supply. It is not just the voices of the Sirens that make them so alluring, but their promise of limitless knowledge:

"No one . . . has ever yet sailed past this place in his black ship
until he has listened to the honey-sweet voice that issues
from our lips; then goes on, well pleased, knowing more than ever
he did; for we know everything that the Argives and Trojans
did and suffered in wide Troy through the gods' despite.
Over all the generous earth we know everything that happens."
(12.186–91)

But there can be no such absolute knowledge for mortals. Among the dead, the most knowing (Tiresias) states little positively, while others know less than the living, their lack of knowledge the correlate as it were of their lack of life.[2] Even among the gods there are disparities of knowledge. The release of Odysseus has taken place only because Poseidon does not know about it, engaged as he is among the Ethiopians, "most distant of men" (1.23). The action of the *Odyssey* itself begins with

Athena capitalizing on Poseidon's absence to plead with her father Zeus on behalf of Odysseus. Even though Poseidon is not to be tricked like his monstrous son Polyphemus, and even though, as the second highest of the gods, he does not really suffer from defects of perception, still he does not choose to pass his days keeping watch on a mortal, and it is this lapse of attention that makes possible Odysseus's return from Calypso's island. If Calypso takes out her resentment of Olympian power on the object of her love, Poseidon takes out on Odysseus his wrath against the gods—he does not name Zeus—who outwitted him behind his back:

> "For shame, surely the gods have rashly changed their intentions
> about Odysseus while I was away in the Aithiopians'
> land, and he nears the Phaiakian country where it is appointed
> that he shall escape this great trial of misery that is now his.
> But I think I can still give him a good full portion of trouble."
> (5.286–90)

Odysseus is both a lightning rod for trouble and a great cause of trouble for others.

With Odysseus's return to Ithaca laid down by Zeus in the opening lines of the poem and his triumph over the suitors similarly decreed in book 5, the element of surprise is effectively absent from the *Odyssey.* The suitors do not know "what was appointed." Never do we as readers of this tale of adventure experience the uncertainty that belongs to adventure itself—the sense of not knowing how things will turn out. "Naturally . . . Odysseus never knows what is going to happen next, nor for that matter do we the readers; but we do know what is going to happen last."[3] In the special case of the adventures recounted by Odysseus himself, like the contest with Polyphemus, the simple fact that they are being recounted means that he cannot have lost his life in the course of them. Originally, however, the outcome of these adventures *was* in doubt, the absence of Athena certifying that Odysseus is on his own, exposed to risk and uncertainty. If Joyce in his transformation of the *Odyssey* makes use of the Cyclops, the Sirens, Scylla and Charybdis, even the Lestrygonians, while passing almost in silence over the entire latter half of the poem where the action is overseen by Athena, this is partly because only in fantastic adventures like these is Odysseus in anything like the ordinary human position of being without divine aid or privileged knowledge.

During his visit to Hades, Odysseus asks the shade of Agamemnon, "What doom of death that lays men low has been your undoing?" (11.398). By this point, the audience of the *Odyssey* has already heard the tale of Agamemnon's murder, in one version or another, many times over. We know the tale but Odysseus does not. Agamemnon for his part has no knowledge of the fate of his son, even though the story of Orestes is so well known on earth that Athena reminds Telemachus of the glory won by Orestes "among all mankind" (1.299). Such a lack of knowledge reflects the misery and loss of power that are the condition of the dead. Again, it is immediately after his remark that he would rather be a slave on earth than king of the dead that Achilles asks Odysseus for news of *his* son.[4]

In the embedded tale of Odysseus's wanderings, there are no conversations among the gods as reported in books 1 and 5. The single apparent exception to this rule turns out to confirm it. Near the end of his narration to the Phaeacian court, Odysseus reports the exchange that took place between Apollo and Zeus after his men slaughtered the cattle of the former: an exchange Odysseus knows of only because Calypso informed him of it. "All this I heard afterward from fair-haired Kalypso, / and she told me she herself had heard it from the guide, Hermes" (12.389–90). By contrast, no explanation is given a few lines earlier when Odysseus reports a speech made in his absence by his troublesome lieutenant Eurylochus:

> "Listen to what I say, my companions, though you are suffering
> evils. All deaths are detestable for wretched mortals,
> but hunger is the sorriest way to die and encounter
> fate. Come then, let us cut out the best of Helios' cattle." (12.340–43)

At the time these fatal words were spoken Odysseus was elsewhere. (Presumably the men could never have been so easily persuaded in his presence to lay hands on the sacred cattle. Nor could they have opened the bag of winds had Odysseus heard the arguments for doing so that he himself reports.) In effect Odysseus has been deputized by the poet—granted a share of omniscience—for the purpose of relaying important information to the audience. But the gods are too great to eavesdrop on in this way, their conferences too far beyond mortal ken. For Odysseus's inferiors but not his superiors in the scale of being, Homer is willing to suspend, at times, the limitations on his knowledge. As long as Odysseus is the narrator, the tale thus lacks the direct access to Olympus it has when Homer or Homer's Muse is doing the telling. From a Homeric perspective, a tale where we as readers knew only what the hero knows at the time—where we ourselves underwent the suspense of adventure—would be one without gods. Visiting Telemachus under the appearance of Mentes, Athena wonders "whether [Odysseus] will come home to his vengeance, here in his household, / or whether he will not" (1.268–69), as though this were a matter of uncertainty. Only if Athena were a mortal with limited knowledge, like Telemachus (whose hope and dread she has dramatized), would the question of Odysseus's return be an open one. Athena has in fact set his return in motion, and the poem itself announced it at the outset: "But . . . in the circling of the years that very year came / in which the gods had spun for him his time of homecoming" (1.16–17). By the time Telemachus, on his way back to Ithaca, worries "whether he would escape death, or be captured" (15.300), we have already had Athena's assurance that the ambush laid for him will fail (13.425–28). Similarly, even as we learn that Penelope, nearing her breaking point, cannot decide whether to remain loyal to Odysseus or accept one of the suitors (16.73–77), Odysseus is already on Ithacan soil plotting the destruction of the suitors. Homerically speaking, what makes a tale interesting is its progress not toward an unknown but a known outcome, and hence the dramatic ironies it creates—the disparities between what is known to us and what is known to the actors themselves, as when Odysseus fails to recognize Ithaca and accuses the loyal Phaeacians of treachery.

And precisely because the Homeric universe is a universe of unequals, it is bound to generate inequalities of knowledge. Possessed with the spirit of resentment, Eve in *Paradise Lost* dreams of "keep[ing] the odds of knowledge in my power" (9.820) by keeping the apple to herself. In the *Odyssey* there really are odds of knowledge, with some at an advantage, others handicapped. Odysseus fails to recognize Ithaca because Athena has disguised it from him. Less powerful than Zeus, Poseidon does not know of the decision to grant Odysseus's homecoming. In a sense, a mist is poured over his perception as well. The exchange between Apollo and Zeus, as a result of which Odysseus loses his entire crew and arrives on Ogygia alone—this is known to Odysseus only because he learns of it after the fact from Calypso, who in turn knows of it only because it was reported to her by Hermes. As noted, Calypso does not know the reason for Hermes' visit in book 5, though the reader does; nor, when he leaves Ogygia, does Odysseus know, though he seems later to intimate, that his homecoming has been sealed by Zeus. Unable to thwart his release from her island, Calypso will at least exercise her right not to inform Odysseus that he will in fact end up in the arms of Penelope. Calypso seems a crux in the Homeric universe—a nymph who recognizes other immortals on sight but knows of their councils only by report; a divinity who cannot charm a mortal and does not rank with the higher gods.

Back on Ithaca Odysseus is subject neither to the hostile will of Poseidon nor the possessive will of Calypso. He is not so much a subject of power as a power himself, and as though celebrating his liberty he uses that power not only to put to death all those who raided his herds and defiled his house (as Apollo destroyed those who laid hands on his sacred herds), but to stage a drama of mistaken perceptions in concert with that higher dramatist, Athena.

If the immortals recognize one another on sight, Athena disguises herself with ease from mortal eyes—a practice rich with possibilities of dramatic irony. With something like the penetration that enabled him to sense the hand of Zeus behind Calypso's change of heart, Odysseus recognizes Athena under the form of Mentor when the latter enters the battle of the palace. No one else, apparently, shares this recognition, and one of the suitors goes so far as to threaten to kill Mentor:

> "When we kill these men, the son and the father, you too
> shall be killed in their company, for what you are trying
> to do here in the palace. You shall pay for it with your own head."
> (22.216–18)

To threaten to kill an immortal would seem to be the last word in human blindness. We as readers see what Agelaus does not, just as we know the outcome of the battle before the first arrow is shot. We know it not only because Zeus decreed it, but because Athena with her superior knowledge and power oversees the event itself.

The gods possess the double ability to recognize one another and to block recognition by mortal eyes. Odysseus, being god*like,* possesses these powers in lesser form: he can recognize Athena in the guise of Mentor when others cannot, and with his fluency in deceit, backed up with Athena's power to transfigure his person, he can conceal his identity. In the most sustained drama of the *Odyssey* the hero employs the disguise of a beggar to mask his identity from friend and foe until the dramatically fitting moment comes to reveal it: hence his disclosure of himself first to Telemachus, then to the swineherd Eumaeus, then, in battle, to the suitors ("You dogs, you never thought that I would any more come back / from the land of Troy, and because of that you despoiled my household" [22.35–36]), then to Penelope, and at last to his father Laertes. There is some show of reason for all this indirection. From the first book of the *Odyssey* to the last, the homecoming of Odysseus is set against that of Agamemnon, who upon his return from Troy walked straight into a trap set by his wife and paid with his life-blood. By means of his undercover return to his own palace, Odysseus makes sure he does not suffer a similar fate. But Penelope is anything but a Clytemnestra, and Athena herself vouches for her loyalty (13.379–81). Similarly, the tests through which Odysseus puts his dearest allies are as gratuitous, practically speaking, as the goddess Athena's tests of him. Just as there is really no compelling military reason for Odysseus, with an invincible goddess at his side, to disguise himself from the suitors for his own safety, so his tests of those most loyal to him go well beyond any practical utility or rationale.

He tests Eumaeus after Athena herself has given him a good character: "always his thoughts are kindly, / and he is a friend to your son and to circumspect Penelope" (13.405–6). He tests his father, whose loyalty is not in question in any case, after the suitors have been slaughtered and any reason for concealment that may once have existed has vanished. "I myself will make trial of my father, / to see whether he will know me and his eyes recognize me" (24.216–17). As strange as it may be to speak of concealment as a mode of exhibition, my sense is that Odysseus conceals himself from those nearest and dearest to him simply as an exhibition of his own godlike power to obscure and reveal his identity. It is done not for any tactical reason but simply to dramatize superior power. In a poem that owes much of its own power to dramatic ironies, those engendered by Odysseus's acts of concealment cooperate as it were with the ends of the work itself. And as I have suggested, a great source of the inequalities of knowledge that make for dramatic irony in the *Odyssey* is inequality as such. When Odysseus tells lies, with considerable virtuosity, to Eumaeus, a master lies to a slave. With Penelope's web resembling her husband's yarns, her "test" of the stranger (19.215) his own practice of verification, and her unconscious recognition of the stranger as Odysseus his own intimation that his release from Ogygia came from Zeus, Penelope is a match for Odysseus, but on the poem's terms she is by no means his equal, and no matter how odd it may seem for Odysseus to defer his own disclosure until after the suitors have been slain (as though Penelope could be trusted only at that point), the poem itself no more questions his right than his power to do so. Neither does it question Odysseus's decision, for some perverse reason, "to make trial of [Laertes] and speak in words of mockery" (24.240) before finally revealing himself as the old man's son. If, nevertheless, his way of toying with Laertes is hard to accept or even make sense of, that is probably because on the poem's terms Odysseus does not outrank his father as he clearly does his swineherd, his son, and his wife, or as Athena outranks him.

Perhaps a second modern epic conceived in opposition to Homer and the epic tradition itself will throw into relief the unequal distribution of knowledge and power in the Homeric world. In Milton's *Paradise Lost* such Odyssean qualities as daring, adventurousness, exile, opportunism, guile, grandeur, the drive for revenge, and indeed the setting of "trials" belong to Satan. Where Odysseus in his hope of returning to his native land and his mortal wife refuses Calypso's offer of immortality, Adam's forfeit of immortality for the sake of his mortal wife represents a betrayal of his God. And in accordance with his subversion of Homeric conventions and ideals, Milton also ironizes the very principle of superior knowledge. It is after she eats of the apple of knowledge and the perverse effects of this act begin to assert themselves that Eve thinks of keeping the fruit from Adam, preserving for herself "the odds of knowledge." Thus she may become "more equal [to Adam], and perhaps, / A thing not undesirable, / sometime Superior; for inferior who is free?" (9.823–25). This is the way Satan talks. Inasmuch as Eve's argument here rests on the fallacious premise that God, "our great Forbidder," is unaware of her crime, we can only suppose that her resentment of Adam is also fallacious, the result of a kind of imaginary inferiority complex. Eve had all the knowledge (and power) needed to resist Satan's temptation; the heightened knowledge ascribed to the apple as to some magical object is another fallacy. As for the reader, it is true that we know the outcome of Eve's adventure before she does, but this advantage does not cancel the fact that we ourselves are Eve's children, given like her to error and the betrayal of our own freedom. With Adam and Eve starting to act like ordinary people prone to resentment and accusation, the domestic drama of book 9 points the way from the tradition of epic to that of the novel. But the modern novel in turn revived an ancient literary form.

2

Callirhoe: *Equal Protagonists*

As a tale that subjects hero and heroine alike to the caprices of Fortune, Callirhoe *departs from the Homeric model of a hero singled out for divine enmity.*

In the last book of the Greek romance *Callirhoe,* as the reunited hero and heroine go to bed, the author marks the occasion with the language of the corresponding scene in the *Odyssey:* "they gladly came to the ancient rite of the bed" (369).[1] Throughout *Callirhoe* the verse of Homer is on display thus, used mainly for purposes of ornament as if to enhance the dignity of prose narrative. In point of fact, *Callirhoe* and the *Odyssey* are constructed on completely different principles. If the *Odyssey* rules out the element of surprise (in the sense that the end of the hero's trials is foretold and foreknown), *Callirhoe* consists of a long train of surprises, which is also to say that the action is governed not by any deity or deities but by the abstract and inscrutable force of Fortune. True, we are told in the prologue to the final book of *Callirhoe* that Aphrodite was responsible for the trials of both hero and heroine, trials she has now decided to bring to an end. Aphrodite

> was becoming reconciled to Chaereas, though earlier she had been intensely angered at his intemperate jealousy; for, having received from her the fairest of gifts, surpassing even that given to Alexander surnamed Paris, he had repaid her favor with insult. Since Chaereas had now made full amends to Love by his wanderings from west to east amid countless tribulations, Aphrodite took pity on him, and, as she had originally brought together this handsome pair, so now, having harassed them over land and sea, she resolved to unite them again. (361, 363)

But that both should be persecuted over land and sea for a fault of the hero's alone doesn't seem to make sense.[2] At the time of Chaereas's original "insult" to Aphrodite in book 1—in a fit of jealousy he kicks his wife, nearly killing her—the text makes no reference to Aphrodite at all. The portrayal of Aphrodite in book 8 as the architect of the tale's action serves simply as a rhetorical way of telling readers that the time for resolution has come.

Throughout the tale to this point, we know no more of what will happen next than the principals themselves, and beyond the hope and expectation that the narrative builds up, we are not even sure of their eventual reunion. Never are we told that Aphrodite's anger is the cause of their troubles and that when that anger is appeased the troubles will come to an end. In direct contrast to the *Odyssey, Callirhoe* keeps the knowledge of the future from the reader, a reader in this respect in the same position as the hero and heroine themselves. (We can be pretty sure, though, that none of their contemplated suicides will take place, for the simple reason that too much of the tale remains.) For narrative purposes we are the protagonists' equals. Few mortals can boast of Poseidon's enmity. That Odysseus won this enmity by the feat of blinding the god's son makes it both a curse and a tribute to his nerve and guile. Among all mortals Odysseus is singled out—if you will, honored—by the second greatest of the gods, as he is singled out by Athena as her favorite. (As the intelligence of Athena takes advantage of the mightier god's distraction in book 1 of the *Odyssey,* we have the sense that the triumph of brains over brute force is being enacted all over again.) Fortune, on the other hand, causes trouble for everyone. In the Homeric universe the enmity of a god is a thing to be propitiated, but there is no propitiating Fortune, the general nemesis of humanity; and while it is true that the greatness of the Homeric hero places him in a kind of exposed position by attracting the notice of the gods, the Homeric universe contains no such equalizing force as Fortune, which overthrows the high and raises up the low.

Just as it plays no favorites, Fortune marks no one as the special object of its enmity. Unlike Poseidon, Fortune after all is not a person with special loves and hates, but merely a personification. And Fortune, not Aphrodite, drives events in *Callirhoe.* "I cannot trust Fortune," says the heroine, "for through her I have already fallen from a happier state, and I am afraid that she is not yet finished with me" (137). Later: "Fortune determined a sequel other than that intended, and started a train of momentous events" (217). Again: "Fortune was now planning a blow as grim as incredible" (361). Only because Fortune, the common enemy of humankind, presides over *Callirhoe* is it a tale of suspense in the first place—a tale that makes both readers and protagonists partakers in uncertainty.

And yet it is true that *Callirhoe* is so constructed that the reader almost always knows more than one of the two protagonists. Separated from one another, they are ignorant, by and large, of the other's state. They are ignorant but the reader is not. Just as Chariton borrows the devices of reversal, discovery, and recognition that originate in the *Odyssey* and later pass to drama, so he makes constant play with dramatic irony (even giving the tale a sort of dramatic character by employing, like Homer, a great deal of direct speech). Some idea of the tale's construction can be drawn from the summary at its halfway point at the beginning of book 5:

> How Callirhoe, the most beautiful of women, married Chaereas, the handsomest of men, through the management of Aphrodite; how, when Chaereas struck her in a lover's fit of jealousy, she apparently died and then, after a sumptuous funeral, returned to consciousness in the tomb; how next grave robbers carried her away from Sicily by night and, sailing to Ionia, sold her to Dionysius; after that, the love of Dionysius and the fidelity of Callirhoe to Chaereas; the compulsion to marry because of her pregnancy; the confession of Theron [the grave robber] and the voyage of Chaereas in search of his wife; how he was captured, sold, and taken to Caria with his friend Polycharmus; how Mithridates identified Chaereas on the point of death and endeavored to restore the lovers to each other; how Dionysius, discovering this from letters, denounced him to Pharnaces, and he to the king [of Persia]; and how the king summoned them both to trial: all this has been set forth in the preceding account. (231)

Through most of this, each of the lovers is in the dark about the other. Even as Callirhoe revives in her tomb Chaereas presumes her dead; when she is carried off by pirates and sold to Dionysius, he knows nothing of it. Only in book 3 does Chaereas learn that Callirhoe's tomb is empty and set off in search of her. As Fortune would have it, he anchors at the beach of Dionysius's estate, discovering there that Callirhoe has become the man's wife. Owing to a twist of circumstance, however, she now presumes *him* dead. Unbeknownst to Callirhoe, Chaereas is taken captive, made a slave, and very nearly crucified. In a refinement of irony, Dionysius, also presuming Chaereas dead, takes the letter from him to be a forgery. The intercepted message never reaches Callirhoe, nor does she know the reason for the trial that marks the dramatic high point of the entire work. Much of the tale's artistry and power is vested in such ironic effects—in the difference between what is known to us and what is known to the lovers themselves, each entangled not only in suffering but error and illusion.

As a tale of two lovers, *Callirhoe* cannot have one character at its center like Odysseus in the poem bearing his name. In fact, it concerns itself equally with Callirhoe and Chaereas—equally, not in a quantitative and still less a political sense (as though it were advancing some radical proposition), but simply in that the tale has two centers of interest. The second book is devoted to Callirhoe, its peak her inner debate over whether or not to abort her and Chaereas's child. Book 3 begins with Callirhoe inviting the lovesick Dionysius to marry her ("so that the line of Hermocrates may have a descendant" [135]), then cuts to Chaereas. The next book opens with Callirhoe performing a funeral for Chaereas, then switches to Chaereas himself, now in slavery. His letter to Callirhoe, intercepted and misinterpreted by Dionysius, sets up the drama of the trial. In that Fortune's perversity has put Callirhoe in the bind of being married to two men at once, some might place her at the heart of the novel. Sentimentally, perhaps, she does take priority—as, dramatically speaking, Chariclea outperforms Theagenes in Heliodorus's *Ethiopian Story*—though between her and Chaereas there is a structural parity. "We have buried each other, yet neither of us possesses even the other's dead body," says Callirhoe (197). She and Chaereas are coordinate figures—joint protagonists. The alternate title of the novel is in fact *Chaereas and Callirhoe*. If not for Chaereas's acts and errors, misfortunes and sufferings, the situation of Callirhoe would not be what it is.

As just noted, the episode of greatest tension in book 2 is Callirhoe's decision whether or not to abort her child. (Immeasurably heightened, such inner debate becomes the pro and contra of Dostoevsky; but where Chariton identifies himself as a lawyer's clerk and views the situation of a woman married to two men as a sort of nice case, Dostoevsky in his great novel of the law, *The Brothers Karamazov*, explodes legal categories.) But if not for a certain equality between Callirhoe and Chaereas, she would not have been carrying a child at all, or so Chariton seems to say. "On the point of consummating their marriage, Chaereas and Callirhoe had experienced identical eagerness to enjoy each other, and the equal ardor of their passion had rendered their union not unfruitful" (119). And only because she is carrying a child does Callirhoe get into the tangle of being married to two men, for as Chariton's summary reminds us, she felt a "compulsion to marry" for the sake of the child. Notice too that it is Callirhoe who performs the novel's critical action, the one that creates the logically impossible, legally curious, and dramatically potent situation of a woman married to two husbands. Through the mediation of a confidante, she invites Dionysius to marry her, provided that he swear an oath never to turn against her and the child he is led to believe his. Though cast in a less active role than her counterpart Chaereas, Callirhoe is not altogether the plaything of external forces. For that matter, Chaereas at one point is taken captive as she herself was, both are mourned alive, and both are given to private outbursts of lamentation. In book 6, for example, Chaereas exclaims,

> How happy I should be if only I had been buried together with Callirhoe in Syracuse! . . . I should now be lying there, spared my subsequent sufferings—enslavement, pirates, chains, the cross, and the king more cruel than the cross. O happy death I might have had before I heard of Callirhoe's second marriage! (291)

and Callirhoe,

> O treacherous beauty, you are the cause of all my woes! Because of you, I was killed; because of you, I was sold as a slave; because of you, I married another

> after Chaereas. . . . To how many ordeals have you surrendered me—to pirates, the sea, the tomb, slavery, the courtroom! But the hardest of all to bear is the king's love. (307)

Whatever the difference in their characters (Chaereas being the more tempestuous of the two) and whatever powers of action are denied Callirhoe, clearly hero and heroine are both of interest to a narrative that shuttles continually from one to the other.

The equality of Callirhoe and Chaereas is the parity between two characters each magnetized to the other and both kept before the reader. As readers, we know more than either of the lovers (being aware of the other's state as they in their separation are not), but the shape of the future we do not know, as no deity has decreed the outcome of the tale as in the *Odyssey.* If you will, our knowledge though greater in degree is the same in kind as that of the principals, and it is by interesting us in the fortunes of these characters in essence like ourselves that the tale builds its tension. Moreover, a tale that has the son of a noble family sold into slavery seems to bear out the principle that "it is not nature but fortune that makes a man a slave." The mind's independence in the face of fortune was in turn affirmed by Stoic thought, an expression of the Stoic belief in "the fundamental equality of men."[3] In Shakespeare's *Winter's Tale* (founded indirectly on Greek romance, and whose plot, like that of *Callirhoe,* is set into motion by an onset of jealousy) the royal child Perdita reveals herself a sort of stoic when she says, "I think affliction may subdue the cheek, / But not take in the mind." She also says, "The self-same sun that shines upon [the] court / Hides not his visage from our cottage, but / Looks on alike" (4.4.576–77, 444–46).

If the tradition of the novel springs in part from a romance like *Callirhoe,* which in turn remembers the *Odyssey,* the later Shakespeare composed, along with *The Winter's Tale,* three other plays now known as romances whose proximity to the sea, generational plots, and separations, reunions, and recognitions all recall the *Odyssey.* It is as if Shakespeare in these tales of wandering and return were himself returning to the beginnings of his tradition. But where no one doubts that Odysseus is the hero of the *Odyssey,* it is hard to say exactly who the hero or heroine of *The Winter's Tale* is, and the hero of *Cymbeline* certainly isn't Cymbeline. And while Homer preserves his hero's distinction even in the face of his suggestive resemblance to a resourceful and long-suffering wife, Shakespeare often introduces resemblances that undercut claims to distinction. Before proceeding to the treatment of "artificial distinctions" in some works of nineteenth-century fiction, I propose a brief discussion of this Shakespearean practice.

3

Notes on Shakespearean Equality

Equality in Shakespeare generally takes the form of qualities shared by occupants of different social worlds.

When Odysseus, disguised as a beggar, puts friend, foe, and even his own father through a series of tests before revealing himself, he does this not to increase suspense or because of any practical necessity, but simply, it seems to me, to dramatize his own godlike power to conceal and reveal his identity. The gods are essentially above necessity, and Athena, his own protector and a kindred spirit, excels in the use of disguise. But by thus imitating the behavior of an immortal, Odysseus neither makes himself ridiculous nor parodies the gods (making *them* ridiculous), nor somehow exalts himself at their expense. He simply confirms his own epithet, "godlike." As a godlike man, Odysseus resembles the gods without being one of them and stands distinctly above the common run of mortals and the other members of his household while still subject to pain, loss, and death. And so when, with Athena's help, he exercises the godlike privilege of concealment, in no way does he call into question or disturb the hierarchy of power in his world. If Homer had been Shakespeare it might have been otherwise, for in Shakespeare if an inferior should mirror a superior, or indeed if gods should conduct themselves like mortals as in *A Midsummer Night's Dream,* such duplications can throw an ironic light on the very ordering of power.

Shakespeare makes abundant use of dramatic irony, putting us in the position of knowing what one on stage does not, his practice in this respect closer to Homer than to a novelist who makes the reader a character's equal in knowledge. In the *Odyssey* Calypso does not know the reason for Hermes' visit, Odysseus does not know what Calypso was told, and, later, others do not know that he is in fact Odysseus. In *A Midsummer Night's Dream* knowledge at times seems distributed like privilege, so that for one to have it another must not. Oberon and Puck know what has come over the lovers, but the lovers themselves have no idea. The mechanicals in *A Midsummer Night's Dream* seem completely unaware of their crimes against language and their folly in general. Theseus does not know of the fairies afoot in the woods and in his very palace. Puck looks down on mortals as one who knows what they do not—"Lord, what fools these mortals be!" (3.2.115)—and Oberon can see what Puck cannot: "That very time I saw (but thou couldst not), / Flying between the cold moon and the earth, / Cupid all arm'd" (2.1.155–57). But through all of this stratification runs a common strain of folly. Oberon himself not only gives Puck a description of Demetrius that, like Cupid's arrow, misses the mark, but is impelled by jealousy—a force that proverbially makes a fool of its own possessor—into humiliating his own beloved. Perhaps his description is sloppy because his mind is elsewhere. (If so, then he like Theseus is "over-full of self-affairs" [1.1.112]—one of many doublings in the play.) As I will suggest later, folly extends even to the voice of rationality, Theseus. As with the community of folly in *A Midsummer Night's Dream*, equality in Shakespeare generally takes the form of common qualities shown, or patterns enacted, by different persons in spite of their differences. After Oberon intervenes in Helena's behalf, but before Theseus overrules the absurd Egeus (thus doing away with the only remaining obstacle to a perfect resolution), Bottom the weaver announces that he has "a device to make all well" (3.1.16). When Dostoevsky makes both the haughty Katerina Ivanovna and the lowly Captain Snegiryov in *The Brothers Karamazov* come close to selling their honor, he writes in the tradition of Shakespeare. Levin in *Anna Karenina* arrives at the realization that king and beggar are bound by the same one truth. Shakespeare in *King Lear* reduces a king to the condition of a beggar and makes him a beggar's fellow.

As an example of ironic mirroring in Shakespeare, consider Falstaff's talk, as well as practice, of thievery in *1 Henry IV*. "We that take purses go by the moon and the seven stars and not by Phoebus, he, 'that wand'ring knight so fair'" (1.2.13–16). "Do not thou, when thou art king, hang a thief" (1.2.62). How can this kind of talk not reflect ironically on a king who not only admits that he "stole all courtesy from heaven" when he was making his political name (3.2.50), but actually stole the throne? Falstaff's doubling of Hal's father, to the point of performing the other in mime, is everything that Odysseus's imitation of a god is not. Odysseus cooperates with Athena in making his own return a drama of disguise and recognition. Power expresses itself dramatically. When Falstaff impersonates Hal's father calling the young truant to account, he not only ridicules the regal accent but, more brilliantly yet, exposes the king's use of stagecraft as an instrument of rule. ("Thus did I keep my person fresh and new," says King Henry, "My presence, like a robe pontifical, / Ne'er seen but wond'red at" [3.2.55–57]—the term "person" deriving from an actor's mask, and a holy robe here reduced to a stage prop.) So potent is Falstaff's parody of the king that when the king actually does call Hal to account in act 3, scene 2, we can't be sure that his tears are not feigned for dramatic effect. "Give me a cup of sack to make my eyes look red," says Falstaff before switching to iambs, "for I must speak in passion" (2.4.384–86).[1] Falstaff's fantastic oaths, too, remind us of the rebels' portrayal of the king as an oath-breaker (as indeed the Percys paraphrase Falstaff in presenting their grievances to the king: "Call you that backing of your friends?" [2.4.150]). Falstaff's famous question, "What is honor?" which might well serve as the subtitle of the play itself, throws into relief the actions of a Machiavellian king as dramatically as his tavern court doubles the king's court. The king of language parodies the king of England.

Falstaff imitates the king explicitly. But it is also possible for characters to echo one another without knowing it. When the newly empowered Angelo launches an anti-vice campaign in *Measure for Measure,* the first arrested appear to be Claudio and Pompey—Claudio a gentleman with "a most noble father" (2.1.7) and Pompey of parentage unknown, employed in a brothel, an unsilenceable voice of license and impertinence. Called on to confess his true occupation, Pompey answers, "Truly, sir, I am a poor fellow that would live" (2.1.223). In the major plot of the play, as we know, Isabella refuses to yield herself to Angelo in order to buy the freedom of Claudio, her brother, now awaiting execution. Told by Isabella how things stand, Claudio after a brief show of courage is flooded with fear. "Ay, but to die, and go we know not where; / To lie in cold obstruction, and to rot" (3.1.117–18). He too seems to be a poor fellow that would live. Pompey's answer is all at once evasion and defiance, simplicity and trickery—a clown's equivocation. Claudio speaks in extremis. The one uses prose, the other verse. But the very correspondence between these cases, as free as it is, cuts across social distinctions otherwise strongly marked, revealing two men with the elementary desire to remain as they are. As Gadshill says in *1 Henry IV,* "*homo* is a common name to all men" (2.1.95).

When one of the gravediggers in *Hamlet* remarks that Ophelia would not have been buried in hallowed ground had she been a commoner, the other agrees, adding that "there is no ancient gentlemen but gard'ners, ditchers, and grave-makers; they hold up Adam's profession" (5.1.29–31). We are close to the language of the Peasant Revolt of 1381: "When Adam delved and Eve span, / Who was then a gentleman?" The gravedigger scene introduces us to a social world antithetical to the upper world of the play, but which nonetheless strangely mirrors that world in some respects. Struck by the callous way one of the gravediggers goes about his work, Hamlet asks, "Has this fellow no feeling of his business? 'a sings in grave-making." "Custom hath made it in him a property of easiness," replies Horatio (5.1.65–68). In a play where people accustom themselves to the most startling disruptions of the moral and political order, these last words have great resonance. Like the good Barnardo who cries "Long live the King!" (1.1.3) as if all his loyalty to King Hamlet had been made over to his successor, the people of Denmark who "would make mouths at [Claudius] while my father liv'd give twenty, forty, fifty, a hundred ducats a-piece for his picture in little" (2.2.364–66). Clearly, though, not just the notoriously fickle people but the court itself has made itself over to the new king, and this in spite of the manifest indecency of his marriage. In the period of a few weeks, the court has somehow managed to accustom itself to this arrangement. Its spokesman, Polonius, acts as though no violation of the order of things ever took place. "Damnèd custom" (3.4.37), "that monster custom" (3.4.161), Hamlet names the power that numbs our moral sense and accommodates us to depravity, as he deems the Danish way of carousing "a custom / More honor'd in the breach than the observance" (1.4.15–16). Hamlet himself may be the author of a great speech in the inset play on time's power to sap resolution and erode loyalty. In *Hamlet*'s world or worlds, it seems people will accustom themselves to anything, and in this context the insensitivity shown in singing in a grave and knocking skulls about with a shovel comments not only on a nature coarsened by work but on all those above work who accept the revolution that has befallen their world as though nothing had happened. Death, of course, is the great equalizer. "Golden lads and girls all must, / As chimney-sweepers, come to dust" (*Cymbeline* 4.2.262–63). But if death equalizes, custom "all sense doth eat" (*Hamlet* 3.4.161), very much like death itself.

Resemblance where we might least expect it appears also in *The Tempest*. While the figure of Caliban troubles a race-conscious age that sees in his story the domination of indigenous peoples, within the play as we have it Caliban's most absurd follies and most violent ambitions are strangely doubled by Europeans supposedly above him in the scale of being. "I prithee be my god," says Caliban to Stephano (2.2.149), identified in the list of players as "a drunken butler." Foolish, but so is Miranda's misidentification of Ferdinand as a god: "I might call him / A thing divine; for nothing natural / I ever saw so noble" (1.2.418–20). And if Caliban's adoption of Stephano as his god is not simply a comical mistake but an act of simplicity and gratitude, these last qualities surely have their place in the human economy. Caliban's most criminal act was to attempt to rape Miranda at the time when he lodged in Prospero's own "cell." Stephano intends to marry Miranda after doing away with Prospero, meaning that he would like to excuse rape by murder, while his dreams of assassination parallel those of Antonio, whose calculating mind is just as distorted as Stephano's drunken one. Characters high and low, European and other, are networked with resemblances we might never imagine among the holders of such different social positions.

In a speech that comports well with the improbabilities of *The Winter's Tale*, the Clown, a shepherd's son, says in act 5,

> I was a gentleman born before my father; for the King's son took me by the hand, and call'd me brother; and then the two kings call'd my father brother; and then the Prince, my brother, and the Princess, my sister, call'd my father father; and there was the first gentleman-like tears that ever we shed. (5.2.139–45)

Somehow class differences are at once marked and erased. The parallels cited above have a similar effect, bringing out as they do a striking resemblance between persons differently placed in the scale of social being. The romance of *The Winter's Tale* reads like a tragedy modified in the direction of comedy, and at this point I would like to turn to a comedy that portrays the hierarchy of power itself with unmatched ironic effect

By definition, each of the lovers in *Callirhoe* lacks the absolute centrality enjoyed by the hero of the *Odyssey*. In Shakespeare's great comedy of love, *A Midsummer Night's Dream,* the same principle is extended. As though love were being at once reduced and multiplied to absurdity, the play features pairs upon pairs of lovers. Duplication in *Callirhoe* takes a second form, with one man after another, up to and including the King of Persia, falling in love with the heroine, giving us the impression that "political power and status become as nothing" in the face of love.[2] In *A Midsummer Night's Dream* love cuts across the scale of being, from Oberon and Titania with their love-war at the top to the mechanicals with their comic tragedy of love at the bottom. In between come pairs of lovers, some in a kind of intoxication that further saps their individuality. In effect, the world of *A Midsummer Night's Dream* is centerless. Theseus, the great critic of the imagination, may imagine himself at its center, but if so he is in error.

Taking into account the fairy world of which he has no cognizance, Theseus—along with his prize Hippolyta—does occupy something like the middle rung of *A Midsummer Night's Dream.* The strata of social being in the play might be mapped as follows: at the low end Bottom and his fellow mechanicals, then the four lovers (evidently of high birth), then the royal couple, above them the fairies, and finally the king and queen of the fairy world, Oberon and Titania. The action shifts freely from one level of being to another, impressing us (but not Theseus, who does not witness these changes) with a vivid sense of the distinctions among them. At the same time, similarities cut across these well-marked differences. The mechanicals and the lovers specialize in making mistakes, Puck in causing mistakes. Oberon's instructions to Puck to anoint the eyes of a certain youth in Athenian garb are faulty in themselves, while his war with Titania is simply folly at the highest level. In contrast to a tragedy set in motion by what Aristotle calls a mistake, the comedy of *A Midsummer Night's Dream* has just about everybody making mistakes, from Oberon's loose instructions and casual management to Bottom's malapropisms, from Hermia's belief that Demetrius has murdered her lover to Helena's belief that all are conspiring against her, from Theseus's denial of the imagination to Pyramus's misinterpretation of a bloody shawl. In the dramatic oxymoron of wooing Hippolyta with his sword, Theseus moreover resembles the mechanicals who contradict themselves to our amusement (as in presenting a "most lamentable comedy" [1.2.11–12]), the lovers he discusses like another species, and Oberon in his love-war with

Titania. Hippolyta, we might say, is Theseus's folly, and it is also she who throws into question his supremacy and his way of bearing himself as though he stood at the undisputed center of things; for Hippolyta, his conquest, is also his equal.

Chaucer's Theseus is a conquering hero, but Shakespeare reproduces very little of this, perhaps because love itself is the hero of *A Midsummer Night's Dream. Amor vincit omnia.* As a comedy of love, *A Midsummer Night's Dream* ends appropriately with a wedding—or three weddings (Theseus having invited the lovers he equates with madmen to share the occasion). By its very form, that is, the play makes the ironic suggestion that marriage is the natural end of love. If love is portrayed in *A Midsummer Night's Dream* as a kind of rapt illusion, elsewhere in literature marriage is portrayed as a great disillusion. It is in keeping with the play's ironic celebration of love and its effects that the lovers, including Theseus, are shown to be hastening toward the very state that constitutes the end of enchantment. The exception might seem to be Oberon and Titania, presiders over a world of enchantment; but are the king and queen of the fairies exactly husband and wife? It is much as though Oberon and Titania had worked out a way to keep the intoxicating power of love in force beyond its natural term, namely by acting like the sovereigns of rival kingdoms. Each with his or her own faction and favorites, haunts and pastimes, Oberon and Titania as they appear before us seem to be unmarried even in marriage—an impossibility, of course, but one that fits well into a play of impossibilities. That neither the king nor queen of the fairies seems to realize that their civil war is their own way of renewing love suggests that even they may be blind.

In his anger at Titania's refusal to surrender her Indian boy (who exists in the play purely as a construct of language and a theme of contention), Oberon daubs her eyes with the juice of the pansy, a drug enthralling her to whatever she first lays eyes on as she awakens:

> The next thing then she waking looks upon
> (Be it on lion, bear, or wolf, or bull
> On meddling monkey, or on busy ape)
> She shall pursue it with the soul of love. (2.1.179–82)

It is Puck who manipulates things so that Titania first spies Bottom the weaver got up in the head of an ass. And only by chance are the mechanicals rehearsing in the woods near Titania's bower in the first place. In other words, the masterstroke of Oberon's revenge—the humiliation of his proud consort—comes about accidentally and without his knowledge. "I wonder if Titania be awak'd," he says at the opening of act 3, scene 2, after we the audience have already seen her enamored of an ass. In a play reminiscent of Chaucer's Knight's Tale, we are reminded of that narrative's successor, the Miller's Tale, whose brilliant outcome is purely the result of coincidence (chance itself devising a resolution more just and even more poetic than all the cosmic machinery of the Knight). The artistry of Oberon's revenge is the artistry of one who does not exactly know what he is setting in motion. An ass doesn't even appear on his list of odious sights.

The conqueror of the Amazons who bears himself almost as though he were Oberon's viceroy on earth (except that he has no knowledge of Oberon), Theseus opens *A Midsummer Night's Dream* with a brief speech also laced with irony.

> Now, fair Hippolyta, our nuptial hour
> Draws on apace. Four happy days bring in
> Another moon; but O, methinks, how slow
> This old moon wanes! She lingers my desires
> Like to a step-dame, or a dowager,
> Long withering out a young man's revenue. (1.1.1–6)

Without knowing it, Theseus himself introduces a practice later to run wild in the play: looking through the eyes of love. From his "methinks" it is no great leap to Helena's "Therefore I think I am not in the night" (2.1.222) and Hermia's "Methinks I see these things with parted eye, / When every thing seems double" (4.1.188–89). "Methinks" points to the realm of things perceived not with the eye but the mind's eye, like the dowager of Theseus's imagination who takes forever to die. Under any circumstances, likening the old moon to this tenacious matron would be strange and extravagant, but all the more when the one offering the simile disbelieves in poetry itself, as in this case. Furthermore, while the sympathies of the simile are all on the side of the young man whose hopes are being balked, as the scene unfolds the author of the simile sides with an old man blocking the hopes of his daughter and her beloved. In act 4 Theseus reverses himself again: "Egeus, I will overbear your will" (4.1.178). No doubt Theseus imagines himself a higher order of being than the mechanicals who contradict themselves so freely ("very tragical mirth" [5.1.57]), but he too contradicts himself freely. Of these ironies Theseus shows no awareness.

If the hierarchy of beings in *A Midsummer Night's Dream* features folly at all levels, at the middle level is a relationship of equality that accords beautifully with the play's impossibilities. How can a woman be the equal of her own conqueror? Nevertheless, Hippolyta is the equal of Theseus. By this I don't mean that she holds the same political power, but simply that she speaks to him with freedom. Hippolyta addresses Theseus not as a subject but a peer one with a mind of her own, unafraid to cross words with him. Throughout the play the two speak in counterpoint. As though love were still being fueled by war, this time a gentle war of words, these lovers have a way of taking contrary positions. Thus, no sooner does Theseus portray the moon as an old woman who lingers intolerably than Hippolyta takes the opposite view. If time is measured subjectively, why shouldn't the same four days that represent sheer delay for one represent a swift interlude for another?

Four days will quickly steep themselves in night,
Four nights will quickly dream away the time,
And then the moon, like to a silver bow
New bent in heaven, shall behold the night
Of our solemnities. (1.1.6–11)

Where Theseus describes the old moon, Hippolyta envisions the new—depicting it as the Amazonian weapon of choice, the bow.[3] Hippolyta's speech, we might say, is the equal and opposite of Theseus's. In the terms of the mechanicals, Theseus says "tedious," Hippolyta "brief." (So too, her image of the crescent is quite literal, his of the wealthy matron fantastically figurative.) Certainly no one else in the scene, or in the play, addresses Theseus with such easy and bold familiarity. Hoping to win his suit, Egeus fawns shamelessly. "Happy be Theseus, our renowned duke!" he says, going on to address the man with obsequious ceremony even as he seeks a judgment of death against his own daughter:

And, my gracious Duke,
Be it so she will not here before your Grace
Consent to marry with Demetrius,
I beg the ancient privilege of Athens. (1.1.20, 38–41)

Even Hermia and Lysander, the disobedient daughter and her disapproved lover, both impenitent, address Theseus as "my lord."

One exchange between Theseus and Hippolyta seems to have been included in *A Midsummer Night's Dream* for no other purpose than to illustrate a lovers' rivalry. "My love shall hear the music of my hounds," announces Theseus after observing the rite of May (4.1.106); but Hippolyta answers that no hounds can match the hounds of Sparta:

I was with Hercules and Cadmus once
When in a wood of Crete they bay'd the bear
With hounds of Sparta. Never did I hear
Such gallant chiding; for besides the groves,
The skies, the fountains, every region near
Seem'd all one mutual cry. (4.1.112–17)

Those were musical hounds. As though ducal dignity were at stake, Theseus replies that his hounds are just as gallant as those of Sparta because they *are* Spartan (giving the contest the aspect of a quarrel over nothing, as in fact it is, because the talked-of hunt never takes place), and the better to sing the nobility of these animals he launches into pure poetry:

My hounds are bred out of the Spartan kind:
So flew'd, so sanded, and their heads are hung
With ears that sweep away the morning dew;
Crook-knee'd, and dewlapp'd like Thessalian bulls;
Slow in pursuit, but matched in mouth like bells,
Each under each. (4.1.119–24)

Hounds like bulls and bells exist in the realm of poetry only. In the manner of the poet who "gives to aery nothing / A local habitation and a name" (5.1.16–17), Theseus sings his hounds into being only to abandon the hunt itself. Hippolyta has brought forth the bard in Theseus even if, in his own view, a bard is an ass.

The complications of the love plot resolved, Theseus cannot bring himself to believe the lovers' story, and in one of the play's most remembered speeches philosophizes on the fallacies of the imagination:

I never may believe
These antique fables, nor these fairy toys.
Lovers and madmen have such seething brains,
Such shaping fantasies, that apprehend
More than cool reason ever comprehends.
The lunatic, the lover, and the poet
Are of imagination all compact. (5.1.2–8)

(Theseus himself is so antique and fabulous a hero that he is mentioned in the *Odyssey* as among the ancients of the underworld [11.631].) This oration seems to make little impression on Hippolyta—as her rejoinders do not seem to register with him, except when she impugns his hounds—for she brushes it aside:

But all the story of the night told over,
And all their minds transfigur'd so together,
More witnesseth than fancy's images,
And grows to something of great constancy;
But howsoever, strange and admirable. (5.1.23–27)

Hippolyta reads the lovers' story very well—admirably. In this case there can be no question of her differing with her conqueror for the sake of differing, either. Hers is not just an excellent mind but one unclouded by resentment at losing herself to Theseus—a noble mind, well matched with the nobility of her position.

Before and during the performance of "Pyramus and Thisby," Hippolyta again addresses Theseus with the freedom of an equal, her words contesting his without rancor. As Theseus announces his choice of entertainment, the two engage in a verbal dance of differences:

> HIPPOLYTA: I love not to see wretchedness o'ercharged,
> And duty in his service perishing.
> THESEUS: Why, gentle sweet, you shall see no such thing.
> HIPPOLYTA: He says they can do nothing in this kind.
> THESEUS: The kinder we, to give them thanks for nothing.
> (5.1.85–89)

The voices clash yet somehow harmonize. In a similar exchange in the course of the performance itself, Hippolyta points out to Theseus the error of his dismissal of the imagination, but does so with such a light touch, such gentle authority that the force of her argument passes almost unnoticed:

> HIPPOLYTA: This is the silliest stuff that ever I heard.
> THESEUS: The best in this kind are but shadows; and the worst are no worse, if imagination amend them.
> HIPPOLYTA: It must be your imagination then, and not theirs.
> (5.1.210–14)

"How shall we find the concord of this discord?" asks Theseus earlier in the scene (5.1.60). His own marriage seems to be a concord in discord: a union between equals with distinctly different minds.

A Midsummer Night's Dream compromises the supremacy of Theseus the conquering hero not only by placing the fairy world beyond his ken, not only by giving Hippolyta but not him the wisdom to credit the lovers' story, but by making him, although an Athenian, a virtual contemporary of his own audience and thus depriving him of the ennobling effect of historical distance. By mingling ancient lore and village imagery, and by setting loose a local hobgoblin in the play's classical world, Shakespeare places this hero of the legendary past on almost the same plane as an audience composed of "men such as men are now." Pip of *Great Expectations,* the subject of the next chapter, sets his tale at a time in the past only to address his equals in the present. If the plot of *Great Expectations* turns on the accidental concurrence of two schemes of revenge, this doubling, involving a woman of wealth and an outcast, each a mystery to the other, is reminiscent of Shakespearean duplications. But it is *Hamlet,* a play filled with doublings and mirrors, that haunts *Great Expectations.*

As noted in the introduction, it is not Shakespeare's way to withhold information from the audience in the interest of raising suspense, as a novelist of a later day might do. The stage is for showing.[4] When in the special case of *Hamlet* Shakespeare does raise suspense, it is by keeping the hero himself in a state of indecision, suspension. Indeed, in the mystery of Hamlet's doubts and delays in the face of a mission that permits neither, it is as if Shakespeare had invented suspense. The very term suggests something "hung up," delayed, uncertain, as if coined with Hamlet expressly in mind. And what we term Hamlet's delays he himself experiences as a mode of ignorance—he does not yet "know [his] course," he dreads the ills "that we know not of," he does "not know / Why yet I live to say 'This thing's to do,'" as he reveals in soliloquies in successive acts (2.2.598; 3.1.81; 4.4.43–44); all of this not-knowing complicated by the irony that he must avenge a crime the world does not know of, while he does. The first of the nineteenth-century novels to be discussed here makes a principle of revealing things to the reader in the order they became known originally to the hero-narrator, which means keeping the reader in the condition of ignorance and uncertainty he himself was in. And the hero-narrator of *Great Expectations* is a kind of diminished Hamlet, an irresolute dreamer and, it turns out, an instrument of revenge. When in a powerful scene of *Great Expectations*—some say the most powerful in all of Dickens—Pip finally comes face-to-face with the one whose will he has been executing, the man's "large brown veinous hands" (39.320) are practically dramatized. "The hand of little employment hath the daintier sense" (*Hamlet* 5.1.69–70).

The hero of what may be the first bildungsroman in English fiction, Thackeray's *Pendennis*, says, "I take the world as it is, and being of it, will not be ashamed of it. If the time is out of joint, have I any calling or strength to set it right?"[5] Hamlet may or may not have the power to set his world right. Pip undoubtedly does not; but his story, a fully achieved bildungsroman, at least vividly dramatizes the incurable condition: inequality. Set some decades after the French Revolution and haunted with images of oppression and captivity, *Great Expectations* takes place in a world almost as stratified as Shakespeare's stage.

4

Great Expectations: *"Absolute Equality"*

Not only does Great Expectations *pose a powerful critique of inequality, but it subjects the reader, the hero, and everyone else in its world to the same condition of ignorance and error.*

Democracy of Ignorance

The Greek romance, of which *Callirhoe* is one, has been called "a latter-day epic for Everyman," the expression of an "equalitarian" age and outlook—and this in the derogatory sense that it adapted itself to "all kinds of values high and low" (as might be said of the mass media today) and addressed itself to readers reduced to an equal degree of insignificance.[1] But for whatever reason—perhaps romance's receptivity to values high and low—more sophisticated fiction has long felt a paradoxical attraction to romance as both its own origin and its favorite object of parody. Beginning with Heliodorus, author of the *Ethiopian Story*, and his ironic play on Chariton, a tradition of parody has shadowed romance like a double.[2] The pinnacle of the tradition is *Don Quixote* with its ridicule of romance, yet the energy of parody also runs through Fielding and Austen, Flaubert and Joyce, as if it were really inseparable from the novel itself. Each of the moderns discussed at length here composed anti-romances. In the case of Tolstoy we leave aside the anti-romance of *Anna Karenina* (its heroine like Callirhoe in the impossible position of being "married" to two men at once) to concentrate on two other works, one of which really is a latter-day epic, the other about a man of no apparent significance whatever. Both *Great Expectations* and *The Brothers Karamazov* are novels in which someone erroneously imagines himself a hero of romance and which draw power from fictions exposed as fictions. It is to the first of these anti-romances that this chapter addresses itself. Romantic visions bring forth in Pip, the hero of *Great Expectations*, the fraudulence, luxury, and loss of independence that Rousseau traces to inequality. Instead of anatomizing some institution like the law courts or the bureaucracy as in *Bleak House* and *Little Dorrit*, Dickens in *Great Expectations* investigates this original evil. Not only the content, however, but important compositional features of *Great Expectations*—in particular, its denial of privileged knowledge to anyone, including the reader—reflect the ideal of human equality.

If in the original romance, the *Odyssey*, knowledge is distributed unequally like a privilege (with the hero enjoying the patronage of a goddess who "know[s] all things" [13.417]), the anti-romance of *Great Expectations* institutes a kind of democracy of ignorance. Late in the novel, as the sun slants in on a group of condemned prisoners as well as the man who sentenced them, Pip remarks that both the judged and the judge "were passing on, with absolute equality, to the greater Judgment that knoweth all things and cannot err" (56.465). No one in *Great Expectations* knows all. Everyone seems in the dark on some critical point. Miss Havisham doesn't know where her ward Estella came from; Jaggers, otherwise so knowing, doesn't know the identity of Estella's father. (He "knew nothing" of Miss Havisham's design to use Pip as a plaything, either [44.363].) Estella herself knows nothing of either parent. Magwitch doesn't know of his daughter's existence.[3] Of Magwitch, Miss Havisham seems to know only the identity of his lawyer (44.363) and the sole condition attached to Pip's legacy, that he keep his name (19.160); of Miss Havisham, Magwitch knows nothing. Neither knows they have a common betrayer. Magwitch, on his return to England, "had no perception of the possibility of [Pip's] finding any fault with [his] good fortune" (41.343), and dies without realizing that his property, his life's work, is forfeited to the crown. Herbert knows the story of Miss Havisham only in part and doesn't know that Pip, and later Miss Havisham, have underwritten him. Asked to relate the story of Jaggers's housekeeper, Wemmick answers, "I don't know her story—that is, I don't know all of it" (48.398). Joe doesn't know Pip's history with Magwitch or, later, his feeling for Biddy. As befits the hero of such a tale of blindness, Pip himself is a sort of concentrated essence of ignorance, unaware of the identity of his patron, unable to fathom Miss Havisham's campaign against a world that made her suffer ("she was perfectly incomprehensible to me," he says after his first visit to Satis House [9.65]), and prey to his own delusions.

Lest Pip's ignorance induce in us the complacency of superior knowledge, however, we ourselves discover things only as he does. The privileges of "Helios, who sees all things" are not ours. In recounting his visit to Circe's island, Odysseus describes the transformation of his men into swine even though he never witnessed the event and received no report of it. As Homer's deputy, he simply assumes a temporary privilege of omniscience. Only after the fact, when it is too late, can Pip put together the tale of his youth, and in so doing he takes pains to reveal only so much as he actually knew at each stage of it.[4] In this respect *Great Expectations* differs from Dickens's other "autobiographical" novel, *David Copperfield*, where "although every scene is brilliantly rendered through David's eyes, as it seemed to him at the moment, there is . . . often a kind of lucid double exposure shading it with the hidden future."[5] Dostoevsky once observed that if an artist imagines an event from the past, he will imagine it "in its completed aspect, that is, with the addition of all its subsequent developments that had not yet occurred at the historical moment in which the artist was trying to depict a person or event."[6] *Great Expectations* resists this fallacy of the historical imagination at every point. Those of us who grew up with the tale and take its construction for granted (and now read back into the unfolding plot what we already know of its outcome, under the influence of the effect Dostoevsky describes) may have lost sight of the subtlety and boldness of Dickens's experiment. The experiment consists in subjecting the reader, Pip, and everyone else in *Great Expectations* to one and the same condition of ignorance, and doing so in recognition of their—our—common humanity. It was Dickens's belief that we are all "connected by fate without knowing it."[7]

In his influential *Theory of Justice,* John Rawls presents a contract theory wherein persons in a condition of equality establish the very principles of justice. But in order for this to take place, each of these founders can have no knowledge of the benefits to be derived from any particular principle.

> For example, if a man knew he was wealthy, he might find it rational to advance the principle that various taxes for welfare measures might be counted unjust; if he knew that he was poor, he would most likely propose the contrary principle. To represent the desired restrictions, one imagines a situation in which everyone is deprived of this sort of information.[8]

Ignorance is the correlate of equality. But how could a person be rich or poor and not know it? This question doesn't really concern John Rawls, as he proposes such conditions as a conceptual device, nothing more. It would take a Dickens to work out situations where someone is rich or poor without knowing it. In *Great Expectations* Pip thinks he is rich until he discovers otherwise, and, as noted, his patron Magwitch dies without knowing that his wealth is not his. In *Great Expectations* the veil of ignorance, as Rawls calls it, is no exercise in abstraction but a given of experience—a condition binding, moreover, on the reader and narrator as though they were themselves parties to a literary contract.

Perhaps the first narrative in our literature where the reader is kept in uncertainty for the purpose of building up interest and suspense is the last of the surviving Greek romances, Heliodorus's *Ethiopian Story,* an artfully constructed tale of the ordeals of love and the revelation of identity. Mindful of the *Odyssey,* Heliodorus begins in the middle of things, but this time we must wait to understand the beginning. Only later do we discover how it is that two lovers, Theagenes and Chariclea, happen to be found by brigands at the mouth of the Nile. But despite its drama and delayed revelations, such a romance as the *Ethiopian Story* is not really a template for *Great Expectations*. I don't mean solely that the *Ethiopian Story* tells a tale of love and *Great Expectations* of love unreturned, or that the former is set well in the past and the latter on the verge of the present, or even that a divine plan governs events in the ancient novel while the plot of the modern is driven by mortals. Chariclea discovers her identity when we do, in book 4 of a tale in ten books, and what she discovers is that she is the daughter of the king and queen of Ethiopia. In Pip there is no royalty, and his way of making the reader his equal in knowledge and fellow in discovery seems connected with the critique of an unequal society posed by his tale. The *Ethiopian Story* has been called a tale of "incomplete cognition."[9] In *Great Expectations* people fail to know not because destiny is written in riddles but because they themselves are fallible and their corrupted world lacks transparency; or as we might say, in an unequal world defective understanding is the last equality. Under the power of this sentiment, Dickens reinvents the novel in *Great Expectations* as the narrative form of imperfect knowledge.[10]

How the world lost transparency Rousseau attempts to explain in the *Discourse on Inequality*. Once "the inequality of fortunes [and] the use and abuse of riches" became an established fact, "it was necessary in one's own interest to seem to be other than one was in reality. Being and appearance became two entirely different things, and from this distinction arose insolent ostentation, deceitful cunning, and all the vices that follow in their train."[11] In other words, it is due to the corruption of moral sentiments as a result of the evolution of property that the world now presents treacherously misleading appearances of the kind that prove so fateful in Pip's story. Of Rousseau's exposé of civilization, John Stuart Mill wrote within two years of *Great Expectations*:

> There lay in [it], and has floated down the stream of opinion along with it, a considerable amount of exactly those truths which the popular opinion wanted; and these are the deposit which was left behind when the flood subsided. The superior worth of simplicity of life, the enervating and demoralising effect of the trammels and hypocrisies of artificial society, are ideas which have never been entirely absent from cultivated minds since Rousseau wrote.[12]

And these ideas are written into *Great Expectations*. The fawning, parasitism, insolence, and insincerity rife in *Great Expectations* are the unmistakable signs of a corrupted and unequal society, just as the different treatment received at the hands of the law by Magwitch and his partner—actually superior—in crime exposes the system of vicious distinctions in the tale's world. At their first meeting Pip and Estella play Beggar My Neighbor. Beggaring your neighbor is the very theme and logic of civilized life, according to Rousseau.[13] When Rousseau goes on to remark that under the regime of corruption even masters are slaves, he chronicles before the fact Pip's relation to his own liveried servant ("the Avenger") in London.

Along with the loss of transparency goes the disappearance of what Jean Starobinski in his study of Rousseau terms immediacy: the state in which nothing comes between self and others.[14] In *Great Expectations* the loss of immediacy reveals itself in the use of agents, intermediaries, pawns, doubles (the two Wemmicks), displacements (as Pip stands in for the male sex in the eyes of Miss Havisham), as well as masks of all kinds. With so much virtually bureaucratic complication besetting their relations, no wonder people in *Great Expectations* labor behind a veil of ignorance. This satiric profusion of false relationships is a symptom of a disordered world. With Joe Gargery, a man who speaks and acts for himself and neither exploits others nor employs masks, we get immediacy, and it is significant that Joe's occupation of blacksmithing is virtually a form of undivided labor in *Great Expectations*. Rousseau associates the inception of inequality with the division of labor.

Once civilization is envisioned as a kind of joint-stock company of hypocrisy, conspiracy theory becomes a possibility, and Rousseau in fact came to believe in the existence of a conspiracy against himself. As Dickens's vision darkened, he "developed a view of the world as almost totally in the grip of a gigantic conspiracy which takes myriad forms but of which the sole effect is to thwart and stifle human freedom."[15] But the critic here quoted applies this observation to *Bleak House* and *Little Dorrit*, among other works, not to *Great Expectations*. It does not apply to *Great Expectations* because, as noted, that novel does not anatomize the institutions of oppression so much as search out the evil—inequality—responsible for oppression in the first place. What is more, while Pip is caught in two schemes that fit perfectly quite as if their authors had plotted it all out like conspirators, the fact is that Magwitch and Miss Havisham inhabit different spheres, never meet, never concert their plans, are too obsessed in any case to coordinate their actions with anyone, and know nothing or next to nothing about one another. Such is the ignorance that runs through this tale of persons linked without knowing it.

Standard Categories and Fixed Distinctions

Considered by many the summit of Dickens's art, *Great Expectations* is the troubled story of Pip—his early and lasting association with a convict, his hopeless love of the marmoreal Estella, his weakness of character in the face of those who prey on his romantic illusions and use him for their own ends. It is a tale of wonders, roughly evocative of the Greek original of the modern novel (which also features orphaned children exposed to the force of events). In the open narrative space of the Greek romance such motifs as the fateful coincidence, the reversal of fortune, and the dramatic recognition figure large, released from the logic and compression of tragedy. In *Great Expectations* it is as though these motifs resumed their tragic significance. Both *Great Expectations* and the ancient romance can be described as an extended tale, told for its own sake, relating "the adventures or experiences of one or more individuals in their private capacities and from the viewpoint of their private interests and emotions."[16]

In one respect, indeed, *Great Expectations* is truer to this definition than the original, for it really is told in the first person. If a Greek romance were told in the words of either the hero or the heroine, the parity between the two, both spiritual and erotic, might well be disrupted. As it is, such concordance exists between these figures that they fall in love at the same moment. As chance would have it (and the factor of chance figures ironically, in one way or another, in all of the nineteenth-century works considered here), Callirhoe and Chaereas "walked headlong into each other at the corner of a narrow intersection—a meeting contrived by the god to make sure that they saw each other. They fell in love at first sight: . . . beauty had been matched with nobility" (*Callirhoe* 31). So it is in the *Ethiopian Story* as well: love comes in at the eye. "At the moment of meeting the young pair [Theagenes and Chariclea] looked and loved, as though the soul of each at the first encounter recognized its fellow. . . . [They gazed] with eyes intently fixed on each other, as if they had had some previous knowledge or sight which they were recalling to memory."[17] While Pip feels a profound affinity with Estella, with whom his memories are bound up, she does not with him.[18] That imbalance alone indicates the tale's ironic attitude toward the ancient conventions of romance that still influence its shape. Pip's hopeless infatuation with this inanimate being might be taken as a darker variant of the sort of imprisonment within a private mental system that makes others in the Dickens world comical. Theagenes and Chariclea, Chaereas and Callirhoe are carried off to distant places; Estella is herself distant, remote, alien.

Besides being told in the first person, *Great Expectations* is distinguished from the ancient romance by a number of factors, one of which claims special notice. In the most dramatic scene of *Callirhoe,* where Chaereas (presumed dead) comes forward in a courtroom, the spectators feel exactly what the actors in the scene do. They rejoice with the defendant, now proven innocent; grieve with the plaintiff; and "about Callirhoe they were baffled" (267), as she herself is. Readers of *Callirhoe* are assumed to have the same set of responses. Dickens is not content that the readers of *Great Expectations* should feel what Pip felt, but additionally, and in contrast to Chariton, makes sure that we know only what Pip knew at each moment. So conscious is Pip of his duty not to smuggle later knowledge into his narration that he apologizes for introducing into his first description of Miss Havisham details that he registered perhaps a minute later.

> It was not in the first few moments that I saw all these things, though I saw more of them in the first moments than might be supposed. . . . It was when I stood before her, avoiding her eyes, that I took note of the surrounding objects in detail. (8.57)

In allowing us to know only what he himself knew at the time, not what he came to know afterward, Pip gives the tale the character of a drama of discovery and makes us a partner in that discovery. Or as we might say, by denying the reader all knowledge except that acquired by the hero in the stages of his experience, Dickens grounds *our* knowledge in experience. Locke in the preface to the *Essay Concerning Human Understanding* likens himself not to Newton but to "an under-labourer . . . clearing the ground a little, and removing some of the rubbish that lies in the way to knowledge." In its modesty and reduced ambition, this statement has something in common with the note of *Great Expectations,* itself a tale of the clearing of illusions. (The Lockean principle that "each individual has a radically private language"[19] yields in Dickens's pages a society of solipsists—people enclosed in their own mental world, whether like Joe, who can read only his own name and really does speak a dialect all his own, or Miss Havisham, a woman of passion forever dwelling on her own injury.) If Locke seeks to ascertain the scope and limits of human knowledge, Dickens brings home to us the imperfect nature of our knowledge not only by denying complete knowledge to anyone in the tale, including its prime movers, but by having our narrator report things as they appeared to him at the time—a fictional version of Locke's historical method. Locke's concern is to settle the foundations of human knowledge, Dickens's to authenticate, as it were, both Pip's knowledge and our own by the living-through of illusion.

The principal source of the young Pip's illusions is his assumption that his life is following the script of romance word for word—that he has been vouchsafed a conventional remarkable destiny. "She reserved it for me . . . to do all the shining deeds of the young Knight of romance, and marry the Princess" (29.234). With the formulas of romance stamped indelibly on his imagination, he misinterprets appearances in a kind of quixotic manner and dupes himself as completely as the grotesques of the Dickens world driven by fictions of their own invention. At the root of his error is the belief that he has for some reason been singled out for the high privileges of romance, and still more fundamentally a belief that conventions of romance laid down long ago govern his life in the present moment. By the time of the tale's telling he has outgrown these delusions of his youth (being capable of change, unlike those Dickensian creations who seem like stuck clocks) and shares his author's sense of the insufficiency of standard formulas and categories. If Wordsworth, transposing the revolutionary critique of artificial distinctions to literature, disputed the categorical distinction between poetry and prose, *Great Expectations* throws into question the social differences that anchor the traditional distinction between comedy and tragedy. The work has both tragic and comic passages. Not even the primary distinction between narrative and drama remains quite secure in *Great Expectations.*

A novel told in the first person, in the voice of "a man speaking to men," possesses something of the charged immediacy, the powerful illusion of presence, of the drama.[20] Moreover, even while telling of change over time (a "pip" after all being a seed), *Great Expectations* employs what we might call dramatic time—the foreshortening that makes for the swift catastrophes of tragedy and the sudden, nonnaturalistic reversals of drama generally. Pip's near-death in the attempt to smuggle Magwitch out of England ushers in a change of character almost as dramatic, in the strict sense of the word, as Hamlet's conversion to a man of action aboard a ship bearing him to England and his own death—a change of the greatest consequence, too, for the Pip who emerges from this disaster is in fact the narrator of *Great Expectations.* At certain points of crisis like this one in *Great Expectations,* time loses the gradualism that otherwise governs a long tale of a boy becoming a man. Events themselves become dramatic. That Pip lives to tell of his trials, and tell of them in the voice of a composed self, means only that *Great Expectations* does not conform to the model of tragedy which dictates that the hero die. A fictional autobiography, a tragedy with comic inflections, an anti-romance that cannot abandon romance itself, *Great Expectations* will not be encompassed by any conventional category, instead fusing different categories into a unity corresponding to that of a person qualified by his unusual nature to speak as a man to men.

According to M. M. Bakhtin, neither can the hero of a novel be fitted into a single category. Such a hero "cannot become once and for all a clerk, a landowner, a merchant, a fiancé, a jealous lover, a father, and so forth," lest he lose both the capacity *for* becoming and the "surplus of humanness" that distinguishes him from a lesser figure.[21] In keeping with his own "surplus of humanness," Pip (who never does become a blacksmith) possesses a mixed nature and an abundance of conflicting potentials. Capable of warmth and frigidity, loyalty and ingratitude, generosity and meanness, impulse and delay, he is characterized by his friend Herbert Pocket as "a good fellow, with impetuosity and hesitation, boldness and diffidence, action and dreaming, curiously mixed in him" (30.251). And just as it is the singularity of his nature, and the unique contradictions of a character "at once effeminate and inflexible"[22] that give the story of Rousseau—the great defender of human equality—its claim to universality, so the curious mixture of Pip's qualities serves to make him an exemplary figure. If Pip is a kind of Everyman, this is not because he is a bare shell of a human being but on the contrary because of his "surplus" of conflicting possibilities. And if he himself were not so overfilled with potential, so indeterminate, his tale would be less charged with uncertainty as well.

Ironically, what qualifies Pip to speak in the first person as the narrator of *Great Expectations* is exactly the lack of that identity certified by tokens like the hero's pin, scar, and bow in the *Odyssey,* or confirmed by trial in the Greek romance—the identity unaltered by events. A mark of Pip's unsettled identity is the multitude of his names and titles, from Handel to Sir to Dear boy to the incongruous Mr. Pip. When Joe calls Pip both Sir and Pip in the same utterance as though addressing both a friend and a superior (27.225), he touches on a division in Pip's being even as he dramatizes his own fantastic oddity. Finally Pip suffers not from an excess of names but from false consciousness—that state of self-delusion known to literature well before it became the malady of those in denial of the political truth. The identity behind the first-person narration of *Great Expectations* is not given from the beginning and does not await the hero at the end as the reward of his labors, but constitutes the record of those labors themselves, the living-through of his delusions. But this is also to say that his is the identity of one at variance with himself.

As Bakhtin writes of the Greek novels, "the hammer of events shatters nothing and forges nothing—it merely tries the durability of an already finished product."[23] Hammer and forge figuring as potent images within its pages, *Great Expectations* tells a different story. Not only is Pip scarred by his ordeals both physically and morally (for events in all their violence register on him deeply), but these ordeals do not test an identity already in place but confound the formation of identity itself. It is Estella who seems to possess the unchanging nature of a constructed thing. She virtually refers to herself as a finished product. ("I am what you have made me," she says to Miss Havisham [38.308–9].) Pip for his part is exposed to pressures from so many sides, and is so liable to delusion, that he barely comes to identity at all, and even that is shattered by the return of Magwitch. Magwitch's scheme is internally contradictory to boot. Bestowing his fortune on Pip because the young Pip "acted nobly" (39.321) but fostering all that is least noble in him by feeding his pretensions, Magwitch deepens the "confused division of mind" (18.147) that was Pip's even before his change of fortune and elicits the conflict of motives that makes Pip the roundest character in *Great Expectations*. One describable as "a good fellow, with impetuosity and hesitation, boldness and diffidence, action and dreaming, curiously mixed in him" is far from a finished identity.

Fittingly for one of so mixed a nature, Pip also seems innocent and guilty in the same measure. He is innocent in the sense of being unaware of others' designs on him at the very time that he loses his innocence to luxury and dissipation. Though he really is the plaything of other wills, caught up in plots he doesn't understand or even know of, in neither his own nor the reader's eyes is Pip blameless. In accordance with its ironic handling of the conventions of romance (conventions that still live in its pages, however), *Great Expectations* thus troubles the question of innocence in ways that romance itself cannot contemplate. Most ironically, Pip is responsible for playing out his role in Magwitch's design in spite of being ignorant of its existence. As further evidence of his "surplus of humanness," innocence and guilt are curiously mixed in Pip.

When his improbable sister is struck down with the shackle once worn by the convict Magwitch, Pip blames himself since he was the one who supplied Magwitch the means to file it off. As the novel progresses and Pip is drawn ever more deeply into the role of unwitting player in others' designs, the guilt here linked so strangely with innocence itself comes into its own. Supposing Miss Havisham his sponsor when in fact his money comes from Magwitch ("I worked hard that you should be above work" [39.324]), he starts to become the spoiled child of privilege that he imagines his appointed character. Guilt preys on him all the same. "I lived in a state of chronic uneasiness respecting my behaviour to Joe. My conscience was not comfortable by any means about Biddy" (34.275). "My lavish habits led [Herbert's] easy nature into expenses that he could not afford, corrupted the simplicity of his life, and disturbed his peace with anxieties and regrets" (34.276). When Magwitch returns and declares himself, he is met with the frigid snobbery he unintentionally helped nurture. Yet Pip's crime of ingratitude, first to Joe and Biddy, then to Magwitch, begins in the naive belief that he is following a script that has been laid down for him. Where innocence in the Greek romance is the seal of identity, now the very innocence of Pip's romantic delusions makes for his betrayal of both others and self. That he really believes himself chosen to rise in life (that is, rise above others), because circumstances conspire against his weak points and play tricks on his mind, makes him invest himself all the more in the role of the chosen one. It is as if Dickens turned innocence against itself, much as Tolstoy turns the blamelessly conventional (and also falsely scripted) life of the hero against him in "The Death of Ivan Ilych," a tragedy in prose. It is tragedy after all that searches the paradox of guilt in innocence, that portrays a hero both sinned against and sinning, blind to his own actions (as with Oedipus) but responsible all the same. All of this is true in some sense of Pip in *Great Expectations*, guilty of much but subjected to fire, flood, and at last delirium, beyond all deserving. And the last of these crises reads like a deprivation of knowledge. "I knew [illness] was coming on me now, and I knew very little else" (57.468). "Whether I had two or three times come to myself on the staircase with great terror, not knowing how I had got out of bed"—this in itself Pip does not know (57.469). Confronted by two men arresting him for debt, he says, "I don't know you." "I don't know what they did, except that they forebore to remove me" (57.469). As though his very knowledge had to collapse like his fantasy of distinction, the purgation of Pip's pride calls for the destruction of his knowledge as well.

Not only, then, does Dickens make an unknown the hero of *Great Expectations*, but he subjects that unknown to overpowering, virtually tragic forces. Naturally, though, this is tragedy with a difference. First of all, simply as a tale that keeps us in uncertainty, *Great Expectations* cannot be a tragedy where fate descends on a hero inevitably—inevitably, if only because known to the audience in advance. In this respect the original tragic figures are the warriors at Troy, caught up in a fate that became legendary. Tragic are the tales of Achilles, who gets his wish that the Greek forces should feel his absence; of Hector, whose death is his city's ruin. In the case of Agamemnon's fatal homecoming we have a tale so completely foreknown that in the first book of the *Odyssey* it is already taken to be common knowledge. In the clarity of retrospect we watch each figure—Achilles, Hector, Agamemnon—somehow achieving his own destruction. The original heroes of tragic drama likewise belonged to the past, their tales in some sense already given. Tragic heroes are also subjected to fatal forces. By making Hamlet so reluctant to execute his father's decree (as though he sought to preserve his freedom in the face of the role imposed on him by tragedy itself), Shakespeare introduces a new suspense into the tragic form. *Great Expectations* is in that tradition, except that Pip receives no decree at all.

Then too, Pip is not the only one in *Great Expectations* to be exposed to overpowering forces. The same principle of equality responsible for Dickens's choice of a commoner to present his autobiography (as Rousseau, a former valet, had done) also dictates that Pip cannot have the honors of tragic distinction to himself. For if Pip seems singled out for suffering, what of Magwitch, his tormentor and patron? Like a tragic figure who undergoes simply too much suffering, Magwitch in the course of his lifelong ordeal undergoes hunger, imprisonment, exile, self-imposed hard labor, recapture, and sentence of death, the greater part of his life being dedicated to the tragic, because self-defeating, passion of revenge. The uncomplaining way in which Magwitch meets his death sentence, and death itself, not only illustrates tragic acceptance but sets a precedent for the ironic but unembittered tone of Pip's very narrative; and just as Magwitch "never . . . tried to bend the past out of its eternal shape" (56.463), so Pip refuses to falsify the past by revealing what became known only later.

As *Joseph Andrews* nears its contrived resolution (whereby the identities of the lovers are established following the ancient conventions of romance), hero and heroine "felt perhaps little less anxiety . . . than Oedipus himself whilst his fate was revealing."[24] In *Great Expectations* Pip really is seized with anxiety as the sponsor of his fortunes reveals himself, and the reader seized with suspense. Here discovery is stripped of the comic character it assumes in *Joseph Andrews* and invested with the power of a tragic effect.[25] (Both Pip and Magwitch, like Oedipus, run into the very thing they are in flight from.) In this scene, of which it has been said that "Dickens seems to draw together lines from the whole of his created universe to make [it] the highest manifestation of his artistic capacity,"[26] the former convict Magwitch, returned from Australia, claims Pip as his foster son, first asking him what property, and whose property, the young man has inherited. "I don't know" is the answer given to both questions (39.323). At that point Magwitch confronts him with indisputable evidence that he, Magwitch, and no one else has been the young man's underwriter. As if Dickens had completely ironized the romance tradition originating in the *Odyssey* of the use of tokens to confirm identity, the returned convict presents his proofs to a "son" overcome with horror and disgust.

> "Concerning a guardian," he went on. "There ought to have been some guardian or such-like, whiles you was a minor. Some lawyer maybe. As to the first letter of that lawyer's name, now. Would it be J?"
>
> All the truth of my position came flashing on me; and its disappoint-

ments, dangers, disgraces, consequences of all kinds, rushed in in such a multitude that I was borne down by them and had to struggle for every breath I drew. (39.323–24)

Maybe it is a flaw in *Great Expectations* that it places Pip in the tragic position of one who experiences a shattering recognition (and "recognition is best when it occurs simultaneously with a reversal," according to Aristotle), when the greater capacity for both action and suffering belongs in fact to Magwitch. But it can be argued that Dickens divides the honors of the tragic position between Pip and Magwitch—that he is too modern, too un-Ptolemaic as a matter of literary practice, to make the tale revolve around a single hero who engrosses all of its tragic potential.

The description of Pip as a kind of impulsive John-a-dreams—one with "impetuosity and hesitation, boldness and diffidence, action and dreaming, curiously mixed in him"—establishes him as a descendant, however remote, of the richest and most enigmatic self in literature, the exemplar of hesitation but also a bold antagonist, Hamlet. At one point Pip attends a farcical performance of *Hamlet* in which, when the Prince asks whether it is nobler in the mind to suffer, "some roared yes, and some no, and some inclining to both opinions said 'toss up for it' " (31.257). For the reader and for Dickens there is a lot more of *Hamlet* in the surrounding pages of *Great Expectations,* with its tale of a young man enlisted into his foster father's campaign of revenge against the destroyers of his life. (So too, when Pip remarks on Herbert Pocket's untroubled way of bearing "all blows and buffets" [22.186], that companion and confidant momentarily becomes Horatio; the troubled mind belonging to Pip-Hamlet.) Hamlet is at cross-purposes with himself, Pip subjected to the conflicting purposes of others and made miserable by a "confused division of mind" (18.147).[27]

If Pip with his erratic shifts between "action" and "dreaming" necessarily brings to mind Hamlet, the convict who makes his entrance among the graves, as though one of the walking dead, and whose Christian name Abel speaks of fratricide, conveys echoes of the Ghost. In the commands of the Ghost, the will of the dead threatens to dominate the will of the living, and had Magwitch been less driven, he might have taken the conventional way of rewarding Pip: by leaving him a fortune in a will, also an instrument by which the dead have their way with the living. That Magwitch seeks in life what is a prerogative of death suggests that he himself exists in a state of death-in-life. And so it proves. Doomed by a society with one law for the rich and one for the poor, Magwitch leads the existence of a living ghost in *Great Expectations,* appearing from nowhere, disappearing for a large stretch of the tale though haunting Pip all the same, then reappearing to Pip and Herbert, whom he swears to secrecy like the Ghost in *Hamlet,* while all but invisible to the world at large. With his return from penal exile for the purpose of seeing Pip, Magwitch is liable to arrest and execution at any moment. Tragedy gravitates to the boundaries of human existence—in *Hamlet,* the edge of a cliff, the verge of suicide, the bank of a fast-running stream, the brink of a grave, the limits of endurance. More than any-one else, it is the commoner Abel Magwitch, living as if in the presence of death, who dramatizes those boundaries in *Great Expectations.*

Unknowns

Driving the plot of *Great Expectations* is not divine providence or the abstract power of Fortune but the designs, the plots, of human agents, especially Miss Havisham's scheme to enslave Pip's heart to Estella and Magwitch's project of making a gentle-man of him, also for purposes of revenge. Miss Havisham tortures him, Magwitch pampers him. (That these two—one born to wealth and one to poverty—are sim-ilarly driven and have the same betrayer, that their lives converge on Pip, that one goes from wealth to self-imprisonment and the other from imprisonment to wealth—this is Dickens's Discourse on Inequality.) Because Pip does not under-stand these designs and because they work together as if their authors conspired, each exploiting a weakness of his constitution (romantic infatuation on the one hand, snobbishness on the other)—their combined effect is to sap his autonomy and confuse him to the core. The dramatic effect of the recognition scene is the greater for his entanglement in this fantastic web.

It is thus the coincidence of two plots—Miss Havisham's revenge against the male sex and Magwitch's revenge against the society that cast him out—that places the young Pip at the mercy of forces he can neither master nor even comprehend, a mariner shaken by two Poseidons. And what makes the coincidence a genuine one (44.363) is that despite their both having been betrayed by one Compeyson, nei-ther Miss Havisham nor Magwitch really knows anything of the other. In a work whose author attended carefully to the question of who knows what, this mutual ig-norance is clearly essential to the narrative design. Knowledge itself in *Great Expec-tations* seems to be qualified with ignorance. When, over their first dinner together, Herbert tells Pip the story of Miss Havisham, he ends with a string of disclaimers.

> "[What was in the letter Miss Havisham received] I can't tell you, because I don't know. . . . Indeed I know only so much, through piecing it out my-self. . . . Mind! I don't know that. . . . I don't know. . . . I know no more." (22.183–84)

When the returned Magwitch delivers his story to Pip and Herbert, in the process mentioning that his nemesis Compeyson "had been in a bad thing with a rich lady some years before" (42.351), he seems not even to know the woman's name. It is Herbert, after the recital, who informs Pip, "Compeyson is the man who professed to be Miss Havisham's lover" (42.356). So too, although Miss Havisham adopts Magwitch's daughter, she has no knowledge that she *is* Magwitch's daughter. She simply informs the lawyer Jaggers

> "that I wanted a little girl to rear and love, and save from my fate. . . . He told me that he would look about him for such an orphan child. One night he brought her here asleep, and I called her Estella." (49.406)

Later, Pip informs Jaggers, "I know more of the history of Miss Havisham's adopted child than Miss Havisham herself does" (51.416). In sum, neither of the revengers who use Pip for their own conflicting ends knows even the name of the other, much less the depths of the other's motivation. So fully committed is Dickens to the portrayal of unknowns that he makes these two movers of *Great Expectations* unknown to one another. Had Dickens (or Pip) made known from the beginning just how events fit together in *Great Expectations,* the reader would have been placed in the position of understanding what no one in the world of the tale does—not even Jaggers, who numbers both Miss Havisham and Magwitch among his clients, and who habitually acts as if he "knew all kinds of things" to the disadvantage of everyone else (18.140; 20.165). In the novel as we have it, such false superiority is precluded.

Pip's ignorance is our own, then; and all of the ignorance in *Great Expectations* seems to converge in Pip—a Hamlet now oppressed by a lack of knowledge. Underlying all the affinities between *Hamlet* and *Great Expectations*—the irresolution of the heroes (each burdened with guilt), the haunting of each by a "father" who somehow returns from the land of no return (in the case of the exiled Magwitch, Australia)—is the reduction of Hamlet and Pip to instruments of another's vengeful will, with the critical difference that Pip doesn't even know he is being used, and used by two implacable wills and not just one. (However, we might regard the two revenge plots of *Great Expectations* as a reflection of the kind of doubling that is everywhere in *Hamlet* itself.) Hamlet of course is subjected to the demand—delivered with the greatest possible rhetorical force—that he avenge the murder of his father. With some two months elapsing between his receipt of this solemn charge and the beginning of act 2, Hamlet's hesitation suggests an attempt to preserve his own freedom in the face of an irresistible force. The drama of the play deepens as Hamlet, even after verifying the Ghost's word, delays the execution of his revenge.

Unlike Hamlet, Pip does not delay the execution of a vengeful command but fulfills only too well, if unwittingly, the role assigned him in Magwitch's vendetta against the society that ruined his life. An unknowing instrument of revenge, Pip also serves as an object of Miss Havisham's vendetta against the male sex (Dickens's concern in both cases evidently being the complete subjection of a life to the purposes of another). Suspense comes with the working out of these cross-plots, the resolution of identities, and Pip's shattering discovery of the truth about his rise to wealth and imaginary distinction. Hamlet's shattering discovery is made in his conference with the Ghost in act 1; later, after considerable intrigue, the Ghost is discovered to be the spirit of Hamlet's father that he appeared to begin with. The suspense of *Hamlet* is not the suspense of awaited discovery. While both Hamlet and Pip are trapped in a riddle, the first suffers from an excess, the second from a deficiency of knowledge. But in a sense, not-knowing is a fit response to a world where the traditional certainties of social position seem to have given way. If Pip had become a blacksmith (as Joe did, following in the footsteps of his father), if Magwitch had never reinvented himself as a sheep farmer in Australia, if Miss Havisham had accepted the role of a spinster that misfortune seemed to consign her to—if the social positions of an unequal world remained stable—Pip's experience would probably never have supported a tale of suspense and surprise in the first place. In this respect it is the shock to traditional distinctions that is responsible for *Great Expectations*.

In the course of Pip's discoveries we ourselves learn just how little we knew about Magwitch, and how viciously he has been dealt with by the authorities whose public face is one of rectitude. Pip himself is unknown to history, and it may be fitting that while tested to the limits of endurance and beyond, he experiences the humble and anticlimactic fate of survival rather than a tragic death. (Somewhat analogously, in *War and Peace* the city of Moscow burns and comes back to life rather than suffering a tragic death like the Homeric city of Troy.) As an unknown, Pip does not have the sort of visibility that makes the godlike heroes of Homer a spectacle for the gods themselves—though at the same time objects of divine enmity—and makes the tragic hero a lightning rod for forces greater than human life can bear. The greatness of tragic figures places them as it were too near the gods for their own good, gods who then remind them that they are merely human. Hamlet's father had

> Hyperion's curls, the front of Jove himself,
> An eye like Mars, to threaten and command,
> A station like the herald Mercury
> New lighted on a heaven-kissing hill (3.4.56–59),

only to die miserably in a state of sin. In the ironic world of tragedy, it is death that sets the final seal of greatness on a human life. There is something of the antihero in Odysseus, not just because he appears before us in rags as one beneath notice but because (according to the prophecy of Tiresias) he will die "in / some altogether unwarlike way . . . in the ebbing time of a sleek old age" (11.135–37).

Only survivors can tell their story. After he and Penelope resume "their old ritual" (23.296), Odysseus tells her the story of his adventures. The hero whose greatness is sealed with death must have his story told by another, as Horatio lives on at Hamlet's request to tell his (Hamlet's) story to the world. To bring out the distinction between Tolstoy and Dostoevsky's views of death, Bakhtin asks himself how the latter would have composed Tolstoy's tale "Three Deaths." He can only conclude that "Dostoevsky would never have depicted three *deaths*" in the first place, for in Dostoevsky's world "death cannot function as something that finalizes and elucidates life," as in tragedy.

> Death in the Tolstoyan interpretation of it is totally absent from Dostoevsky's world. Dostoevsky would not have depicted the deaths of his heroes, but the *crises* and *turning points* in their lives; that is, he would have depicted their lives *on the threshold*.[28]

Death itself cannot be depicted because events in the Dostoevskian world are presented as though in the words of the characters themselves—the author having renounced the pretense of standing above them and writing about them—and no one can narrate his or her own death.[29] Autobiography cannot end in death; and Pip, as a fictional autobiographer, cannot have a classically tragic fate. (In this he is upstaged by Magwitch, who dies in a state of acceptance, beyond all excuses, defenses, and arguments.) Like a character in Dostoevsky, who in fact has a definite affinity with Dickens,[30] Pip is shown in crises and at turning points; and in accordance with the prosaics of the novel, the humble task of telling his story falls not to Horatio but to Pip himself.

Tragic and Comic

Among the great ironies of the *Iliad* is that between the two warring armies there is no distinction in ethos or valor, which is to say that they are each worthy of the other—equally heroic. Heroism itself, it seems, implies a certain standard of equality. At one point in book 12 of the *Iliad,* the well-matched armies are likened to equal weights of wool in the hands of a woman laboring for her children (12.430–36). To say that the *Odyssey* lacks the tragic character of the *Iliad* is to note, among other things, that it contains no equal or rival against whom Odysseus can be tested. (For that matter, neither does it feature the contest of god against god, as in the *Iliad.*) But if heroes are to be measured against one another on the field of war, does this not imply that heroism itself is in some way self-negating?

In the twelfth book of the *Iliad,* the middle of the poem, Hector leads a counterattack against the Greek forces. He does not know—although we do, privy to the intentions of Zeus and the vision of the future—that the Trojans' success will be temporary and in fact self-defeating, as it will rouse Achilles from his tent; that Troy itself will perish as a result; and that the race of heroes that includes both Achilles and Hector will pass from the earth by the will of Zeus.[31] All of these ironies generate a complex music akin to that of a tragedy where one greater than ourselves knows less than ourselves, if only because his very story is already known. Greatness revealed in its human weakness makes for poignancy and paradox. The tragic irony associated with the Homeric view of heroes blind to their own future and the purposes of Zeus is transformed in *Great Expectations.* In accordance with the dictate of equality, we share Pip's blindness. At no point in *Great Expectations* is the future revealed to us but not to him or any other character; indeed, it is not revealed to anyone. (Even the official ending of *Great Expectations*—"I saw no shadow of another parting from her" [59.493]—does not amount to a revelation of the future. It is the statement of a person, that is, one subject to error.)[32] Discussing the cardinal literary distinction between force and fraud, Northrop Frye associates the first with the violence of tragedy and the second with the ruses of comedy. "As *forza* is open violence, tragedy seldom conceals anything essential from audience or reader," while in comedy (Frye seems to be thinking of New Comedy in particular) identities may be concealed from the audience.[33] In *Great Expectations* the identity of Pip's sponsor is concealed from the reader because it was concealed from Pip, and its disclosure—the tale's peripateia—approximates a tragic effect. At the same time, the strain of comedy in *Great Expectations* seems to tell us that the hereditary distinction between the tragic and the comic—the one concerned with lofty and the other with common persons and matters—no longer applies. The warriors on the plains of Troy and the woman weighing her wool exist in separate worlds; but in *Great Expectations* the tragic and comic live practically side by side.[34] Dickens in fact conceived the novel as a tragicomedy.[35]

And the mixing of tragic and comic tones in *Great Expectations* in defiance of traditional literary decorum implies a rejection of the social orderings on which literary classification was grounded. Depicting a fall from a political height, tragedy centers on the great, while comedy concerns itself with the inferior, according to Aristotle. A century before Dickens wrote *Great Expectations,* it was already apparent to some that the fixed distinction between tragic and comic subjects rests on nothing more solid and creditable than a double prejudice, a hereditary error of the brain that works in favor of the great and against the poor.[36] To Dickens, the system that stands on such fallacies is itself false, and particularly in the story of Magwitch, whose life was ruined by one who knew exactly how to play on the prejudice against the poor, he explodes the social presumptions underwriting tragedy and comedy as literary categories.

Systems and Prisons

In *Gulliver's Travels* the hero's habit of assimilating himself to his masters, even to the point of adopting the gait and neigh of a horse, makes for a satiric illustration of the way a mind without innate moral sense falls captive to whatever system it finds itself in. "Any system can become a prison," writes Denis Donoghue.

> *Gulliver's Travels* is only superficially about big men and little men: it is really about entrapment; and the most disturbing episode in the book deals with the Struldbrugs, those people in Luggnagg who are immortal in the appalling sense that they get older but can't die. They can't leave the system.[37]

Upon hearing that the Struldbruggs are immortal, Gulliver naively assumes that being exempt from death they "have their Minds free and disingaged."[38] In point of fact, they become the hopeless prisoners of their own deformed passions, envying those lucky enough to die. The grotesques of Dickens are like mortal Struldbruggs, speaking a sort of private language where the Struldbruggs lose the use of words. Even Pip has something of the Struldbrugg in him: where they are mocked by their own desires, he is condemned to live in a perpetual state of desire he himself understands to be futile. Like the tale of the Struldbruggs, the Dickens world is ruled by the irony of captivity. Not long before *Great Expectations,* Dickens devoted *Little Dorrit* to the paradox of the willing prisoner, illustrating the theme unforgettably in William Dorrit, who wears mind-forged manacles when free and can only expand his spirit, it seems, when immured in the safety of the Marshalsea; in the willed paralysis of the Miss Havisham-like Mrs. Clennam; in the entrapment of Miss Wade within her own resentment of imagined injuries; even in a kind of abdication of sexual being by Arthur Clennam, another hero divided in mind and haunted by failure.[39] These, however, are but special cases of characters locked within their own constructs. The Dickens world abounds with beings who can't leave the system—not necessarily the system they find themselves in, but one they author, the warped expression of their own powers. In the manner of Prince Vasili in *War and Peace,* who "like a wound-up clock, by force of habit said things he did not even wish to be believed" (4), the grotesques of the Dickens world have become human mechanisms. Much of the comedy of *Great Expectations* is vested in these inhabitants of a private system, these creatures of habit whose "humors" in the satiric sense—their oddities—have taken possession of them. In this respect, and in keeping with the author's practice of mixing moods, the very comedy of *Great Expectations* is serious: a comment on minds entrapped in some illusion of their own creation, like Mrs. Joe in the fantasy of her oppression, and entrapped the more completely for that reason. (By contrast, Mrs. Pocket's delusions of nobility were instilled by her father, "who had invented for himself a conviction that his deceased father would have been made a Baronet" but for opposition in high places [23.190]. In a parody of hereditary privilege, Mrs. Pocket inherits a fiction.) In portraying those who immure themselves in their own mental Marshalsea, Dickens is as concerned with the renunciation of freedom as Dostoevsky in his legend of the Grand Inquisitor. As to

Pip, had he remained a prisoner of his own ignorance and pretension, he might never have been able to tell a tale in good clear language in the first place. His tone itself speaks to us of experience gained and illusions surrendered. Others in *Great Expectations* remain so locked in their own mental world that they speak a kind of language of one that would never do for telling a tale. Presumably these distortions of language support and are supported by the grotesque social relations that are evident to the reader from the first pages of *Great Expectations.*

If the grotesque shuts himself in the system of his own "humor," a Miss Havisham—shut in her room as well as in the mania of a consuming passion—brings out the more tragic side of the forfeiture of freedom. The tragic figure, writes Northrop Frye, uses freedom "to lose freedom. . . . This happens to . . . Hamlet when he accepts the logic of revenge."[40] Imprisoned of her own free will and, even worse, surrendering in rapture to the logic of revenge, Miss Havisham dramatizes the perversion of freedom. While plotting revenge employs Odysseus's powers so fully as to constitute a mode of self-expression, vengeance makes a grotesque of Miss Havisham; and while in the Homeric world revenge serves as a way of making one's name (as in the case of Orestes) or making oneself known (as Odysseus reveals himself to the suitors when he sets about slaughtering them), Miss Havisham's revenge is indirect and secretive.[41] It is an aggravated form of the "deceitful cunning" and the "dark propensity to injure" associated by Rousseau with the evils of inequality.[42] Miss Havisham's sole rival in obsession in *Great Expectations* is Magwitch, who also sacrifices his freedom to the will to revenge. "Singlehanded I got clear of the prison-ship; I made a dash, and I done it. I could ha' got clear of these death-cold flats likewise—look at my leg: you won't find much iron on it—if I hadn't made the discovery that *he* [Compeyson] was here. Let *him* go free?" (5.36). And these two powerful, perverse wills, each too wrapped up in itself to recognize the other, converge on the young Pip. In an important sense, he too loses freedom. He does so by enslaving himself to Estella—the link between Miss Havisham and Magwitch if only they knew it—in spite of her inanimate nature and in fact her own warning. Like a grotesque, Pip too is trapped in the absurdity of obsession. It was presumably because this fate was too dark that Dickens rewrote the ending of *Great Expectations* to raise the prospect of his reunion with Estella. ("I saw no shadow of another parting from her.") For Dickens, the image of a human being locked in a mental system can be comic or tragic or perhaps both.

If a system is said to be rational when all of its parts are disposed "in accordance with a unifying central criterion," a Dickens character commanded by some single fiction of his own invention becomes a sort of Swiftian figure lost in a private system.[43] In its very composition, *Great Expectations* disputes the rationality that subjects all to a single criterion. Being a romance and a satire *on* romance, and heightened with color both tragic and ludicrous, the work seems to repudiate uniformity itself as if that too were the result of confinement in a single perspective. Dickens is a Shakespearean novelist, and it bears remembering that in the playwright's time tragedy, history, and comedy were not hard-and-fast categories. In Shakespeare's problem plays these genres bleed into one another notoriously, yielding in *Measure for Measure* an enigmatic comedy acted out in the shadow of the executioner's block, and in *Troilus and Cressida* an indeterminate composition that was originally classified now as history, now comedy, now tragedy. But *Hamlet* too is a problem play, the hero himself being the problem; and *Great Expectations* takes place under the shadow of this figure who resists our efforts to understand him because he never seems identical to himself. Even *Hamlet* has a dash of dark comedy. To Dickens a strictly "tragic" version of *Great Expectations*—a *Great Expectations* with no admixture of the comic—would have seemed rigid and one-sided. To the closed logic of system, he opposes a work of abundant life that overflows literary divisions and categories. To the grotesque who reads everything in one way, he opposes a work bound to no single literary perspective in spite of being told by one person.

"Man is born free; and everywhere he is in chains": a principle with both comic and tragic applications in *Great Expectations.* On the one hand are minds manacled to absurdities of their own creation, like Mrs. Joe's image of herself as a woman oppressed. On the other hand is the brute oppression of Magwitch, victim of society's double standard. Magwitch, it seems, was not many years in this world before he was locked up. "When I was a ragged little creetur as much to be pitied as ever I see . . . I got the name of being hardened. 'This is a terrible hardened one,' they says to prison wisitors, picking out me" (42.349). From the fastening of this epithet on Magwitch to his leg-iron in the marsh to the very linkage of his story to Pip's, the fact of the chain figures powerfully in *Great Expectations.* And arguably, the character in *Great Expectations* who breaks out of his own mental system most dramatically is the very man we meet shackled, the one whose tale is bound to Pip's for good and with whom Pip divides the laurels of tragic experience: Magwitch. Toward the end of *Great Expectations,* even before capture and conviction force resignation upon him, Magwitch accepts his lot with a peace of mind nothing like the resentment that possesses him for most of the tale—a state of both rest and readiness akin to the tragic wisdom that lies beyond rationalizations and the fury of argument. "I'm quite content," Magwitch says after his arrest (54.454). To the judge who condemns him as a "scourge of society"—the very description he once resented so bitterly—he replies, more in sorrow than in anger, "My Lord, I have received my sentence of Death from the Almighty, but I bow to yours" (56.465). Guilty of murder but also sinned against, Magwitch takes on a resemblance to those tragic figures including Hamlet's father, a victim of murder with sins on his head, who confound the categories of guilt and innocence governing the romance world. His story adds a dimension of depth to *Great Expectations.* Like Pip and like the work itself, he too is a curious mixture, at once victim and victimizer, remembering both kindnesses and injuries, passing from obsession to peace.

Literary Leveling

The novel, it has been said, "is always expanding to meet the new and widening interests and outlook of its time, tending to absorb and to supplant in popular favor all other forms, especially poetry and drama and whatever in artistic literature is intense or concentrated, and to become for the open society of the cosmopolitan world what the old epic was for the closed society of tribal and patriarchal days—everything."[44] We cannot fail to be struck by the epic length of some of Dickens's novels, as well as their ambition to mirror a world in its entirety. In *Great Expectations* the drive to encompass all makes for prose with the heightened quality of poetry and the immediacy of drama, for a certain crossing of tragic and comic moods, and for both the fulfillment and frustration of the original romantic conventions of the novel itself. The literary name given to the power that flows through all of the divisions of literature almost as if they weren't there is satire. Confined to no single tradition, indifferent to drama and narrative, prose and verse, and capable of adapting itself to both tragic and comic expression, satire has strong anti-generic potential.[45] Satire turns the act against the actor, revealing us as the captives of our own folly, pretense, and delusion, like Pip in *Great Expectations* and others to come on our list of "heroes."

In *The Dialogic Imagination* Bakhtin unearths a tradition of comical satire that poses "a critique on the one-sided seriousness of the lofty direct word" and reminds us that reality "is always richer, more fundamental and most importantly *too contradictory and heteroglot* to be fit into a high and straightforward genre," an opinion Dickens would have seconded.[46] Belonging to this tradition is "the comic Hercules," identified by Bakhtin as "one of the most profound folk images for a cheerful and simple heroism, and . . . an enormous influence on all of world literature."[47] The comic Hercules of *Great Expectations*, as already noted, is Joe Gargery, "a sort of Hercules in strength, and also in weakness" (2.6). A vivid example of cheerful simplicity, Joe is also the human image of the spirit of equality in *Great Expectations*, not only in his lack of snobbery but in the more positive sense that he acts like the equal of the child Pip (7.49) and speaks for "equal justice betwixt man and man" (7.46). But even as he carries the "direct word" of equality into *Great Expectations*, Joe Gargery embodies a "contradictory and heteroglot" mix of qualities—not just strength and weakness, or manhood and childhood, but wisdom and folly. Pip refers to the abundance and wealth of his nature (57.474).

Also suggesting abundance, "satire" comes from the Latin word for "full," as though at root it referred to something overflowing, not to be contained within any single vessel or category. Dickens is drawn to satire as a disbeliever in the literary laws marking off one domain from another: satire cuts across literary differences roughly as the principle of equality cuts across differences in social position. The next novelist before us was not so much an antinomian as an iconoclast, possibly the most complete in literature, and among the idols he shatters is the form of the novel itself. It has been said of *War and Peace* that it "satirizes all historical writing, and all novels."[48] Tolstoy does not satirize for the joy of destruction, or not solely for that reason, but because only satire can expose the insufficiency of systems and tear away the pretenses of the great and the falsehood of artificial distinctions. And with these ends Dickens might have agreed.

Late in his life, Tolstoy wrote to a correspondent (in English), "I think that Charles Dickens is the greatest writer of the nineteenth century, and that his works, impressed with the true Christian spirit, have done and will continue to do a great deal of good to mankind."[49] Such was his esteem of Dickens that it survived his rejection of art. His early works *Childhood* and *Boyhood* were written under the immediate influence of Rousseau and the Dickens of *David Copperfield*. Perhaps by the time Tolstoy wrote *War and Peace* he was beyond literary influences. Nevertheless, there is still an affinity with Dickens. Inasmuch as the adult Pip, like David Copperfield, carries within him the child he was, we see things in *Great Expectations* to some extent through the eyes of a child not yet accustomed to the imbecility of human conventions and the practices of a grotesque world. Of Tolstoy too some say that he reveals things in their strangeness, as if the reader were seeing through the eyes of one unfamiliar with human practices—a strategy that serves Tolstoy's satiric purposes.

5

War and Peace: *The Presence of the Unknown*

Satirizing the illustrious and the heroic, War and Peace *offers a study of the unknown, including the unknown causes of events and the role in these events played by persons unknown to the historians.*

Known and Unknown Outcomes

Having journeyed to the underworld on Circe's instructions to consult the prophet Tiresias, Odysseus receives the mysterious message that he might just possibly reach home despite Poseidon's enmity, but that after he kills the suitors he must undertake another journey. Critical to Odysseus's prospects, it seems, is his visit to the island of Thrinakia. To this event Tiresias attaches several conditions: if Odysseus and his men leave the cattle of Helios untouched he might see Ithaca again, although if the cattle are harmed he still might see Ithaca (albeit without his companions), if he manages to escape. Any mortal who received such a bewilderingly conditional message would be in knots of uncertainty over it, but never is Odysseus shown asking himself what the words of Tiresias mean—this even though they echo most suggestively the curse hurled at him by Polyphemus and are echoed in turn by Circe's warning (12.137–41). Homer will portray his hero in nakedness, but not the nakedness of uncertainty; nor will he allow the audience, which already has the word of Zeus for Odysseus's homecoming, to experience the uncertainty of the prophet's prediction. In direct contrast, Dickens keeps both the reader and the hero of *Great Expectations* in ignorance, builds up suspense, allows no one in the world of the tale the comprehensive knowledge of a Tiresias. Readers of *War and Peace* are able to look back on historical events already complete, but this does not mean they are in possession of comprehensive knowledge. Far from it: they discover that such knowledge eludes them.

While the hero of the *Odyssey* is technically the same person as the Odysseus of the *Iliad,* he is shown in circumstances and lights foreign to the *Iliad,* as if released from the constraints of "history" into the freer world of romance. The Greek novelists, in inventing tales of adventure for characters who already nominally existed, both followed and extended the Homeric precedent. As if he needed no precedent, Tolstoy in *War and Peace* mingles historical characters with those of his own invention—not because he believes himself under no obligation to the truth, but because those unknown to the historians are in truth the source of history. And only because it tells of persons unknown to the historians does *War and Peace,* a historical novel, advance toward an outcome also unknown. If Napoleon really believed in his own "inevitable progress toward the achievements and rewards that both history and eternity had decreed to be necessary," and if he termed that decree his destiny,[1] Tolstoy destroys the myth of destiny written in the stars not only by commemorating Napoleon's defeat, and tracing that defeat to an event (the burning of Moscow) that appears inevitable only in retrospect, but by making *War and Peace* completely unpredictable. The singular construction of this novel thus represents one application of the principle that the elevation of unknowns to literary prominence inspired new ways of telling a tale.

In Tolstoy's hands, then, the history of events already complete becomes a tale moving toward an undetermined ending. Indeed, *War and Peace* is and was designed to be potentially endless. (Tolstoy once thought of calling the novel *All's Well That Ends Well,* but discarded the idea. Shakespeare's *All's Well* has itself become known as a problem play.) It is precisely to put an end to the hero's interminable sojourn on Calypso's island that Athena intervenes at the start of the *Odyssey* and sets the action of the poem going. Up to that point, Odysseus has been caught up in a series of adventures leading nowhere and landing him in what seems a permanent impasse; not coincidentally, Athena has been absent throughout this period, leaving him without the benefit of special favor and protection like any other mortal. The *Odyssey,* then, is predicated on Athena's decision to bring a potentially endless exile to an end. Tolstoy took care to provide no definitive ending to *War and Peace* and even to make an ending impossible in principle by keeping alternate outcomes always in play, because "not just one but many potential futures spring from any given moment."[2] Although *War and Peace* "ends" on a domestic note like the *Odyssey,* we still feel we are in the middle of things, where the *Iliad* begins. History does not tell a story with an ending like Odysseus's homecoming, and in the final analysis the sort of superior knowledge possessed by Athena (such as the knowledge that Odysseus "will not long be absent from the beloved land of his fathers" [1.202], as she tells Telemachus in book 1) is denied to characters within *War and Peace,* to the reader, and even, if he is to be believed, to the author himself.[3]

Heroes and Eminences

"Without false modesty, it is like the *Iliad*," Tolstoy said of *War and Peace*.[4] As if this likeness left room for conflict, however, Tolstoy contradicts Homer's portrayal of the heroic even as he rivals the poet's breadth of vision and dramatization of a world-historical event. For Tolstoy, history is made not from above but on the ground, and it is not made by heroes, no matter how noble they may be or how much they engross our interest. Only the historians and their dupes believe in "some special animals called 'heroes'" (1143). The really decisive actions do not take place in the glare of history at all. Tolstoy's epic thus illustrates with unusual force the difference between the hero as a performer of exploits and a hero in the diminished sense of the central figure of a literary work, with the added irony that *War and Peace* divides the honors of centrality among three protagonists. The work is too large for any character to dominate. And although their way of life is portrayed in great and loving detail by one who knows it from within, nothing done by any of the three noblemen at the center of *War and Peace* alters the course of events. Unlike the Trojan War, the duel fought over Pierre's wife Hélène, that sardonically diminished Helen, is of no historical consequence. Those who believe themselves important to history draw the author's contempt. Even in the "Peace" sections of the novel, figures of eminence are somehow demoted. Count Rostov places his affairs in the hands of his steward, is rebuked by his huntsman, is upstaged by his young daughter, and upon his death leaves debts amounting to "double the value of the property" (1220), in all demonstrating a kind of Dickensian incompetence. The great Count Bezukhov suffers his sixth stroke "while in the Rostovs' ball-room the sixth *anglaise* was being danced" (72). Prince Bolkonsky is "convinced that there were no political difficulties in Europe and no real war, but only a sort of puppet-show at which the men of the day were playing, pretending to do something real" (103). These three monarchs all pay dearly for their own position. The formidable Marya Dmitrievna, whose "whole bearing seemed a reproach to others for any weakness, passion, or temptation—the possibility of which she did not admit" (589), arranges for Natasha to go to the opera where, as it happens, she meets temptation.

If the Greeks and Trojans of the *Iliad* possess a common language and ethos, the members of Russian high society who adopt the ways of the French and imitate their salons are shown to be out of touch with the Russian people, the real authors of their nation's victory. For all his admiration of Homer, the author is too patriotic to make the French the equals of the Russians like the Trojans and Greeks—two armies infused with the same spirit, possessed of the same ideals, one side favored by this Olympian, the other by that. (If the Greeks and Trojans were not equal in the sense of being well matched and fully worthy of one another, the contest between them would not be heroic.) Homer does not satirize, whether because he has already shown his heroes from on high and has no need to diminish them further, or because satire would threaten the spell of epic seriousness, or because the free energy of negation just has no place in the Homeric world. *War and Peace* can be taken as one vast satire, a work that exceeds all more definite literary categories just as human life defies the explanations contrived to make sense of it. (In this respect the conventional dictum about *War and Peace,* that it is the image of life itself, holds quite true.) Finally, while events in both the *Iliad* and *War and Peace* move toward an outcome already known, in Tolstoy this powerful irony is compounded by two others: as noted, the stories of Prince Andrew, Nicholas Rostov, and Pierre wind toward an unforeseeable conclusion, while the essays interleaved in the novel inform us that it is the unknown, not the illustrious, who really determine the course of history. And it is for this reason, in part, that the causes of events lie concealed from human understanding.

For the reader or hearer of the *Iliad,* it is not just the destruction of Troy and the death of many heroes that impend over the poem, but the annihilation of the heroic race itself, to be replaced by "men such as men are now." The inhabitants of the post-heroic world possess what the original heroes did not: a vision of history explaining the eventual disappearance of the great ones by the will of Zeus. If we take up Tolstoy's suggestion and compare *War and Peace* to the *Iliad,* we find that it disputes this relation of past to present in its entirety. Not only does Tolstoy demystify the past and negate the myth of the heroic, but he argues that even though we latecomers can see what no one in 1812 could—namely, that the cause of Napoleon's defeat was his "advance into the heart of Russia late in the season without any preparation for a winter campaign, and on the other [hand], the character given to the war by the burning of Russian towns and the hatred of the foe this aroused among the Russian people" (731)—still the learned world has managed to blind itself to this plain truth. And instead of the vision of history that Homer's audience receives as a kind of consolation for its own belatedness, the readers of *War and Peace* receive the mocking revelation that the war of 1812 "had to occur because it had to" (647).

Homer writes of a war in the legendary past when heroes still walked the earth; and like Homer, we commonly glorify the past. In the world of Shakespeare's histories

> it is only the past that can be idealized or thought of as heroic or peaceful. The *Henry VI* plays look back to the great and victorious Henry V; the play of *Henry V* looks back to the time of Richard as a time when there was no curse of usurpation on the royal house; and in [*Richard II*] we have John of Gaunt idealizing an earlier time, apparently the reign of Edward III, the reign that saw the Black Death and the beginning of the Hundred Years' War with France.[5]

But if only the past can be so fondly imagined, the literary form of the novel, concerned as it is with the present (as its English name suggests), implies a certain disenchantment of the world. Tolstoy writes of a recent war already mythologized, but he writes as a novelist, that is, portrays it as a present still unfolding, not a past heroically remote. Not only does he seek to correct the distortions of retrospect, but to illustrate, to make present, in the several fates of the tale's central characters the same mystery shaping historical events.

Unknown Causes

Tolstoy has the ancient epic before him in *War and Peace*—as an example not to be followed but shunned. "The ancients have left us model heroic poems in which the heroes furnish the whole interest of the story, and we are still unable to accustom ourselves to the fact that for our epoch histories of that kind are meaningless" (808). Later in his life Tolstoy would write in the same vein about the entire tradition of literature and the arts, rejecting it in the name of human equality. In effect, he came to abandon satire as a literary force—one that dissolves systems and overflows conventional categories and definitions—in favor of pure wrath, scorn, and negation.

As we just saw, the two great causes cited by Tolstoy for the defeat of Napoleon's army are the Russian winter and the Russian people. No mention of military heroics. Later on, again without citing Homer by name, Tolstoy observes in the critical spirit of a modern that

> in historical events (where the actions of men are the subject of observation) the first and most primitive approximation [to a cause] to present itself was the will of the gods, and after that, the will of those who stood in the most prominent position—the heroes of history. But we need only penetrate to the essence of any historic event—which lies in the activity of the general mass of men who take part in it—to be convinced that the will of the historic hero does not control the actions of the mass but is itself controlled. (1055)

So it is that Napoleon, imagining himself making history, is portrayed satirically as the dupe of his own celebrity and the puppet of history itself. (We might think of Orwell in "Shooting an Elephant": "Here was I, the white man with his gun, standing in front of the unarmed native crowd—seemingly the leading actor of the piece; but in reality I was only an absurd puppet pushed to and fro by the will of those yellow faces behind.") History is made from below, by "the activity of the general mass of men who take part in it," by the army and not the commander. The polemical character of such comments is itself foreign to Homer. As for the Homeric similes scattered through *War and Peace,* these are neither mere embellishments of the text nor perhaps even demonstrations of "the oneness of the world" as said of Homer's own,[6] but returns to the soil of everyday life where history originates—a field of existence antithetical to the court, the salon, even the headquarters—or else illustrations of a rigorously natural causality quite contrary to the Homeric vision of divine causation. The guests at the English Club dinner in honor of Bagration—one of those commanders who do not make history—are possessed of a strong sense of their own importance, but when the guest of honor arrives all suddenly crowd together "like rye shaken in a shovel" (324). Suddenly they are reduced to anonymity, their self-importance cut down as by a scythe.

Earlier, the same guests were likened to those Homeric insects, bees. When, unlike the ruined city of Troy—from whose ashes Rome would be born, according to the heroic lore of the West—the ruined city of Moscow returns to life, the thousands streaming back to the great center after the departure of the French forces are likened not to bees but ants:

> It would be difficult to explain why, and where to, ants whose heap has been destroyed are hurrying . . . and it would be equally difficult to explain what caused the Russians, after the departure of the French, to throng to the place that had formerly been Moscow. But when we watch the ants round their ruined heap, the tenacity, energy, and the immense number of the delving insects prove that, despite the destruction of the heap, something indestructible, which though intangible is the real strength of the colony, still exists; and similarly though in Moscow in the month of October there was no government, and no churches, shrines, riches, or houses—it was still the Moscow it had been in August. All was destroyed, except something intangible yet powerful and indestructible. (1186)

What could be more contrary to the heroic cult of distinction than a colony of ants, all of them identical to the human eye? The analogy has more than merely illustrative force, too. The activity of the ants really corresponds to "the activity of the general mass of men" responsible for history.

The exact causes of the great reversal of the war of 1812, the burning of Moscow, remain unknowable just as the identities of all the "ants" who fled Moscow in the first place cannot possibly be known. It was the desertion of Moscow by its own inhabitants that placed the city in the position where for one reason or another—the actual cause is undiscernible—it had to burn. "A town built of wood where scarcely a day passes without conflagrations when the house-owners are in residence and a police force is present, cannot help burning when its inhabitants have left it and it is occupied by soldiers who smoke pipes, make camp-fires of the Senate chairs in the Senate Square, and cook themselves meals twice a day" (961). Credit for the burning of Moscow goes not to patriotic defenders of Russia but to nameless persons who went about deserting the city as unmindful of the historic significance of their action as the history books are unmindful of them. But this is ironic credit, of course, for the very word "desertion" speaks of the opposite of glory.

Tolstoy believes that Moscow burned for causes unknown—a spark from a soldier's pipe, perhaps—but as a result, ultimately, of the actions of ordinary persons unknown to history. He believes that victories are won by nameless soldiers on the battlefield itself, and not by strategists, theorists, or generals. He also believes that "only unconscious action bears fruit" (1007), as those who fled Moscow had no idea of the result their action accomplished. He believes that those the history books ignore author history itself, and that the wise do not know their own wisdom. What is the relation between these two kinds of not-knowing? Evidently it is Tolstoy's belief that the common people perceived by the more illustrious merely as background are the ones in touch with the truth of things, a truth deeper than words or indeed knowledge. This thesis comes to life in the person of a peasant who emerges, some feel unconvincingly, into a kind of brief prominence late in *War and Peace.*

The comparison of human beings to a disordered army of ants is not very complimentary to the human beings, but Tolstoy's portrayal of the Russian peasant in Platon Karataev—kindly, beautiful, and as round and full of proverbs as Sancho Panza—is affirmative. Pierre, himself a Quixote, meets this natural miracle of a human being when taken prisoner by the French in Moscow. Though idealized, Platon Karataev is no saint. He was conscripted after being caught, tried, and flogged for stealing wood. In a way he never foresaw, however, his arrest was the salvation of his family, for if he had not entered the army, his brother, the father of five, would have had to go instead.

When asked by Pierre if he feels sad, Platon Karataev first introduces himself and then says,

> "How is one to help feeling sad? Moscow—she's the mother of cities. How can one see all this and not feel sad? But 'the maggot gnaws the cabbage, yet dies first'; that's what the old folk used to tell us," he added rapidly. (1036)

The proverb appears inexplicably, as if from nowhere, like Platon Karataev himself, and just as inexplicably Platon Karataev seems to understand that Moscow, the cabbage, will survive the French. Perhaps he understands this because he himself is one of the common people who are the movers of history.

In Homer everyone speaks alike. In *War and Peace* Platon Karataev's speech is, and is meant to be perceived as, the direct antithesis of the sort of epigram composed in advance in order to sparkle in the salon or the drawing room and be quoted thereafter. He himself quotes "the old folk," and his words are so far from preconceived that they seem to flow of themselves. He doesn't even keep track of them. When Pierre, with his genius for incomprehension, asks what Platon Karataev means by the maggot and the cabbage, he is responding to the authentic unpredictability of the other's speech. Appropriately, Platon Karataev answers the question not by explaining himself but by adding something even more mysterious.

> "What? What did you say?" asked Pierre.
>
> "Who? I?" said Karataev. "I say things happen not as we plan but as God judges," he replied, thinking that he was repeating what he had said before. (1036)

More than once Tolstoy calls our attention to the specific quality of Platon Karataev's speech, so fluid it cannot be predicted even by him.

In contrast to the studied performances and affectations of the salon, the artless Platon Karataev "when he began to speak . . . seemed not to know how he would conclude" (1040). Again,

> The chief peculiarity of his speech was its directness and appositeness. It was evident that he never considered what he had said or was going to say, and consequently the rapidity and justice of his intonation had an irresistible persuasiveness. (1039)

As we know, Platon Karataev expresses himself in proverbs—"folk-sayings which taken without a context seem so insignificant, but when used appositely suddenly acquire a significance of profound wisdom" (1039). His speech has the power to stun, the unpredictability marked by the word "suddenly."

Platon Karataev does not know how he is going to conclude, and just this quality of openness Tolstoy sought to write into *War and Peace* itself.

> Most novels, [Tolstoy] pointed out, tend to a conclusion that the author has planned from the outset, which means that the ending is silently present in the beginning. But this is not the case with *War and Peace,* in which both the beginning and ending are arbitrary. . . . [Tolstoy] selected a possible stopping point (1856) that he knew he could never reach, so that however much he might write, he could still write more. There would never be a moment at which all threads would be tied up.[7]

Remarkably direct and unpretentious in style, continually surprising, and not aimed at a preconceived conclusion—as noted, the work seems to end in the middle of things—*War and Peace* as a whole reproduces in its own way the striking quality of Platon Karataev's speech.[8] A story the peasant loves to tell Pierre would later be told by Tolstoy himself under the title "God Sees the Truth, But Waits" (one of only two of his own works not disowned by Tolstoy in *What Is Art?*). And in Tolstoy's version it becomes a tale of not-knowing: a merchant does not know how a bloody knife made its way into his belongings; his wife does not know whether to believe in his innocence; he himself, now in Siberia, does not know for what sins, exactly, he is being punished; he does not know what to do when by chance he meets up with the actual murderer; he does not know what to say when the latter begs his forgiveness. Platon Karataev, whose version of the tale will be discussed presently, seems to have mastered the art of not-knowing as well.

The embodiment of the ideal of human equality, Platon Karataev does not know exactly where his speech is going, and this fact of not knowing Tolstoy cherishes in him. Not only is Platon Karataev an unknown in the eyes of a world mesmerized by leaders and heroes—above all Napoleon, who declares characteristically at one point in *War and Peace,* "I know everything!" (665)—but he is in touch with the unknowable, the mystery of things. He is in touch with the unknowable because he lives outside the glare of history in the element of truth. Neither the ants nor even the observer of the ants could say why they race about. "It would be difficult to explain why, and where to, ants whose heap has been destroyed are hurrying." The ants, then, constitute a living demonstration of the unknowable. The human beings figured by the ants have no idea that by attending to their own diverse interests, all of them entirely "personal" (1186), they advance the higher purpose of returning a great city to life. (The argument here bears a family resemblance to Mandeville's satiric contention in the *Fable of the Bees* that the pursuit of entirely selfish interests makes for a powerful, bustling hive.)[9] When he set out to steal wood, Platon Karataev had no idea that he would end up in the army in place of his brother. If "only unconscious action bears fruit" as Tolstoy maintains, Platon Karataev was certainly unconscious of performing an act of heroism when he went about an act of theft. He simply did what he had to do. Of his arrest he says to Pierre, "We thought it was a misfortune but it turned out a blessing!" (1037). As in the case of the burning of Moscow, the reader of *War and Peace* sometimes doesn't know whether to mark down an event as a victory or a reverse, a misfortune or a triumph. The captive Pierre has his life spared only to be led away to be shot, only to survive.

Platon Karataev goes where he has to go, and according to Tolstoy so does history itself. Taking full advantage of the openness of the novel as a literary "form," Tolstoy introduces into the latter half of *War and Peace* polemics on the false interpretation of the past, in the first of which the case is made that the war of 1812 resulted not from Napoleon's ambition or any similar cause but from causes beyond number converging in a way that passes human comprehension. History is a web of coincidence. "Myriads of causes coincided to bring [the war of 1812] about" (647), a point later reaffirmed:

> To the question of what causes historic events, another answer presents itself, namely, that the course of human events is predetermined from on high—depends on the coincidence of the wills of all who take part in the events, and that a Napoleon's influence on the course of these events is purely external and fictitious. (839)

This being the case, no one who plays a part in events, and least of all those who suppose themselves the authors of events, can possibly understand the larger design of history itself. By analogy, Platon Karataev could not possibly have foreseen the connection between stealing wood and saving his family, or unriddled the coincidence that saw him arrested just as a conscription was taking place. Not only, then, does Tolstoy believe unknowns like Platon Karataev to be the movers of history, but he envisions history itself as an expression of the unknowable in whose presence Platon Karataev lives. Not only does "the impossibility of knowing historical laws" guarantee "the potential significance of even the most ordinary action of the most ordinary person," but history, as a tale of the unknown, bears the very image of this person.[10] In effect Tolstoy agrees that "things happen not as we plan but as God judges."

Ignorance, Incomprehension, Wonder

If "he who plays a part in an historic event never understands its significance" (1007), then in a work of fiction that aims to portray history as it occurs, and so correct the fictions of the historians, human action will have to be portrayed ironically. Often in *War and Peace* we see what those engaged in events do not, so that their actions are enveloped in a kind of dramatic irony. Homeric irony it might be called, for in the *Iliad* the mortals who fulfill Zeus's triple intention of embarrassing the Greeks, destroying Troy, and extinguishing the race of heroes have no idea of that intention and no access to the conferences of the gods. In this respect they too are "unconscious." It seems that Tolstoy is Homeric after all, depicting events taking place over the heads of their performers.

After the rout at Austerlitz has already begun, Nicholas Rostov, unaware of what is happening, rides full of hope with a message for Kutuzov. We learn exactly what Pierre does not know about his own estates; his ignorance is our revelation:

> He did not know that the priest who met him with the cross oppressed the peasants by his exactions, and that the pupils' parents wept at having to let him take their children and secured their release by heavy payments. He did not know that the brick buildings, built to plan, were being built by serfs whose manorial labour was thus increased, though lessened on paper. He did not know . . . (401)

Again, Pierre "did not know that Natasha's soul was overflowing with despair, shame, and humiliation" (631) after betraying her engagement to Prince Andrew. (The words "did not know" seem to follow Levin through *Anna Karenina*.) French cavalrymen gallop into a river and drown themselves proudly before Napoleon, who at that moment happens not to be "even looking at what they were doing" (651). A peasant does not know that the French have paid him in counterfeit money. Nicholas Rostov "had no idea that the village he was entering was the property of that very Bolkonsky who had been engaged to his sister" (783). Napoleon "could not know the course of the battle" of Borodino (839). Pierre doesn't know that he has stumbled onto the battlefield itself. Natasha doesn't know that Prince Andrew lies in one of her family's carts as they flee Moscow. The French army in *its* flight from Moscow "resembled a wounded animal which feels it is perishing and does not know what it is doing" (1077). In such moments of dramatic or even cosmic irony, it is as though the power of sight had passed from those within the tale to the author, leaving them blind and deluded and him with supreme knowledge. We may recall the *Odyssey,* whose cast of characters ranges from the all-seeing Helios to a blinded Cyclops, and where it often seems that in order for one to know, another must not. Tolstoy's vision is the correlate of others' blindness.

Not only Tolstoy's prose but also, of course, its readers survey events from this higher perspective; and in a world where even the wisest (a Platon Karataev or on the other hand a Kutuzov) know that they do not know, and where all are bound by "the rule forbidding us to eat of the fruit of the Tree of Knowledge" (1007)—a surprising allusion in one who was such a demystifier by nature—such revelations of irony run the risk of making us too knowing, of inducing a deeply false sense of superiority to error.[11] In point of fact, to derive from Tolstoyan irony a feeling of looking down on the ignorance of others would be a serious misreading—a misinterpretation worthy of being viewed with irony—for Tolstoy does not confine himself to the conventional argument that eyes blinded by vanity and self-deceit fail to see things as they are. He advances the more disturbing proposition that no one, least of all the historians and (by implication) their cousins the novelists, can really see down to the true causes of things. Exactly how it is that Moscow burned no one knows or will ever know. As for the priest who oppresses the peasants behind Pierre's back, we would not even know of his existence had we not suddenly been notified of it. In this case we don't have the time, as it were, to look down on Pierre.

Throughout *War and Peace* we marvel at Pierre's aptitude for incomprehension, but on reflection it would seem that a genuine lack of understanding is better than all those pretensions to understanding, those systems and theories the human intellect employs to deceive itself, exploded by Tolstoy. In bringing to life the absurdity of the German schoolroom in his journal *Yasnaya Polyana*—and it was his belief that bad education was at the root of inequality—Tolstoy emphasized the pedagogue's inane pretense of knowledge: "He casts a look round the class, and knows already what it is that they ought to understand; he knows this, and he knows what the children's souls are made of, and much else that the seminary has taught him."[12] Better the humility of not understanding than the self-delusion of this impostor. As Isaiah Berlin observes of Pierre's bewilderment on the battlefield of Borodino (and the same could be said of other displays of incomprehension), "That, at any rate, is concrete, uncontaminated by theories and abstractions; and Pierre is therefore closer to the truth about the course of events . . . than those who believe them to obey a discoverable set of laws or rules."[13] (When Tolstoy reports of the married Natasha that she "positively did not understand" theories about women's rights [1238], the remark could just as well be taken as a compliment to a mind unclouded by theories as the notation of a mental limit. Tolstoy's own observation that Russians do not know how to write novels in the European manner[14] also constitutes a compliment.) No doubt Pierre Bezukhov is a fool; but the fool is a figure of great literary potential. Among the manifestations of foolery cited by Bakhtin in his discussion of the art of not understanding are Montesquieu's impersonation in the *Persian Letters,* Swift's complex play in *Gulliver's Travels,* and in fact Tolstoy's own "description of the battle of Borodino from the point of view of an uncomprehending Pierre."[15] And yet the fool cannot be reduced to a human device employed to achieve certain literary effects. Who would want to say of Lear's Fool that he is a device to expose falsehood and fraud? Tolstoy himself dreamed of becoming a Fool of Christ, a wanderer living on the alms of the people.

Things really do happen that leave us uncomprehending. Two prisoners being led to their execution by the French cannot comprehend what is about to happen to them (1031). Only with time does Pierre himself come "to understand the news he had been given after his rescue, about the death of Prince Andrew, the death of his wife, and the destruction of the French" (1179–80), and this is like him, but how could such news be taken in at once? In *The Brothers Karamazov* the good doctor Herzenstube admits to Madame Khokhlakov that he "can make nothing of" her daughter's case (181); but how much wiser is this ignorance than the shows of knowledge put on by the doctors of Ivan Ilych. In his dream of the baby, Dmitri simply cannot understand why such suffering exists. Alyosha for his part comprehends scarcely more of the storm swirling around him in his own household than Pierre does of the battle unfolding before his eyes at Borodino—"I know nothing" about the affairs of men and women, he says at Madame Khokhlakov's (188)—but if we as readers see through his failures of understanding (after the event), the fact is that the novel continually reveals to us our own failures in this department. So too *War and Peace.* Of the three protagonists of *War and Peace* Pierre seems the dearest to the tale itself (as Alyosha is identified as the particular hero of *The Brothers Karamazov*), and from this we might guess that his incomprehension in the face of events, as foolish as it is, exemplifies the sort of response the tale solicits in ourselves. If we already knew the devout and deep-souled Princess Mary, the attempt of Anna Pavlovna Scherer in the opening scene of *War and Peace* to interest Prince Vasili in marrying off his wastrel son to her—as though Princess Mary were nothing but a valuable piece of human livestock, and one, moreover, that Anna Pavlovna Scherer disposed of—would strike us as an impudent fraud. But because this *is* the opening scene, we do not and cannot know Princess Mary (any more than we know that the matchmaker's efforts will not and cannot come to anything); and so we cannot make much of this business. Necessarily we are in the position of a Pierre, "observant" (9) but somehow unseeing. Nor do we perceive that even as Anna Pavlovna Scherer opens up this (false) possibility of financial rescue, the tale itself is preparing Pierre's conquest by the prince's daughter Hélène. Pierre's marriage to Hélène is proof that you can have eyes and not see. But of course no one can see the future. Who would imagine that the little princess, pregnant in the opening pages of *War and Peace,* and "very pretty and rosy" (11), would die in childbirth? Who, before the fact, would have supposed or believed that for Napoleon victory would literally turn to ashes?

At some point in *Anna Karenina,* say the twenty-fifth time we are told something one of the characters doesn't know, we lose the feeling of superior knowledge that seems to radiate from Tolstoy's prose and recognize that we do not know either. In *War and Peace,* a work that warns of the fallacies of superior knowledge even as it induces the experience of such knowledge, the figure of Pierre dramatizes not only our own defects of perception, but our wonder before the mystery of events. In a stunning scene at the end of book 2 of *War and Peace,* the master of bewilderment, "amazed at his own words," tells Natasha,

> "You have your whole life before you. . . . If I were not myself, but the handsomest, cleverest, and best man in the world, and were free, I would this moment ask on my knees for your hand and your love!" (640–41)

Having once made the fatal error of assuming that his engagement was scripted before it even took place, Pierre here reminds the suffering Natasha that the end of her life has not been written. The reader of *War and Peace* learns, similarly, that the future remains unwritten, that no eye can possibly discern its shape in the present, and even as it unscrolls itself before us, we can only look on in wonder like Pierre.

Such is the economy of knowledge in the world of the *Odyssey* that for one who knows there seems to be another or others who do not know. It seems that for everything we ourselves have come to know about the characters of *Anna Karenina,* there is something else as yet unknown. Our knowledge is never complete. Having run off to Italy with Anna, Vronsky suddenly reveals a dilettante's interest in painting. Only when Levin receives a second letter from his brother's wife (a prostitute) do we learn of the first (487). We are deep in the middle of the novel when we discover that Karenin grew up an orphan and how it is that he now has no friends. As readers we are always just catching up with the present, always in expectation, always awaiting. So do the events of *War and Peace* flow into the future. When he utters his words to Natasha, Pierre cannot say where they come from (a quality that helps explain his bond with Platon Karataev), nor can we say where the future comes from. Virtually as a corrective to the feeling of superior knowledge induced by his own ironies, Tolstoy has threaded through *War and Peace* tales of courtship so winding and knotted that even knowing the ending (which no reader can possibly foresee), we get lost in their turns almost as in a great carpet of flowing design. Regarding the future of Prince Andrew and Princess Mary, Nicholas Rostov and Natasha Rostov, and Pierre, we know at the beginning and even the middle of *War and Peace* no more than Platon Karataev knew when he went out to steal wood. These characters after all are unknowns, historically speaking, not figures like Napoleon whose end has already been written. Of them we read not with a feeling of Olympian knowledge but a strangely exhilarating sense of possessing no advantage of knowledge whatever. Their future will become known to us only as it becomes known to themselves. The very format of a novel about a war already concluded on the one hand and the private lives of some members of the Russian nobility on the other accentuates the difference between events whose outcome is already known (which encourages in those with the benefit of retrospect all kinds of illusions of understanding) and events whose outcome no human eye can see until it takes place. It is as if Tolstoy had combined in one work an *Iliad,* the tale of a war whose outcome was not just known but legendary, and an *Odyssey* telling of the return from the battlefield to private life. The *Odyssey,* however, advances toward an ending decreed from above and revealed to the reader, and rather than taking an unknown for a hero, Homer explores the private side of the life of one of the heroes of the Trojan War. Only later did it become possible to write stories about private persons without historical significance. Even Callirhoe is introduced as the daughter of a historical figure, the Syracusan general Hermocrates. "What Thucydides did for the Peloponnesian War, that Chariton has done for the daughter of Hermocrates!"[16] The public and private sides of existence, separated at birth in Western literature, are reunited in *War and Peace.*

Tolstoy and His Mentor

"In our time," wrote Tolstoy, a man of imperial temper, some years after *War and Peace,* "everyone is at least dimly aware of the equal rights of all people."[17] Eventually he made an absolute of equality, rejecting his own art, including *War and Peace,* in its name. Within *War and Peace* itself the conflict between Tolstoy's focus on the nobility and his belief in the Russian people produces the feeling that the makers of history are not the novel's principal persons, however brilliantly portrayed, but those outside the light of glory, the ken of the historians, and to an extent *War and*

Peace itself. Those who imagine themselves history's authors or leading actors—Napoleon above all—delude themselves, subject as they are to the law that "he who plays a part in an historic event never understands its significance" (1007).

Whether or not Napoleon is the epic hero of history, within *War and Peace* he is less charismatic than Natasha at age thirteen. Natasha comes from a household that is itself somehow upside down, with a servant managing "all [the] affairs" (58) of Count Rostov, a kind of moneyed Micawber. When the wolf makes its appearance in the great hunting scene of *War and Peace,* the serf Daniel who is the head huntsman actually curses the count. "'Blast you!' he shouted, holding up the whip threateningly at the count. 'You've let the wolf go!'" (531). The count is described as "frightened and shamefaced." As brilliant as the moment is, within a few pages normalcy returns and Daniel recedes into the background that is also his element. In general in *War and Peace,* with the exception of Platon Karataev, peasants and servants remain, like Daniel or the steward Dmitri who manages affairs the count no longer understands, a felt presence in the background of a tale whose well-lit places belong to members of the nobility.[18] And despite his awareness that the priest who met Pierre oppressed the peasants and that Platon Karataev stole out of need, Tolstoy seems to concern himself very little with political reform. In what way, then, does he manifest a feeling for equality? For one thing, by exempting no one from the force of events. Because the factor of chance plays a critical role in human affairs according to Tolstoy, chance is written into the construction of *War and Peace,* producing the seeming randomness of the narrative which has dismayed and amazed its readers, but chance could not operate if people were not equally exposed to its power. For some unknown reason—by chance—the French general Davout and his captive Pierre recognize one another as fellow human beings.

> Davout looked up and gazed intently at him. For some seconds they looked at one another, and that look saved Pierre. Apart from conditions of war and law, that look established human relations between the two men. At that moment an immense number of things passed dimly through both their minds, and they realized that they were both children of humanity and were brothers. (1029)

But perhaps what actually saves Pierre is that he finds himself sixth and not fifth on the list of prisoners to be shot.

Not at all ambiguous is Tolstoy's portrayal of high society and everything associated with it—salons, theaters, amours—as a counterfeit of human existence. Tolstoy's hatred of salon culture, his preference for rural life, his eye for insincerity, all correspond with the Rousseauian sentiments that flowed into the modern discourse of equality in the age of the French Revolution. Particularly corrupt in Rousseau's judgment is the "brilliance that dazzles the eyes"—the sort of pretentious display that accompanies the cultivation of false distinctions.[19] Reminding us as he does of the illusory centrality of heroes, the falsity of dazzling amours, the importance of things disregarded, background conditions, the presence of the unknown, Tolstoy makes the rejection of brilliance a principle of art. If one attended a salon "to know and be known,"[20] in the Tolstoyan world the unknown shadows the known, and celebrities like sopranos, actresses, renowned doctors, and Napoleon are reduced to players in a masquerade of deceit. And like Tolstoy's rejection of social brilliance, his belief in the limits of knowledge recalls Rousseau's. Among the first reflections in the Savoyard Vicar's profession of faith are the following:

> We do not know ourselves; we know neither our nature nor our active principle. We hardly know if man is a simple or a compound being. Impenetrable mysteries surround us on all sides; they are above the region accessible to the senses. We believe we possess intelligence for piercing these mysteries, but all we have is imagination. Through this imaginary world each blazes a trail he believes to be good. None can know whether his leads to the goal. Nevertheless we want to penetrate everything, to know everything. The only thing we do not know is how to be ignorant of what we cannot know.[21]

Rousseau speaks of "the heavy veil that [Nature] has drawn over all her activities"; convinced that ultimate truth lies hidden from us, he maintains that "the reasonable and modest man [is of] finite understanding. . . . Full of respect, he therefore stops short and does not touch the veil, content with the knowledge that an immense Being lies beneath."[22] In *War and Peace* we glimpse the immensity of moral Being even as we acknowledge its mystery.

The young Tolstoy once made a list of the literary works that had the greatest influence on him. Rousseau is the only author credited with two works of "immense influence"—the *Confessions* and *Emile,* the treatise on pedagogy in which we meet the Savoyard Vicar. (Tolstoy eventually published his own *Confession,* as well as teaching peasant children and becoming at last a Sage, that is, a teacher of humanity. It was his hope that his *Primer* would instruct "two generations of *all* Russian children, from the tsars' to the muzhiks'.")[23] Rousseau himself is a kind of background condition of *War and Peace.* The awareness of the false conventions of narrative and the duplicity of language itself that is everywhere in *War and Peace*—even this has a counterpart in Rousseau. "Marvelous writer that he is, Rousseau is constantly protesting against the art of writing," as might also be said of Tolstoy, who later protested against literature in full.[24] Like the sincerity that saves human expression from falsity and insignificance because it is deeper than words, a belief in equality preserves *War and Peace* from the artifices of more conventional fiction. In any case, Tolstoy need not orate equality in a work that breathes equality, a work imbued from its first pages with the sentiments animating the *Discourse on Inequality.* That the author of *War and Peace* was a nobleman jealous of his rights, proud of his birth, and scornful of upstarts; that he despised liberalism—this doesn't mean that he could not assent to the principle of equality, or could only do so hypocritically. (In effect, Tolstoy himself anticipates the charge of hypocrisy by attributing to Prince Bolkonsky, who tyrannizes his daughter unmercifully, "the theory that all men are equals" [101].) It means that he could not go along with the Western currents that carried the ideal of equality following the French Revolution. By the same token, he *could* go along with much of Rousseau, who died before the revolutionaries of France appropriated his name, and who no more conformed to the tone and tenets of what came to be called liberalism than Tolstoy himself. The split composition of *War and Peace* that strikes every reader—its shifts from narrative to essay—in itself recalls "the two Rousseaus, the political theorist and the autobiographer and novelist."[25] As the singularity of Rousseau is so great as to transcend the genres he writes in (they are many; he is one), so does the singularity of *War and Peace,* imbued with the spirit of Tolstoy, transcend conventional literary distinctions.[26]

That the history books ignore the real authors of history, as Tolstoy argues in *War and Peace,* is a Rousseauian paradox in itself. Even Tolstoy's portrayal of war is as Rousseauian as it is Homeric. Tolstoy:

> On the 12th of June 1812 the forces of Western Europe crossed the Russian frontier and war began, that is, an event took place opposed to human reason and human nature. Millions of men perpetrated against one another such innumerable crimes, frauds, treacheries, thefts, forgeries, issues of false money, burglaries, incendiarisms, and murders, as in whole centuries are not recorded in the annals of all the law courts of the world. (645)

Rousseau:

> [Once nations came into being] there arose wars between nations, battles, murders, reprisals which make nature tremble and offend reason, and all those horrible prejudices which count the honour of shedding human blood a virtue. The most decent men learned to regard the killing of their fellows as one of their duties; and in time men came to massacre one another by thousands without knowing why, committing more murders in a single day's battle and more atrocities in the sack of a single city than were committed in the state of nature over the whole face of the earth.[27]

And in an irony fully consonant with Rousseau's inverse view of social distinctions, Tolstoy claims of the participants in historic events that "the higher they stand in the social hierarchy the less are they free" (731). When Pierre, in his captivity, forgets that

> a superfluity of the comforts of life destroys all joy in satisfying one's needs, while great freedom in the choice of an occupation—such freedom as his wealth, his education, and his social position had given him in his own life—is just what makes the choice of occupation insolubly difficult (1082),

he forgets, in effect, the lesson of the *Discourse on Inequality*. When, also in his captivity, Pierre loses himself in the pleasure of eating potatoes, his innocent selfishness corresponds precisely with Rousseau's "amour de soi-même" (as opposed to corrupt "amour-propre"), which has been described as "an instinctive self-protective, self-regarding disposition . . . to stay alive, enjoy life and avoid injuries."[28]

Rousseau presides, too, over the union of Pierre and Natasha.

> Pierre one day told her of Rousseau's view, with which he quite agreed, that to have a wet nurse is unnatural and harmful. When her next baby was born, despite the opposition of her mother, the doctors, and even of her husband himself—who were all vigorously opposed to her nursing the baby herself, a thing then unheard of and considered injurious—she insisted on having her own way, and after that nursed all her babies herself. (1240)

As though Rousseau's entire theory of education were founded on this principle, within the first few lines of *Emile* he writes, "The first education is the most important, and this first education belongs incontestably to women; if the Author of nature had wanted it to belong to men, He would have given them milk with which to nurse the children."[29] What Pierre assents to in theory, Natasha realizes in practice.

But it is in depicting salon society as a kind of collective self-deception that Tolstoy most resembles Rousseau. The *Discourse on Inequality* ends by postponing as if for another work the question of

> how, as a result of always asking others what we are and never daring to put the question to ourselves in the midst of so much philosophy, humanity, civility, and so many sublime maxims, we have only façades, deceptive and frivolous, honour without virtue, reason without wisdom, and pleasure without happiness.[30]

War and Peace opens in the drawing room of Anna Pavlovna Scherer, a world infected with the malady diagnosed by Rousseau. Tolstoy begins where Rousseau ends. In these opening scenes we are also introduced to Pierre, who is markedly different from the others and whose difference, it turns out, resides above all in his capacity to put honest questions to himself. After stumbling into marriage with one whose beauty dramatizes the meaning of "façade," Pierre goes on a quest for virtue, wisdom, and happiness amid the simulacra of these things. And I read of his quest not as one looking down from the heights of superior knowledge on error, still less with an affected superiority to life itself like some in *War and Peace,* but as one held fascinated, not knowing where the quest will end.

In and of itself, Pierre's blunder in marrying the odious Hélène illustrates how it is that man, born free, finds himself in chains. Imagining what it will be like "to be looked upon as a sort of Paris possessed of a Helen" (220)—a note of the mock-heroic—Pierre married not because he really wanted to but because he somehow felt that it was expected of him and that the story of his union had already been written. "So it is all finished!" he thinks to himself before he has even decided to propose (220). In his belief that the history of his life has already been written for him, Pierre resembles the misguided hero of *Great Expectations* who imagines himself cast in the role of a knight delivering a maiden (Estella) from captivity; except that Pierre walks into captivity. And much as Pierre succumbs to a false sense of the inevitable and assumes his part in a fiction, so Natasha at the incomprehensible opera comes to believe that "'it has to be like this'" (599) and soon thereafter assumes her part in a love intrigue that also, she believes, has to be. The Natasha and Pierre who eventually unite have each learned from bitter experience the falsity of love as a conqueror that takes the will captive and lays down its own laws, like some Napoleon in the world of the heart. That Natasha's crisis originates in the opera house is another Rousseauian touch. As Rousseau said, and as Tolstoy would demonstrate again in "The Death of Ivan Ilych," the theater is a source of corruption.

Like Pierre, Ivan Ilych walks into captivity; like Pierre, he takes the fatal and irreversible step of marrying because everyone seems to expect it. His is a tale of missteps. But if these characters betray their own freedom and delude themselves into believing their lives already scripted, the author himself reminds us of the openness—what Bakhtin terms awkwardly the "unfinalizability"—of human life by giving Pierre at the "end" of *War and Peace* a new and surprising life with Natasha, and by closing the novel with Pierre primed for a new role as a Decembrist. In "The Death of Ivan Ilych" reminders of the openness of life are written into the text—obscured, however, by the author's portrayal of souls in chains. In *War and Peace* we learn of the unknowable in language supremely clear and intolerant of obscurity; of the equality of souls in a work often imperial in tone (a work Homeric in scale, too, even while argumentative and satiric as Homer is not). Though as a work of rigorous concentration it little resembles *War and Peace,* "The Death of Ivan Ilych" is similarly riven with contradiction, and similarly probes the distinction between things publicized, noted, celebrated, and things unseen and unknown.

War and Peace opens with the "well-known" Anna Pavlovna Scherer greeting Prince Vasili,

> a man of high rank and importance, who was the first to arrive at her reception. Anna Pavlovna had had a cough for some days. She was, as she said, suffering from *la grippe*; *grippe* being then a new word in St. Petersburg, used only by the *élite*. (3)

Tell me the news, she asks the prince. "The Death of Ivan Ilych," after a scene concerning an item in the newspaper, conducts us to a kind of funeral soirée put on by the hero's wife, a stage on which she can dramatize her own fictitious suffering ("Oh what I have suffered!"). According to the *Discourse on Inequality*, as we know, at a fatal moment in human history being and seeming "became two entirely differing things, and from this distinction arose insolent ostentation, deceitful cunning and all the vices that follow in their train."[31] The memorial service for Ivan Ilych makes for a kind of theater of dissimulation, as does the gathering at Anna Pavlovna Scherer's in its own way. The prince has a motive in visiting Anna Pavlovna: to secure an appointment for one of his sons. Ivan Ilych's wife has a motive in taking aside Peter Ivanovich for some private conversation: to investigate the possibility of a larger pension. Inasmuch as the published notice of her husband's death has made the visit of such men as Peter Ivanovich socially obligatory in the first place, Tolstoy in the opening pages of "The Death of Ivan Ilych" ironizes distinction and public notice as rigorously as he does in attaching the epithet "well-known" to Anna Pavlovna Scherer. As early as *Childhood*, Tolstoy had marked the difference between sincere (as we might say, Rousseauian) grief and a simulated grief that makes itself noticed. In a stunning moment in the middle of *War and Peace*, two girls seek to *avoid* being noticed by Prince Andrew after stealing some plums from his hothouse. He does catch sight of them, but pretends not to. "A new sensation of comfort and relief came over him when, seeing these girls, he realized the existence of other human interests entirely aloof from his own and just as legitimate as those that occupied him" (754). Thus does a fleeting revelation of human equality come to a man little prepared to receive it. Like the visit of pilgrims to Bald Hills while Prince Bolkonsky is away; like the secrets her children keep from the Countess Rostova, who imagines they have none (43); like the theft of wood by Platon Karataev, which led to his conscription—the theft of the plums reminds us of all that exceeds our field of vision. In the middle of the novel Natasha herself reports that she was "punished once about some plums" (554), but as we know nothing about it, we can only say that this too surpasses our field of vision.

At this point it may be fitting to look back to the story Pierre loves to hear from Platon Karataev, which Tolstoy himself was later to tell in his own manner as "God Sees the Truth, But Waits." A nameless merchant wrongly convicted of murder and doing hard labor in Siberia discovers the actual murderer to be one of his fellow convicts. Penitent, the murderer confesses to the authorities, who in turn send a written petition to the tsar.

> The place was a long way off [says Platon Karataev], and while they were judging, with one thing and another, filling in the papers all in due order—the authorities I mean—time passed. The affair reached the Tsar. After a while the Tsar's decree came: to set the merchant free and give him a compensation that had been awarded. The paper arrived and they began to look for the old man. "Where is the old man who has been suffering innocently and in vain? A paper has come from the Tsar!" So they began looking for him . . . but God had already forgiven him—he was dead! That's how it was, dear fellow! (1135–36)

If God saw the truth, why did he wait?

If God adhered to the human principle that justice must not only be done but be seen to be done, he would have taken a different course in this case that gives every appearance of injustice triumphant, but God did not care to make a public demonstration of his justice to satisfy human demands (as both Ivan Karamazov and the Grand Inquisitor would have had it). The God of this fable does not traffic in the spectacular. His justice is like the sincere grief that does not advertise itself. Not only is he the God of those who live faithfully a hidden life (among them the nameless merchant), but so are his own ways hidden. The epigraph of *Anna Karenina*, "Vengeance is mine; I will repay," seems to imply, likewise, that justice will not be meted out in conformity with human fashions and demands.

At the mundane level, though, what delays the release of the innocent merchant is a bureaucratic system that requires all the paperwork to be "in due order," or that somehow gets lost in its own fantasy of restoring the merchant to freedom with full honors all around. Ivan Ilych, a bureaucratic expert, is the agent of such a system; in their own way, however, so too are his doctors, who pretend to be treating him to their own great honor and credit while he dies under their eyes.

6

"The Death of Ivan Ilych": Text vs. Author

If Ivan Ilych is a tragic hero, then so potentially is everyone.

A Negative Hero

As we know, near the end of the *Discourse on Inequality* Rousseau observes that we socialized people "have only façades, deceptive and frivolous, honour without virtue, reason without wisdom, and pleasure without happiness." "Social man lives always outside himself; he knows how to live only in the opinion of others."[1] The hero of Tolstoy's "The Death of Ivan Ilych" is portrayed in these terms exactly. His very existence seemingly a façade, Ivan Ilych squares all that he does with the opinions of others. On his deathbed he realizes, "I was going up in public opinion, but to the same extent life was ebbing away from me. And now it's all over and there's only death" (161). Fittingly if ironically, the tale opens with the hero's colleagues coming upon his obituary. He who lives by public opinion dies in the newspapers. As though Tolstoy had dedicated the tale to Rousseau, Ivan Ilych's world is one of "superiors and inferiors," too (135). Only when he suffers the superiority of the physicians who pretend to treat him does he begin to awaken to his own pretense. Depicting as it does such one-sided relations as judge to defendant and physician to patient (and these are conceived as analogous), "The Death of Ivan Ilych" offers a study in inequality. Of it Isaiah Berlin once wrote that it cannot be understood without an appreciation of Tolstoy's ideal of "a society of free and equal men, who live and think by the light of what is true and right, and so are not in conflict with each other or themselves."[2]

A hero leading the false life anatomized by Rousseau—a life of imitation and inauthenticity, envy and emulation, quite opposed to the Tolstoyan ideal—stretches the meaning of "hero" itself. Even Ivan Ilych's status as a hero in the modest sense of a protagonist is tenuous, for he possesses a kind of accidental centrality in his own story, a story that would never have been written had he not lost his footing momentarily on a stepladder. (A *War and Peace* equivalent of a minor mishap, scarcely even perceptible at the moment but full of fatal consequences, would be a pipe ash going astray in a city ripe for burning.) We might view "The Death of Ivan Ilych" as one in a line of Tolstoyan experiments in doing away with the institution of the hero. *War and Peace* drips irony on certain "special animals called 'heroes'" (1143) and has no central character. From the title of *Anna Karenina* we might suppose Anna herself to be its central character, but that distinction could equally go to Levin, whose life is so completely independent of hers that the two meet but once over the course of the novel. In operatic terms Anna Karenina is certainly the heroine of *Anna Karenina,* but Tolstoy does not subscribe to those terms and does not credit the delusions of one who imagines herself at the center of things. As though Tolstoy had taken his campaign against the hero as a literary institution to the limits of the possible, in "The Death of Ivan Ilych" the hero lacks all the expected characteristics of the kind and acquires his central position purely by chance. Though filled with the acid of scorn, the tale is not as dogmatic an act of negation as a tract like *What Is Art?* where the author's hatred of inauthenticity (and inequality) is released from the frame of fiction. And in elevating a nonentity to a genuinely tragic position, "The Death of Ivan Ilych" almost in spite of itself bears out the rising literary potential of commoners over the course of literature's history.

Tragedy with a Difference

According to Aristotle, comedy is "an imitation of inferior people."[3] By the nineteenth century, however, it had become possible to portray commoners not only with high seriousness but even in a tragic light. Yet the same realism that brought commoners to the fore of literature in the first place also subjected these newly tragic figures to conditions undreamed of by Aristotle. The heroes of tragic drama suffer, but they do not suffer

> the encumbrances of material contingency. Where men speak verse, they are not prone to catching colds or suffering from indigestion. They do not concern themselves with the next meal or train time-tables. Like wealth, in the poetics of Henry James and Proust, verse relieves the personages of tragic drama from the complications of material and physical need.[4]

In the tragic tale of Ivan Ilych, whose illness first manifests itself as something like indigestion, the ordeal of physical disease is depicted with a power seen perhaps neither before nor since. By the same token, "The Death of Ivan Ilych" departs radically from the Aristotelian model of tragedy, more radically perhaps than Tolstoy himself allows. By following out the tale's implications we arrive at conclusions in conflict with those imposed by the author's imperial language. The heroes of Dostoevsky possess such life and voice that to many they seem independent even of their author. In "The Death of Ivan Ilych," by contrast, the author's intention bears down on the tale with great force, so that any independence it might achieve will be against his will.

"The Death of Ivan Ilych" begins with reports of the hero's death in the form of a pretentious obituary published by his wife and interested comment by friends eyeing his now-vacant post.[5] The atmosphere of sordid insincerity carries over to the memorial service in the hero's home, with the wife exploring the possibility of a fatter pension and the friends going through the motions of mourning, disturbed by the proximity of death and eager to resume their card games. The hypocrisy of these proceedings is laid bare by the author with the severity that distinguishes the entire work. We are so repelled by the sight of mourners profaning the solemnity of death with their parodies of grief that we cannot imagine the dead man himself was equally shallow and self-centered, all the more because "the expression on [his] face said that what was necessary had been accomplished, and accomplished rightly. Besides this there was in that expression a reproach and a warning to the living" (125). As it happens, in life Ivan Ilych was morally indistinguishable from his false friends, and, had he been the survivor, he could easily have put in an appearance at a memorial for one of them on the way to an evening of cards, instead of the reverse. As Gary Saul Morson has argued, Tolstoy is the master of "sideshadowing," the intimation of what might have happened if things had taken another turn.[6] The fragility of the outcome of events in "The Death of Ivan Ilych" is itself a powerful fact whose significance dawns on the reader only slowly. In the reconstruction of the life of Ivan Ilych that follows the observance of his death, the turning point of the story—the onset of his reversal of fortune—is in fact the merest contingency, his slip on a stepladder hanging drapes.

In another work, such a misstep might be read as a symbol of the false path the hero has taken, or the perils of the ladder of success, but here the event is recounted so incidentally, with such a complete absence of portent, that only in retrospect does it stand out as the origin of the hero's illness. If his overreaching himself on a stepladder constitutes a tragic act, it also dramatizes his unfitness for the tragic role itself in the classical sense. Was there ever a more derisively prosaic height from which a tragic fall occurred? Anyway, Ivan Ilych's careerism is plain enough without being italicized for the knowing reader by the special language of symbols. The son of a civil servant described in Dickensian terms as a "superfluous member of various superfluous institutions" (129), Ivan Ilych follows the fashions of his class, attending law school, securing an official post, indulging in a little dissipation, and with the reform of the courts in the 1860s becoming an examining magistrate. It is in this position that he learns the art of professionalism, screening out all but the official aspects of the case before him. He marries; almost at once, the marriage curdles. Just as he separates his personal views from official duties, he flees an odious domestic life by throwing himself into his work. Promoted to public prosecutor, he holds the position for some seven years, enjoying his power and more particularly the illusion of relief from the misery of his marriage. Three of his children have died.

His career stagnating, Ivan Ilych journeys to St. Petersburg "with the sole object of obtaining a post with a salary of five thousand rubles a year" (136). By good luck he finds such a place in his former department, where as an added delight he is now the superior of his old colleagues—a detail that brings out the atmosphere of petty comparisons in which he and his set live. It is at the zenith of his fortunes, while decorating a new house for his wife and daughter, that Ivan Ilych suffers the bruise in his side that marks the starting point of his ordeal. Like Everyman in the medieval drama, who also devotes himself to false goods and suffers the desertion of his friends, he has been arrested by Death: the judge will himself undergo trial before the sentence is carried out. Over and beyond his physical pain is the moral torture, first of being treated by medical charlatans with the same haughty air he puts on in court (he too has become a case), second of being unable, practically until his last hour, to comprehend how it is that on his very deathbed he should be surrounded by pretenders. At the end comes realization. Recognizing that his own life was the fraud he can now perceive so clearly in others, he is set free by the truth, and as compassion even for his wife overcomes him (she is not so much worse than himself, after all), he dies to ease his family's sufferings as well as his own. Perhaps the look on the dead man's face said he had done his dying well because that is exactly what took place. A prisoner of false consciousness breaks through to the truth. A petty man performs an act of nobility. While for us, as readers, these events are of great significance, in the tale all goes on as before. As though Tolstoy had bitterly ironized the return to normalcy at the end of a tragedy, the death of Ivan Ilych leaves everything unchanged—the nonsense of the law courts, the falsity of the bureaucratic system, the play-acting of social life.

In some plain sense of the word corresponding to the work's own repudiation of technical language, the story of Ivan Ilych is indeed a tragedy. He rises to a position of power and prosperity only to undergo the most complete humiliation and the most grueling suffering. The state of acceptance in which he dies, and which appears to be written on his face in death, constitutes tragic knowledge. However, tragedy in this tale is subject to a double qualification. First, contrary to the tradition of drama itself, nothing happens suddenly in the tale, nothing disrupts the natural pace of time or violates the norms of common experience. Second, a mediocrity like Ivan Ilych, a mid-level civil servant, does not possess classical tragic stature. On his way to recognition, Ivan Ilych asks himself if it can really be possible that "I lost my life over that curtain as I might have done storming a fort" (151). A tragic hero by any canonical definition does not hang curtains, still less give up his life doing so. That Ivan Ilych does meet his fate in an accident on a stepladder—the contrary of a dramatic catastrophe, a non-event of the same order as his widow's shawl catching on the edge of a table—vividly illustrates what Lionel Trilling calls the "absurdly *conditioned*" nature of daily life, so mortifying to human pride, as well as the folly of "the small concerns of this world."[7] On the other hand, there is no getting away from daily life, and if Ivan Ilych deludes his own intelligence in decorating a house as though the life lived within its walls were not itself indecorous, he also deludes himself time and again by supposing he can shake off the prosaic facts of his domestic existence like dust off his feet. (After telling off her husband, Anna Karenina imagines making a clean break with her former life only to discover her inability to do any such thing. Even if Karenin represents in her eyes only a detestable code of "lies and propriety" [208], much like the code of Ivan Ilych, this does not mean she can shake off the facts of her domestic existence.) If we find our circumstances absurd and humiliating, this is precisely because they permit no escape. Only a Quixote dreams of attacking castles. Considered in the light of the prosaic, the idea of storming forts may in fact be just as hollow as that of beautifying an ugly life with the right drapes. An incongruous hero, Ivan Ilych is both more and less free than a classically tragic figure: more inasmuch as he is not subject to Fate or otherworldly agents (making his ruin absolutely his own doing), less inasmuch as he is subject to material necessities, embarrassments of the body, absurd conditions, traps of prosaic existence from which the other is exempt.

The result is a tragedy that conforms but roughly to the literary norm of tragedy itself.[8] There is much in the tradition of drama as such—not only its improbable reversals but its spectacular contrasts between the high and the low, master and man, figure and ground—that offends Tolstoy's belief in the equality of souls and is repugnant to the ethos of "The Death of Ivan Ilych." What is most detestable about Praskovya Fedorovna is precisely her dramatics. If "The Death of Ivan Ilych" constitutes a tragedy, then, it must be a tragedy of its own kind, unlike any in existence. Certain of the Aristotelian conditions of tragedy are in fact fulfilled inversely in "The Death of Ivan Ilych." "The preparations for marriage and the beginning of married life, with its conjugal caresses, new furniture, new crockery, and new linen, were very pleasant until his wife became pregnant" (133). A man who experiences his wife's pregnancy as a reversal of fortune, as though it were an unexpected outcome, is himself somehow the reverse of an Aristotelian hero.[9] What of Aristotle's requirement that the hero be "one of those people who are held in great esteem"? As Ivan Ilych himself eventually recognizes, his concern with reputation, his dependence on "esteem," was itself the flaw that precipitated his fall from happiness to misery. "I was going up in public opinion, but to the same extent life was ebbing away from me. And now it's all over and there's only death" (161). What Aristotle terms the "serious error" committed by a man enjoying the good fortune of public esteem becomes, in the case of Ivan Ilych, subservience to public opinion itself.

Similarly, while the best tragedies, according to Aristotle, "are constructed around a few households," it is as a householder in the sorriest sense of the word that Ivan Ilych mounts the fatal stepladder.[10] We wonder, too, if the tale does not begin at the end, with the hero already dead, to confound the Aristotelian framework of beginning, middle, and end. It is as if Tolstoy had distilled literature down to tragedy in "The Death of Ivan Ilych," preserving from Aristotle, however, only the outline of the tragic plot as a terrible reverse suffered on account of a serious error.[11] Arguably Ivan Ilych's most serious error is his marriage to the "thoroughly correct young woman" (133) who very soon reveals herself a repulsive nag.

If the truth uncovered by Ivan Ilych in the course of his ordeal compares in horror to Oedipus's discovery that his entire life has been plotted, this is in part because his own life was scripted as well. Where Tolstoy's art shatters the model of tragic composition, Ivan Ilych follows the way of life laid down by his class as implicitly as if he were obeying an edict of destiny, even marrying because it seems the correct thing to do. Like Oedipus, that is, he walks blindly into the lethal trap that has been prepared for him, except that it has been prepared not by Fate but by the human beings whose ways he imitates, the members of good society. That the story line he follows to his own ruin was written not by the gods but by mortals as deluded as himself makes his subjection to it all the more absurd and pitiful.[12]

Walking straight into a cage "from which there was no way of escape" (133), Ivan Ilych provides an illustration at once prosaic, tragic, and ridiculous of the dictum that man, born free, is everywhere in chains. According to J. S. Mill, one who sells himself into slavery enters into an invalid contract because "the principle of freedom cannot be that he should be free not to be free. It is not freedom to be allowed to alienate his freedom."[13] Unlike the disappointed slave, Ivan Ilych in plunging into marital bondage has no idea of what he's getting into and yet enters into a perfectly valid contract, making his position in a sense even more grotesque. And it is his marriage that sets the course of the rest of his life. The consequences of an absurd union descend on him as inexorably as, later, the consequences of disease, and prompt the same attempt to ignore and escape his own condition as that disease. In fact, if Ivan Ilych hadn't been in the habit of draping the ugliness of his domestic life, drapery per se might not have been so important to him and he might never have suffered his injury. First as a husband, then as a patient, Ivan Ilych veils the truth from himself. Although in the eyes of literature, marriage to a shrew would ordinarily make you a comic figure, with Ivan Ilych it is otherwise. The comic potential of his situation comes to nothing, realizing itself instead as the bitter mockery of tragedy.

The tragedy of *Great Expectations* is laced with humor. "The Death of Ivan Ilych" is laced with what might be called potential humor. The sheer unlikelihood of the hero calls to mind the diminutive heroes of the mock-epic, figures absurdly out of proportion to the heroic scheme itself. That Ivan Ilych was mortally wounded not on the field of battle but on a stepladder seems even to him ridiculous, though bitterly so. At the time of the decorating accident, Ivan Ilych and his wife were "at one in their aims and moreover saw so little of one another, they got on together better than they had done since the first years of their marriage" (137), a remark that might elsewhere be taken as a witticism but here serves as a straight description of fact. The marriage itself is if anything even worse than that of Don Jóse and Donna Inez in *Don Juan,* who

led
For some time an unhappy sort of life,
Wishing each other, not divorced, but dead.
They lived respectably as man and wife.[14]

Donna Inez "saw *his* agonies with such sublimity / That all the world exclaimed, 'What magnanimity!'"[15] Praskovya Fedorovna pretends to bear her husband's suffering with heroic fortitude. The differing opinions the sick man himself receives from medical experts are potentially as comical as the conflicting pronouncements in the courtroom on the question of Dmitri Karamazov's sanity. The very chamber pot is a traditional comic prop.[16] The cranky springs of a sofa make for a kind of slapstick during Ivan Ilych's memorial.[17] The height of the ridiculous proves the vanishing point of the ridiculous in "The Death of Ivan Ilych."

Indeterminacy

"The practice of the romancer in the matter of invention differs from that of the tragedian, not in kind nor in theory, but only in the extent to which it is carried," which is to say that action in the romance is multiplied for its own sake and spun out to indefinite length.[18] With this in mind, arguably the primary feature of "The Death of Ivan Ilych," its powerful concentration, its omission of all but the essential, indicates a rejection of romance and a kinship with the tragic mode. If you strip away everything false and ornamental from fiction, this novella seems to say (and its hero undergoes such a correction), you arrive at tragedy. So it is in the tale itself: it does away with all of the tricks of romance. So emphatic is Tolstoy's repudiation of artifice, so strong his will to return fiction itself to the soil of truth, that a revolutionary possessed of ideals like these might dream of clearing out a capital city and forcing its population into the countryside. Mercifully, Tolstoy's violence is purely literary. The destruction of the idols of fiction dictates the complete negation of the original romantic conventions of the novel.

In a coincidence reminiscent of traditional romance, Nicholas Rostov comes to the rescue of the endangered Princess Mary. Over the course of "The Death of

Ivan Ilych" there seems but a single coincidence—namely, that Ivan Ilych runs into an acquaintance and discovers an opening in the Department of Justice as he sets out for St. Petersburg to look for a new post—but on the other hand, a coincidence once in a while is itself in the natural order of things. With the exception of the fact that a fatal illness begins with a knock on the side (though in the novella's own terms this too is in the course of nature), nothing in the narrative offends probability. No author ever took more seriously Dr. Johnson's admonition that it is modern fiction's task "to bring about natural events by easy means, and to keep up curiosity without the help of wonder; it is therefore precluded from the machines and expedients of the heroic romance." As Johnson says in the same paper of the protagonist of a modern novel, Ivan Ilych is "leveled with the rest of the world"—the imagination of Tolstoy awakening the full latent force of the word "leveled."[19] Things do not simply happen to Ivan Ilych like some hero of romance buffeted by the wind of the extraordinary. For the most part, in fact, the implications of his own actions descend on him in the inexorable way that suffering follows crime in the logic of tragedy—except that in this case all is the work of natural causality, not of avenging furies or the decrees of Law. Try as he may to escape his wife, Ivan Ilych must return to her vulgarity sooner or later and reckon with the humiliations he brought on himself when he married her. Try as he may to ignore, arrest, or even palliate his disease (the result of another misstep, in this case literal), it returns with full force. That he experiences at the hands of his physicians exactly the sort of almightiness he himself radiates in court may seem the work of a retributive god but, as I will argue, is actually the rigorously natural consequence of his own fascination with illusory goods like celebrity and prestige. Instead of haunting specters and inescapable edicts, Ivan Ilych is subjected to the haunting returns of his own actions and the bitter futility of the attempt to escape from himself.

So it is that the horror of his story as he himself comes to understand it lies not so much in how he dies as in how he lived. Even his decorating accident would not have happened had he not been so intent on outfitting his house with "all the things people of a certain class have in order to resemble other people of that class" (138). The accident itself is the kind of thing that could well happen within the ordinary course of events—something, as it were, minimally improbable. Like the machinery of the supernatural, the wonders of the romance plot are rigorously excluded as violations of the work's intent to bring the hero to an examination of his own life without distractions or excuses. The expedient used to achieve this end is the most natural one possible, the furthest from the artifices of fiction: illness. Immobilizing him, isolating him from practically all souls but the loyal servant Gerasim, illness leaves Ivan Ilych with no release from suffering and nothing to do but think. (In *War and Peace* two prisoners about to be executed by the French cannot comprehend what is about to happen to them, "because they alone knew what their life meant to them, and so they neither understood nor believed that it could be taken from them"

[1031]. Ivan Ilych experiences a similar terror and incomprehension but is not granted a quick release.) That his doctors prove his mirror image is anything but a coincidence. The allure of social brilliance that drew him to his wife in the first place (and draws her to Sarah Bernhardt as he lies dying) also makes her insist on his consulting "a celebrated doctor" (142) at the onset of his illness, and it is this notable who treats him with the same show of superiority he himself puts on in court. From Ivan Ilych's experience of this impostor come the first rays of enlightenment—not only a sense of what the wretches in his own power might feel but a dim perception of his own falsity, now glimpsed in another. Precisely in their arrogance and fraud, the doctors in "The Death of Ivan Ilych" serve as the catalysts of the hero's awakening. Ivan Ilych is linked to these tormentors as closely as a man and his own reflection, almost as closely as the terms of a syllogism. Were their resemblance to him purely incidental, it could never have produced such a profound, if gradual, effect of recognition.

Only in seeking again and again to evade his condition does Ivan Ilych learn that it cannot be evaded, and only by entangling himself over and over in delusion is he brought face-to-face with his capacity for self-deceit. In any event, Ivan Ilych could not possibly have understood the truth of his case from the moment of the mishap ("he felt particularly bright and well just then" [138]), and even if he had, he would have remained in ignorance of the more important truth arrived at in the course of his long crisis. So it is that he is denied the quick and glorious end of one storming a fort and is subjected to the inglories of illness and the torment of a slow passage toward death. Time itself is the most fundamental of forces in "The Death of Ivan Ilych." When Magwitch pours out his gratitude to the twenty-three-year-old Pip because of the kindness Pip did him many years before—"You acted nobly, my boy. Noble Pip!" (321)—he neglects to account for the passage of time and the possible erosion of the boy's nobility. As Ivan Ilych comes to realize with the approach of death, time eroded the authenticity that was his in childhood. Time qualifies the spark and fire of life. Time does not possess a purely negative character, however. Compelled by the sheer protraction of his ordeal to search his soul, Ivan Ilych uncovers a truth never glimpsed before.

As his illness takes hold, Ivan Ilych visits a renowned doctor at his wife's insistence:

> He went. Everything took place as he had expected and as it always does. There was the usual waiting and the important air assumed by the doctor, with which he was so familiar (resembling that which he himself assumed in court), and the sounding and listening, and the questions which called for answers that were foregone conclusions and were evidently unnecessary, and the look of importance which implied that "if only you put yourself in our hands we will arrange everything—we know indubitably how it has to be

> done, always in the same way for everybody." It was all just as it was in the law courts. The doctor put on just the same air towards him as he himself put on towards an accused person. (142)

Though written in the third person, this passage reflects in some degree the hero's own perceptions.[20] In the consultant's air of professional detachment and competent authority Ivan Ilych recognizes his own manner, even as he senses that this man is of no possible use to him. The experience is repeated with other doctors, all of them mirroring back his own demeanor in court, none of them able to treat or even understand his disease, or much reduce his pain. Faced with his own fraudulence, the judge himself is put on trial, by analogy with the physician challenged to heal himself. In the eyes of satire, after all, the physician and the lawyer are twins, both swollen with the pride of false learning, both given to lying, both plagues to those unlucky enough to find themselves in their power.[21] That Ivan Ilych can discern his resemblance to these masters of sham indicates the dawning of vision, though only the dawning. To bring him to full understanding all at once, to have recognition flash upon him instantly, would violate Tolstoy's principle of doing nothing by jumps. Ivan Ilych perceives readily enough that he is just like his own physicians and furthermore that these men are impostors, but not until the end does he bow to the inescapable conclusion that he too has been an impostor. It is as though even a syllogism took time to sink in. As a student he indeed learned that "Caius is a man, men are mortal, therefore Caius is mortal," but this "had always seemed to him correct as applied to Caius, but it certainly didn't apply to himself" (149). Human equality, however, dictates that it does apply. Experience also confronts Ivan Ilych with the syllogism, "The medical experts are pretenders, I am just like them, I too am a pretender," a conclusion even more difficult to accept than the fact of his mortality.

Guilty of killing his father and marrying his mother but without the knowledge that these are his parents, Oedipus defines the tragic conundrum of guilt-in-innocence that applies as well to Ivan Ilych. The guilt of Ivan Ilych is of a different kind, however, in that he commits no crime, no real act of turpitude, nothing that seems to justify the ordeal of his slow death. "But I'm not guilty!" (162) he cries out some weeks before the end, his struggle not yet concluded, and in a narrow sense he is correct. As a judge he never took bribes or threw people in jail for no reason, "never abused his power; on the contrary he tried to soften its expression" (132). Scrupulous and incorruptible even as he tempers justice with mercy, Ivan Ilych seems more like a textbook example of a good judge than one who deserves to be tried and convicted himself. He lives by the book of propriety as well, marrying because it is what decent people do and following the social code in all things. In point of fact it is the outward irreproachability of Ivan Ilych's life that constitutes his guilt in the author's eyes and at last in his own.[22] Though passing at his ease through crowds of supplicants in the enjoyment of his power (again somewhat in the manner of Oedipus) violates no statute, the act is indecent. Under the sanction of legal propriety, Ivan Ilych treats those in his power with a kind of majesty whose fraudulence he can appreciate only when he is reduced to a position equally miserable; under the cover of social convention he leads a domestic life so sordid it verges on the obscene. In either case it is the knowledge that he is abiding by an established code of conduct that allows him to act so unreflectively. Innocence underwrites indecency and fraud. As if in a free interpretation of the intermediate character of the tragic hero, Ivan Ilych is neither admirable nor depraved, and suitably to the satiric logic of tragedy, the very principles in which he found his safety prove his ruin.

On many grounds, then, "The Death of Ivan Ilych" qualifies as a tragedy. The hero endures not only great suffering but a kind of absolute abasement, an experience so rending it destroys the seeming unity of his being. Subjected to tragedy's mocking logic, he finds his own power of action turned against him and must try himself where before he tried others. The reversal of his fortunes brings with it recognition—in this instance, recognition of his own hollowness. As with a tragic hero, in spite of his sins Ivan Ilych is by no means the worst of men, and his torment seems in excess of justice. Again, however, this is tragedy with a difference, Tolstoy having eliminated the most axiomatic quality of the tragic hero, the ground of all his other qualities, his singularity. In the world of Oedipus there is none like him. Another of his magnitude would be a second sun in the heavens. Like a figure raised above the ground, tragic greatness stands out against everything else, now reduced by contrast to a single plane.[23] The same sort of naturalism that leads Tolstoy to allow no jumps in "The Death of Ivan Ilych," but instead to trace the gradual working of great changes, prohibits a hero who has himself vaulted beyond the ordinary range of human character and experience. In high tragedy the hero "in a very real sense . . . lets the servants live for him. It is they who assume the corrupting burdens of hunger, sleep, and ailment."[24] Ivan Ilych knows ailment in his own person. He stands not above the common plane, but on it. At least until the onset of his crisis, nothing sets him morally apart from the friends who hasten from his memorial to their card game (he himself loved cards), the doctors who impose to the very end, possibly even the wife who leaves him on his sickbed to take in the performance of Sarah Bernhardt.[25]

As it turns out, the warning written on Ivan Ilych's face in death is therefore directed at those like himself—his equals. First meeting him as he lies in state, we cannot imagine that the life he led was completely out of character with his postmortem dignity. The sage in death was a fool in life. That he did break through his own delusions means, however, that the power of sham over him was not absolute. According to Max Weber, the bitter result of the rationalization of the world is the entrapment of human beings in an "iron cage" of their own making.[26] Ivan Ilych pries his way out. Is it not then possible that some other trifler or opportunist will one day do the same, even if it be in the shadow of death? So stereotypical are Ivan Ilych's false friends and insincere wife that we cannot begin to envision them awakening to their own disgrace as he does, but he did awaken, and who is to say they cannot? It is true that they seem the very definition of hypocrisy, as though hypocrisy summed up their entire being and they could never become other than they are. But a careerist is all Ivan Ilych gave any appearance of being. For Schwartz with his false cheer or Praskovya Fedorovna with her addiction to acting and aversion to truth to look into themselves is not so much more unlikely than the thought of Ivan Ilych, a man of no originality, disowning the script he lived by. Having come to the realization that "the further he departed from childhood and the nearer he came to the present the more worthless and doubtful were the joys" (161), Ivan Ilych is visited with fragmentary memories like those more fully rendered in Tolstoy's own beautiful evocation, *Childhood.* If it was as a result of his childhood that some flicker of truth remained with Ivan Ilych in adult life, had not others a childhood? In spite of his escapism, there is already a momentary glint of awareness, a stirring of possibility, in Peter Ivanovich, distressed as he is at the "consciousness of his own and [Praskovya Fedorovna's] dissimulation" at the dead man's memorial (128). The detail appears incidentally and passes quickly, as the report of Ivan Ilych's misstep does also.

In Tolstoy's powerful fable of human equality, "Master and Man," the former, an unremarkable figure, suddenly finds it in himself to warm his servant with his own body when the two, lost in the snow, face death. He seems to depart from the being he was. So does Ivan Ilych defeat prediction; but if he possesses the spark of moral capacity, others equally unpromising might as well. In this tragedy in defiance of Aristotle, precisely because the hero is quite ordinary (as is the incident that triggers his crisis), someone else could conceivably occupy his position. The aristocratic character of tragedy accommodates the modern principle of equality. And where "tragedy seems to lead up to an epiphany of law, of that which is and must be," "The Death of Ivan Ilych" reminds us of what might be—the possibility of awakening.[27] The tale speaks of the contingent, not just the necessary. Unlike a Freudian slip determined by an underlying compulsion, Ivan Ilych's slip on the stepladder was after all genuine—determined by nothing. If Oedipus, the exemplar of tragedy, was condemned to murder his father and marry his mother, the tragedy of Ivan Ilych takes place in the absence of Fate and its modern equivalent, irresistible causal forces. As though to confound the tragic precept that character is destiny, the tragic figure in this case is a man of small character and destiny does not exist. The iron cage is not perfect, unexpected outcomes are not precluded, critical issues are undetermined. A tragedy where so much is left open to the play of possibility is itself something no one would have predicted.

For Dostoevsky "man is not a final and defined quantity upon which firm calculations can be made, man is free, and can therefore violate any regulating norms which might be thrust upon him," as Bakhtin remarks in a discussion of the Underground Man and his contest with the words of others.[28] In the first chapter of his *Notes* the Underground Man identifies himself as a man of forty, once a civil servant, who now seems to have something wrong with his liver. Ivan Ilych in the middle of his tale could be described in terms quite similar, and by the end, as if to prove that he too is no "final and defined quantity," he defeats the norms he lived by. The better to realize his heroes in all their indeterminacy, Dostoevsky shifts the center of consciousness to them, making *The Brothers Karamazov* a structure with several focal points, a *Hamlet* with more than one prince. While Tolstoy concentrates in "The Death of Ivan Ilych" on change over time rather than the moment of crisis (as when Hamlet unsheathes his sword over the kneeling Claudius, or when Dmitri brandishes a weapon as he peers in on his father), he takes indeterminacy to perhaps even greater lengths than Dostoevsky in *The Brothers Karamazov* by making the hero's status *as* hero practically a matter of chance and leaving open—by implication—the possibility of others some day undergoing a transformation of their own. What of the schoolboy Vasya, "who looked extremely like his father" (129)? Or even the fop engaged to his daughter, like himself an examining magistrate? In this world the center of consciousness can be anywhere.[29] Though he does not probe the limits of Euclidean reality like his mighty opposite Dostoevsky, Tolstoy does open up the Aristotelian framework by depriving the tragic hero of his primary possession, his uniqueness.[30]

According to Aristotle, tragedy excites pity and fear, pity for unmerited suffering and fear for "the person like us." In Ivan Ilych this latter condition becomes virtually absolute. Tolstoy has fashioned one so much like us as to shatter the Aristotelian paradigm, a man indistinguishable from any other of his sort until he literally stumbles onto tragic experience. Ironized in Ivan Ilych is the very salience of a hero, that quality in virtue of which all eyes fasten onto him. Hanging drapes in an attempt to give his new house a touch of salience, he succeeds only in making it look "so like others that it would never have been noticed " (138). Thinking himself a figure, Ivan Ilych proves himself a nobody. In one sense, however, this lack of singularity may be a virtue. Those in "The Death of Ivan Ilych" who play up their own distinction, whether eminent doctors or the great Sarah Bernhardt or the also theatrical Praskovya Fedorovna in her role as the queen of suffering—all appear as corrupt and fraudulent as the theater itself in the opinion of Rousseau. Such is the originality of "The Death of Ivan Ilych" that it constitutes a tragedy, and a great one, even as it rejects theatricality per se and exposes the dramatization of the self as the cultivation of a false distinction.

At the time of his accident, no sign appears of what is truly remarkable in Ivan Ilych, his power to question and reflect. But if this man seemingly without distinction carries within himself the seed of tragic capacity and the potential for enlightenment, may not others as well? What if the tale contains stirrings of meaning we do not register as yet, just as Ivan Ilych's stumble reads as his "downfall" only after the fact? Before the significance of that event was perfectly obvious it was perfectly invisible. On his deathbed it occurs to Ivan Ilych that "his scarcely perceptible attempts to struggle against what was considered good by the most highly placed people, those scarcely noticeable impulses which he had immediately suppressed, might have been the real thing, and all the rest false" (164). Maybe other signs in the tale go unrecognized as well. After all, Gerasim, who rises into prominence in the latter part of the work, barely attracts our notice in its first section. Another background figure, Ivan Ilych's son Vasya, is a kind of crux of indeterminacy, possessing as he does something of the beauty of childhood even though, at his father's memorial, his eyes have the look of "boys of thirteen or fourteen who are not pure-minded" (129).[31] What will this schoolboy become? We might think of "The Death of Ivan Ilych" as a detective story with no crime in the conventional sense, with clues of the highest subtlety, but most importantly—and in accordance with Tolstoy's own distrust of the neatness of narrative—with an open solution. If we never find out exactly how Moscow burned or what exactly happened on the battlefield of Borodino but only, in both cases, what might have taken place, still less can we speak with knowledge of what might take place in the future.

Word and Deed

One evening, while Ivan Ilych lies dying, his wife enters the room dressed to the nines, "her full bosom pushed up by her corset, and with traces of powder on her face. She had reminded him in the morning that they were going to the theater. Sarah Bernhardt was visiting town" (158). In her shallowness and grotesque sensuality, Praskovya Fedorovna serves as a living illustration of Rousseau's thesis of the depraving effect of the theater and of good society itself. Just as Ivan Ilych's loss of happiness and entrapment in falsity pick up Rousseau's theme of the fatal effect of dependence on public opinion—and it is Rousseau, after all, whose maxim "Man is born free; and is everywhere in chains" presides like a sort of warning inscription over "The Death of Ivan Ilych"—so it was the purely social brilliance deplored by Rousseau that attracted Ivan Ilych to this woman in the first place (132). Tolstoy, we are reminded,

> remained an admirer of Rousseau, and late in life still recommended *Emile* as the best book ever written on education. Rousseau must have strengthened, if he did not actually originate, his growing tendency to idealise the soil and its cultivators—the simple peasant, who for Tolstoy is a repository of almost as rich a stock of "natural" virtues as Rousseau's noble savage. Rousseau, too,

must have reinforced the coarse-grained, rough peasant in Tolstoy with his strongly moralistic, puritanical strain, his suspicion of, and antipathy to, the rich, the powerful, the happy as such.[32]

The simple peasant is exemplified in "The Death of Ivan Ilych" in the butler's assistant whose kindly offices to the dying man contrast so sharply with the selfishness of his wife. For their part, had the doctors in "The Death of Ivan Ilych" heeded Rousseau's admonition to "give up the attempt to strip the veil from nature once and for all," they would have spared Ivan Ilych many a useless test and many a false exhibition of knowledge.[33] (As Rousseau records in book 6 of the *Confessions*, he himself was subjected to nonsensical explanations and vain measures at the hands of the doctor when he fell seriously ill. "I can well say that I did not begin to live until I looked on myself as a dead man,"[34] which holds true, more or less, of Ivan Ilych as well.) The doctors' disrespect for the unknown seems of a piece with their cultivation of false distinction. As to Praskovya Fedorovna, in attempting to parlay her husband's death into a bigger pension, she like the friends interested in the dead man's post displays a glaring lack of Rousseauian virtue, for it was a principle with Rousseau "never to profit in any way by the death of anyone dear to me."[35] Praskovya Fedorovna stands before us fully defined, the very type of vanity and luxury in the complete Rousseauian sense. That is what she is and that is all she will ever be. One who appears at her husband's deathbed with "her full bosom pushed up by her corset" has provoked the "puritanical" criticism leveled at her. Confirming to the letter Rousseau's portrayal of the falsity of those goods that exist only in the eyes of society, she possessed charm as a girl and is drawn to prestige in the person of renowned doctors and to celebrity in that of Sarah Bernhardt. In complaining, during the memorial for her husband, of how greatly she suffered at the end, her theatrics are of one piece with the falsity she displayed in quitting him for the theater in the first place. This woman is a known quantity. She is the human image of insincerity and will never be anything other than that. It is impossible to read "The Death of Ivan Ilych" without a strong conviction that this is the interpretation the author intends.

But the tale itself plays the fox to the author's intention.

For much as Ivan Ilych outgrows what seems like his own fixed nature, achieving tragic stature and insight, so the tale itself transcends the ideological framework so forcibly stamped upon it by the author's Rousseauian program. If Praskovya Fedorovna stands fully defined, her husband once seemed locked into his definition as a nonentity—a man of no depth, a hopeless prisoner of false consciousness—and that impression proved false. Whatever the intent of the teller, the tale itself shows that our experience cannot be predetermined, our moral capacities known with finality in advance of experience. The *Odyssey* rules out surprise. "The Death of Ivan Ilych" brings forth surprise in a world where surprise seemed excluded—where the ending is given before the tale even begins, and everyone, including the hero, seems fully known.

This appearance proves deceptive. No one is really an open book. Of none can it be said with certainty: this person is forever incapable of enlightenment. Given woman's special reputation for false display, we assume the theater is Praskovya Fedorovna's idea and hers alone, but as we learn in a brief passage of considerable import, actually Ivan Ilych is the one who demanded that the children see the legendary actress.

> They had a box, which he had insisted on their taking. Now he had forgotten about it and her toilet offended him, but he concealed his vexation when he remembered that he had himself insisted on their securing a box and going because it would be an instructive and aesthetic pleasure for the children. (158)

That Ivan Ilych still thinks the theater an edifying institution, even while perceiving the falsity that envelops him for exactly what it is, constitutes another proof of the reality of time in this tale. Enlightenment does not come to Ivan Ilych all at once. Enlightenment is not absolute, and neither perhaps is ignorance. At any rate, when mother and daughter head for the theater with Ivan Ilych on his deathbed, it is not exactly the act of desertion it appears. In the end the imagination of Tolstoy is simply too honest to portray Ivan Ilych as a victim of his wife's fraudulence.

Admittedly, it is hard to imagine a Xanthippe like Praskovya Fedorovna, who complains of her husband's suffering when she doesn't ignore it, achieving tragic dignity and depth. But who would have imagined Ivan Ilych capable of breaking through the lies in which he lived? Moreover, he himself at one time turned his back on the ailments of his child and the possibly real ailments of his wife, indifferent to both as they would later prove toward him. In one of those telling episodes related in passing like his slip on the stepladder, the new father recoils from illnesses he is neither concerned with nor understands:

> With the birth of their child, attempts to feed it and the various failures in doing so, and with the real and imaginary illnesses of mother and child, in which Ivan Ilych's sympathy was demanded but about which he understood nothing, the need of securing for himself an existence outside his family life became still more imperative. (134)

That Ivan Ilych deepens in the course of suffering does not mean that his also obtuse and indifferent wife will deepen as well; it means that we dare not rule out the possibility. Time, the subtlest of forces, will perhaps work some change in Praskovya Fedorovna. That Ivan Ilych dies asking his wife's forgiveness, overcome with pity at the sight of her suffering, establishes Praskovya Fedorovna in any case as more than a caricature of a human being. Throughout the tale she has figured as a kind of degrading circumstance Ivan Ilych cannot escape—the shackle on his foot. Finally the richly prosaic imagination of Tolstoy cannot reduce this daughter of commonplace beneath the level of humanity. Through the last act of Ivan Ilych, the definition of Praskovya Fedorovna as a common shrew, and nothing but that, is retracted.

It is said that Tolstoy in *War and Peace* "wanted to change our habit of viewing our lives as if they resembled conventional narratives. Our lives have not been authored in advance, but are lived as we go along. They are process, not product."[36] The iconoclastic spirit of this project—the revolt against conventional narrative as if it were one more means of bewitching human intelligence, like the mysteries of freemasonry or priestcraft—is probably responsible for the independence of "The Death of Ivan Ilych" itself, that is, the complete freedom with which it handles the principles of tragedy. But if lives are not authored in advance, neither is the outcome of the life story of Ivan Ilych's false friends, or even his detestable wife, given in advance. Tolstoy indeed categorizes relentlessly, so much so that even characters at the fringes of the tale, like the various unnamed "shabby friends and relations" who descend on Ivan Ilych at one point "with much show of affection" (140), seem to wear their definition on their brow. Tolstoy's word renders summary judgment. But as the tale of Ivan Ilych unfolds, Tolstoy's deed contradicts his word. Here is a man displayed before us like a specimen in a case, categorized as a blind fool, who transcends his own typicality in the ordeal of coming to consciousness. If Dostoevsky grants his heroes rights against himself, renouncing as it were the advantage of authorship, Ivan Ilych is given the power to refute his definition as a man lost to the truth. The extraordinary fact of his awakening calls into question the dismissive characterization of all the others in the tale categorized scarcely more summarily than himself. Their history remains unwritten. Under the tale's non-Aristotelian conditions, no one figure engrosses all tragic potential. Others too may achieve the dignity of tragic stature—who, how, and when we cannot say. "Contingency always reigns," as it reigned over Ivan Ilych's mishap in the first place.[37] If Ivan Ilych—Anyman—is cast into the heroic position by chance and achieves, over time, insight of which he could never have been imagined capable before the fact, one equally improbable may also at some time be enlightened by suffering. And if we ask, "What does it matter if someone is transformed by suffering when his place in the social mill is simply filled by another and all goes on as before?" the answer can only be that, whatever its utility, the act of awakening matters in itself, as the story of Ivan Ilych's own awakening powerfully demonstrates.

Others possess the same potential as Ivan Ilych: so at least the evidence of the tale implies. And that evidence overrides the power of the author's intent (a possibility Tolstoy himself allowed for in his reading of Chekhov's tale "The Darling").[38] If Ivan Ilych breaks through his own confines, "The Death of Ivan Ilych" overcomes the rigidity of the author's own position—his hatred of good society, his harsh caricature of woman, his cold wrath. By analogy with the "surplus of humanness"[39] that makes it impossible to reduce Ivan Ilych to an overpaid bureaucrat, the tale as such possesses a profound humanity that takes it out of conformity with the narrow views behind it.

Though Dostoevsky, the psychologist of envy, envied Tolstoy's leisure; though *War and Peace* deals with the historical and *Crime and Punishment* with an imaginary Napoleon; though Tolstoy slighted *Crime and Punishment* and Dostoevsky *Anna Karenina*—for all of this, and all of the differences that heightened their rivalry, Dostoevsky and Tolstoy had a mutual friend, Nikolai Strakhov, a critic of the spiritualist movement. In his 1878 monograph on "Basic Concepts of Psychology," which he presumably discussed with both novelists, Strakhov asserts the unknowability of the self, meaning that the subject "is not susceptible to being known as an object." It has been said that both Tolstoy and Dostoevsky develop the implications of this principle.[40]

In "The Death of Ivan Ilych" it is the unknowability of the person that allows Ivan Ilych himself to develop in ways that would never have been predicted or even imagined, and that preserve similar possibilities for everyone else in the tale despite the author's use of language that seems to know all there is to know. In effect, "The Death of Ivan Ilych" teaches what Rousseau's Savoyard Vicar considers the thing most needful: "The only thing we do not know is how to be ignorant of what we cannot know."[41] In *The Brothers Karamazov* readers are continually reminded of the limits on their knowledge, as if only so could they understand the mystery of the world.

7

Quixotism in The Brothers Karamazov

In the tradition of Don Quixote, Dmitri Karamazov imagines himself a hero of romance, singled out by and for the extraordinary; but in this case a reader may not be able to know a giant from a windmill.

Equality as a Literary Principle

If, as M. M. Bakhtin argues, the hero of a novel cannot be "a clerk, a landowner, a merchant, a fiancé, a jealous lover, a father," and nothing more,[1] in the person of Fyodor Pavlovich Karamazov we meet a landowner who "hardly ever lived on his own estate" (7), a businessman who pays no attention to his taverns, a father who more or less forgot the existence of his sons and stands as a kind of antithesis of fatherhood as such, and a possessive lover who does not in fact possess the woman of his affections and probably never could. Neither, however, does *The Brothers Karamazov* itself slot into existing categories. Whether the author's genius was just too original to fit a model or his interest in boundary conditions extended even to boundaries of a literary kind, the fact is that *The Brothers Karamazov* blurs the lines that set off one literary domain from another. It redraws the map of literature; or imagines one where the continents haven't yet drifted apart. In view of its strongly dramatic character, even cataloging *The Brothers Karamazov* as a novel, the most open and least defined of literary forms, is somehow misleading. *Joseph Andrews* is bewilderingly classified by its author as a "comic epic-poem in prose."[2] *The Brothers Karamazov* might be termed a drama in prose, a drama both comic and tragic.

It is of course strictly impossible for narrative to become drama, inasmuch as stage action is not related to the audience but realized in its presence. This impossibility does not daunt an author unwilling to sacrifice either the immediacy of drama or the unlimited range of narrative. Parallel lines do meet, more or less, in *The Brothers Karamazov.* The elementary distinction between drama and narrative loses much of its force in a work where by far the greater part of the telling is done directly by the characters themselves—the only description of the murder comes from the killer—and where the narration is hedged with disclaimers as if to keep it from intervening too positively between the reader and events. Such narration as there is, moreover, is deeply infiltrated by the direct speech of the characters. The novel opens conventionally enough, with information about the brothers' childhood—all were abandoned by their father and taken in by others, like the exposed infants of romance—but not until the scandal scene in the elder's cell do we learn of current affairs in the Karamazov family, and then not through narration but direct speech. So knotted and tense is the situation that emerges that it could work itself out in a dozen ways.[3] Much as a character might be endowed with a surplus of potential, the conflict in the Karamazov household is of such intensity that it could drive different novels. We first learn of Dmitri's rivalry with his father, and his disloyalty to his betrothed, in the heat of dialogue.

The foreword to *The Brothers Karamazov* identifies Alyosha as the hero, and it is true that readers enter into a special bond with Alyosha in the sense that we go through the tale in a state of half-perception resembling his own. When Alyosha voices astonishment at Rakitin's prediction of a crime in his household, we may be struck with his lack of perception, but until a moment before we ourselves didn't even know what was going on in that household. Somehow we had gotten several chapters into this great novel before stumbling on the information that father and eldest son happen to be colliding over a certain woman, and two brothers are potentially in conflict over another. When Dmitri makes his passionate confession to Alyosha, neither Alyosha nor the reader knows that he has not in fact told all. No more than Alyosha do we ourselves know what Dmitri means by striking himself on the chest "as though [his] dishonor was lying and being kept precisely there" (156). Alyosha never considers that Smerdyakov might actually be his brother, and indeed Smerdyakov barely enters his field of consciousness, but at the same time readers never really hear from Smerdyakov in the way we do from Dmitri, Ivan, and Alyosha himself. One book of *The Brothers Karamazov* is entitled "Alyosha," another "Dmitri," another "Ivan"; none is entitled "Smerdyakov." It is as if we had been made to partake of Alyosha's own defects of perception. (Had Smerdyakov been treated as a brother, that is, an equal, rather than a menial by the other three, events might have taken a different course.) Denied the comfort of superior knowledge, readers of *The Brothers Karamazov* are in fact placed again and again in a position like that of the least knowing of the brothers. As noted, Alyosha sometimes seems to understand as little of the events crashing and swirling around him as Pierre does of events on the battlefield. "Despite the incessant firing going on there, he had no idea that this was the field of battle" (847). The Karamazov family is a field of battle in its own right, but this is also to say that the conflict has many centers, not just one.

Being so intricate, the drama of the Karamazov household revolves around no one brother exclusively. But while none occupies the central position of a tragic hero, for the title of tragicomic hero of *The Brothers Karamazov* there is only one candidate: Dmitri. In part this means simply that Dmitri, and he alone, possesses a rich mix of tragic and comic qualities. His every word and deed recoiling against him, he finds himself by the middle of the novel in the classically tragic position of one who brings his fate upon himself but whose suffering is in excess of his deserts. At the same time, however, Dmitri is magnificently comic, something akin to a swaggering soldier who blows the bubble of his bravado so large it finally pops.[4] His jealousy alone appears in both tragic and comic lights. Intense suspicion of his own father as a sexual rival renders Dmitri all at once an extreme danger to himself and others and a clownish dupe who sees things that aren't there and misses things that are. Jealousy is a comic passion under whose dominion men sink to base and ludicrous actions like spying, even while consumed with thoughts of their own honor; it is also, in Dmitri's case, a terrible error and a cause of ruin.[5] But as this may already suggest, Dmitri is in fact more than a collection of qualities, some tragic and some the opposite. In him we are reminded of a figure who embodies the tragic and the comic in a profound human unity: Don Quixote. The things Dmitri does under the influence of his passion for Grushenka—his fixed idea, his Dulcinea—can only be described as quixotic. Certainly Dmitri cannot just be labeled a rake, a bully, a military officer, a victim of temporary insanity, or for that matter a specimen of jealousy, all such terms containing some fatal inaccuracy and all of them far too limiting, too "finalizing" as Bakhtin would say. The reason he *can* be labeled a Quixote—himself a man without a role—is precisely the unlimited richness of that great archetype.[6] Don Quixote's preoccupation with relieving distress reappears in the urge "to do something" to relieve human suffering that wells up in Dmitri's powerful dream of the baby following his interrogation (508), and what makes this urge truly quixotic is that it *is* bound up in a dream.

Noble in dreams, foolish in reality, Dmitri earlier in the novel is seized with the idea of turning a piece of bad legal paper into 3,000 roubles—an ambition no less visionary than Parson Adams's hope in *Joseph Andrews* (a work of homage to *Don Quixote*) of getting a hundred pounds for "nine volumes of manuscript sermons."[7] Adams for his part appears in a comic light, the object of jokes and receiver of knocks as well as the voice of benevolence, his indignities reminding us that comedy delights in humiliation. Humiliation also, however, lies at the core of tragic experience: Lear's reduction to a beggar, Ivan Ilych's physical helplessness, Michael Henchard's retreat to a hovel in *The Mayor of Casterbridge.* There are scenes in *The Brothers Karamazov,* notably Dmitri's interrogation and the taunting of Ivan by his private devil, where humiliation appears in both aspects at once, as though the author sought the common root of the tragic and comic modes. Where Dickens explodes the social distinctions that ground the traditional literary categories of tragedy and comedy, Dostoevsky scrambles those categories themselves (as in Dmitri's tragic antics) while keeping clear of anything that could be mistaken for a program of

Jacobinism or political leveling.[8] He prosecutes his argument with tradition in literary, not political terms. In the opinion of Bakhtin, this archconservative was in fact the greatest innovator in the history of the novel.[9] If Bakhtin is correct and Dostoevsky endows his heroes with rights against their own author, and other characters with rights equal to theirs, then in fact he has translated the most incendiary ideal of the French Revolution, the Rights of Man, into literary innovation.[10]

Dostoevsky wrote of the insulted and the injured and entered into a dialogue of differences with those radicals who espoused a social religion of equality. In his vision of a perfect society, ordinary people would freely serve the great like Shakespeare, proving by the act of service that "I am in no way beneath thee in moral worth and that, *as a person,* I am equal to thee."[11] In the words of Father Zosima's brother, "we must all serve each other" (289). Here I am concerned with equality less as a political than a literary principle. If by virtue of being human we cannot be known like objects (as Dostoevsky's friend Strakhov maintained and he himself believed), then *The Brothers Karamazov* ought to be composed accordingly. According to Bakhtin, it is. Dostoevsky's heroes, he says, are in truth the opposite of known quantities—never can it be said of them that "all of you is here, there is nothing more in you, and nothing more to be said about you."[12] I think it is this factor of the unknown, or the incompletely known, that not only distinguishes these heroes from the more transparent characters common to fiction but gives them a resemblance to living persons. But if unknowability belongs to the heroes of *The Brothers Karamazov* as an endowment of their humanity, then not even the author possesses complete insight into them, and if not him, still less us. We read *The Brothers Karamazov,* therefore, not as possessors of superior knowledge (as though we had been let into the councils of the gods) but as novices willing to give up the pride and pretension of knowledge itself. "I am not a doctor," says the narrator of *The Brothers Karamazov* before launching into an account of Ivan's delirium (634).

The argument has been made, and I think made well, that early readers of *War and Peace* offended by its violation of conventional practices came closer to the truth than those today who read the work with no sense of shock.[13] The original readers of *The Brothers Karamazov,* that is, the literate public of Russia, read each successive installment of the novel with rapt attention and great expectation. Today first or second or third-time readers of *The Brothers Karamazov* may come closer to its truth than professional readers who, in retrospect, can discern in the narrative the clear signs of foreshadowing. (Such retrospective prophets remind me of Polyphemus in the *Odyssey,* who after he is blinded by Odysseus remembers the prophecy that he would be blinded by someone of that name.) While the novel was still coming out in serial form, a woman wrote the author asking who the murderer of old Karamazov was. A modern edition of the novel refers to the questioner as a real-life Madame Khokhlakov, as if she were tormented by a featherbrained curiosity. Dostoevsky answered her patiently. In point of fact, all readers of *The Brothers Karamazov* have found and at one time or another still find themselves in the same position as this ridiculed inquirer: the position of not knowing. As Dostoevsky takes the mystery tale to a higher level, so too does *The Brothers Karamazov* induce the tension of uncertainty not only for the sake of suspense but to dispel in the reader every assurance of superior knowledge and to remind us of our fallibility and our limits. When Ivan tells Alyosha in his famous indictment of divine indifference to human suffering, "I confess in all humility that I can understand nothing of why" the world is arranged as it is (243), his spirit is prosecutorial, his humility a pose. Every reader of *The Brothers Karamazov* experiences the humility of not understanding.

To Dostoevsky the epigraph to *Anna Karenina*—"Vengeance is mine; I will repay"—meant that only God can judge because "only to Him is known the *entire* mystery of this world."[14] Human beings lack knowledge. What is more, if all things were known, faith would lose meaning, inasmuch as faith as Dostoevsky conceives of it means belief in the absence, and without the comforts and assurances, of positive knowledge. Not Dostoevsky but Ivan's creation the Grand Inquisitor makes the argument that Jesus should have proven his divinity to the world so that humanity would know for certain who he was. Later in *The Brothers Karamazov* the jury is unable to credit Dmitri's innocence with all of the evidence on the other side. Dmitri's guilt can be "proven" but not his innocence. As in this case, human knowledge falls short, and by keeping the reader's knowledge always incomplete Dostoevsky remains true to the conditions of human life as he understands them.

Only when the Karamazovs meet in the elder's cell and words fly do we begin to understand the forces at work in the family, and then only in outline. When Alyosha somehow fails to heed his elder's warning to watch over Dmitri, we ourselves lose sight of Dmitri as well. At the point we learn that Dmitri was "unaware . . . of what had happened with" Grushenka, that he "could make nothing out of her intentions," that he knew only in part of the contents of the letter from her former lover (364–65), our own knowledge of these matters is sketchy; and of the money worn on his very chest we know nothing. When, in a jealous fury, Dmitri races to his father's house with a blunt instrument in hand, we do not know Grushenka is not there. On this crucial matter it might be said that we and Dmitri are equals in ignorance. Only well after the fact do we learn from Dmitri that he drank and brawled perhaps "just because unknown ideas were storming within me" (592). They were unknown to us as well. Not until Grushenka opens her heart to Alyosha do we understand why she toys so recklessly with both father and son, and perhaps not even then. If Dostoevsky had been Cervantes, however, we would have known more than the characters themselves.

The Quixotic Dmitri Karamazov

When Pierre in *War and Peace* imagines himself "a sort of Paris possessed of a Helen" (22) as he dreams of marriage to Hélène, he shows an infatuation with romantic illusion that marks him a kind of Quixote, though the smile of irony has been replaced with a bitter grin of negation. Quixotism makes its appearance in *The Brothers Karamazov* as early as the novel's second paragraph, in the story of a romantic who drowned herself as, and because, Ophelia did. (Actually, this version of Ophelia's end is itself a romantic distortion. Ophelia did not hurl herself into a stream.) Where Don Quixote devotes himself to the imitation of imaginary examples, this copyist imitates the Ophelia of her imagination even at the cost of her life. Of the river bank she leaps from, Dostoevsky writes, "If this cliff . . . had not been so picturesque, if it had been merely a flat, prosaic bank, the suicide might not have taken place at all" (8). For Dmitri Karamazov there is no escape from prosaic existence—as is true of Don Quixote as well.

Once caricatured by Turgenev as the "Knight of the Rueful Countenance,"[15] Dostoevsky cites Don Quixote more often than any other literary figure in *A Writer's Diary,* remarking at one point of Cervantes' masterwork, "There is nothing deeper and more powerful in the whole world than this piece of *fiction.* It is still the final and the greatest expression of human thought, the most bitter irony that a human is capable of expressing."[16] The bitterest irony is of course tragic irony, though the comic energy of *Don Quixote,* as well as its disregard of the conventions and formal requirements of tragedy, precludes us from viewing the work as tragic per se. If *Don Quixote* were less tonally ambiguous, it might have seemed to Dostoevsky less profound. It is his striving to realize the ideal on an earth antithetical to the ideal that makes the story of Don Quixote so comic and tragic. Dmitri Karamazov too sees his passion for the ideal crossed and mocked.

> I can't bear it that some man, even with a lofty heart and the highest mind, should start from the ideal of the Madonna and end with the ideal of Sodom. It's even more fearful when someone who already has the ideal of Sodom in his soul does not deny the ideal of Madonna either, and his heart burns with it, verily, verily burns, as in his young, blameless years. (108)

This passage resonates with a comment in the author's notebook of 1864 that has been identified as "perhaps philosophically the most important line in all his work. . . . 'Man strives on earth toward an ideal that is *contrary* to his nature.'"[17] In the story of the broad-natured Dmitri Karamazov and his longing for the ideal—a story at once intensely ironic and highly ridiculous—a double tonality similar to that of *Don Quixote* is at work.

Smeared with blood (though not his father's), flaunting a suspicious sum of money (also not his father's), Dmitri professes astonishment when arrested for the murder of a man whose life he threatened for all to hear but whom he did not kill after all. If his interrogation, trial, and conviction make for a tale of terrible irony, his belief that fate has somehow conspired against him is nevertheless as ludicrous as

Don Quixote's belief that he is being persecuted by magicians. The truth is that one who acts as blindly as Dmitri Karamazov is a fool of comic proportions. One of the great fools of literature, Dmitri is a hero of the ridiculous, blinded by visions of Grushenka and given to the belief that a kind of sorcery is at work against him. "It's a wonder, fantastic!" he exclaims to his captors (479). Quixotic in the complete sense and the subject of a "fate" that is indeed most bitterly ironic, Dmitri finds himself incriminated by his own actions and struggles against his plight in a manner both tragic and ludicrous. As Dr. Johnson notes, it is one thing to read romances, with their "heroes and . . . traitors, deliverers and persecutors," another to read of persons like ourselves, "leveled with the rest of the world."[18] Dmitri, like one who has read too many romances, has visions of deliverance and falls into the delusion that he has been singled out for persecution by the power of the extraordinary. If he really were targeted by the malice of fate, or indeed if he were to walk away scot-free from his own actions, he would have to be some special category of person, subject to conditions that do not apply to humanity in general. Dmitri does not belong to a special category. He has no exemption from the conditions of prosaic existence. He is level with—equal to—his fellow beings, not in a category apart. Says Folly in *The Praise of Folly,* "I am the only deity who embraces all men equally."[19]

Where Don Quixote belongs to the lowest rank of the Spanish nobility, Dmitri, son of the lowest sort of landowner, demands to be treated under arrest as a man of honor and hopes to serve out a short prison sentence "without loss of the rights of my rank" (567). (That, contrary to his fantastic hopes, the guards "talk down" to him is more than he can bear [763].) Also under interrogation, Dmitri reveals himself, like his Spanish ancestor, as "markedly obsessional, but only on a defined and limited range of matters," the special object of his mania being the rag he wore around his neck containing 1,500 roubles.[20] It is next to impossible for Dmitri to convey to third parties the significance that rag holds for him, destroying as it does his own image of himself as one too uncalculating and romantic to put away one woman's money to finance his escape with another. His Dulcinea, again, is the commoner Grushenka, and much as Don Quixote under the inspiration of romantic ideals is apt to see things that are not, Dmitri can practically see and feel Grushenka in his father's house when she is not there. (Recall, however, that the reader has no more idea than Dmitri that on the critical night she is literally and figuratively somewhere else entirely.) It is his suspicion that Grushenka is with his father that takes him to the house on the night of the murder and thus makes possible the crime itself. In the comic figure of Don Quixote who nevertheless dramatized for Dostoevsky "the most bitter irony," as well as in his descendant Dmitri, we have an image as it were of the multi-tonality of *The Brothers Karamazov.*

What could be more extravagantly misguided, more quixotic, than Dmitri's frantic search for the 3,000 roubles that to his brain represents salvation? Though not a knight, Dmitri certainly has a quest, and it takes him first of all to the old merchant Samsonov. As the common-law partner of Grushenka, however, old Samsonov is no more likely than his own father to give Dmitri the means to run off with her, nor is such a classical miser going to send good money after bad by purchasing financial paper from a Dmitri Karamazov. But while Dmitri is on the verge of complete despair, the scene itself takes place at the border of hilarity. From Samsonov's giant of a son to his own mighty but suppressed rage, the entire event is a comedy, if only Dmitri realized it. Perhaps no one but a Dmitri Karamazov would place his hope in the ogre described toward the opening of the scene in all his Dickensian ugliness.[21] And from here Dmitri takes his suit to two others maybe even more improbable than Samsonov himself. As we discover later when the seal of silence is broken and Dmitri reveals the story of the money around his neck, half the magic sum of 3,000 roubles is all this time on his own person. Why then does he seek it at all? Because he is intoxicated with the fantasy of carrying away Grushenka in triumph, which he cannot do on another woman's money. But if standard roles ill suit a true novelistic hero like Dmitri Karamazov, what of a script so standard, a story so overtold (as though it appeared in a thousand old books of knight-errantry) that we wonder how it could take possession of an intelligent brain? In the manner of a Quixote, Dmitri has become enthralled to a fantasy of honor: honorably paying off one woman so that he can chivalrously carry off another. Seeking a sum of money that will purchase his release from Katerina (impossible) and finance his escape with Grushenka, he succeeds only in building up the case against himself in the eyes of the law. In the full quixotic sense of the word, Dmitri's quest for 3,000 roubles is an errand of folly—all the more because his money isn't really needed at all to carry away a woman, Grushenka, who has money of her own in abundance.

While no one is going to mistake Father Zosima for Rousseau, still the elder's indictment of a corrupt and unequal society in which people enslave themselves to superfluous desires is consonant with the sentiments of Rousseau's *Discourse on Inequality*. "Taking freedom to mean the increase and prompt satisfaction of needs," says Zosima, discussing a world divided into rich and poor,

> [moderns] distort their own nature, for they generate many meaningless and foolish desires, habits, and the most absurd fancies in themselves. They live only for mutual envy, for pleasure-seeking and self-display. To have dinners, horses, carriages, rank, and slaves to serve them is now considered such a necessity that for the sake of it, to satisfy it, they will sacrifice life, honor, the love of mankind. (313–14)

The young Zosima, a well-regarded military officer, was himself an "absurd creature" full of imaginary notions of honor and precedence (295). Dmitri Karamazov as an officer seems to have been much like this, but even now he acts like Zosima's moderns. Given to display, Dmitri has a theatrical personality, throws ostentatious parties, and, as we saw, is touchy about the privileges of rank, but as revealing as any of these symptoms is his subjection to a "meaningless," "foolish," "absurd" need for money, the idol of the modern world. From one point of view a romantic fantasy, his dream of bearing Grushenka away with his own financial power can also be read as the sort of mania to which men abandon their freedom in a highly class-conscious society, according to Zosima. Zosima describes those so distorted by the world they live in that they do not know what to do with their own freedom. Dmitri seems to have trouble with the freedom he possesses because he is no longer in uniform, and over the course of the novel he succeeds in forfeiting it. Certainly the need driving Dmitri's quest for 3,000 roubles is imaginary; and yet the consequences of the adventure are real enough, as it is cited against him by the authorities as proof that at the time he had no money to speak of, and that the money that appeared in his hands on the night of the murder can therefore only have materialized as a result of the murder. The man who spends the first half of *The Brothers Karamazov* obsessed by a dream later finds himself trapped in a nightmare.

Captivated as he is by the foolish and the absurd, Dmitri, like his great original, Don Quixote, believes himself, or would like to believe himself, a hero in a romance, a lightning rod for the power of the marvelous. If only by portraying Dmitri as one who imagines himself at the mercy of events like the hero of a Greek romance, or subject to the black magic of coincidence like a Don Quixote, *The Brothers Karamazov* takes its place in a tradition inaugurated by *Don Quixote* itself, that of ironizing the romantic foundations of the novel.[22] Dmitri feels that circumstances conspire against him, that he is at the center of a "plot." While there is a certain fractional truth to this, it could more justly be said that the plot of *The Brothers Karamazov* has Dmitri bringing about his own ruin, knotting his own noose; everything he says and does comes back to incriminate him, with an effect at once bitterly ironic and tragically ludicrous. As though Dostoevsky sought to surpass even the irony of Cervantes, he denies Dmitri the escape to the road that he yearns for and that constitutes the very condition of adventure. In fact, Dmitri's most quixotic delusion may be his fantasy of one day clearing all debts, cutting the bonds of his entanglements, and betaking himself to a new life like Don Quixote taking to the highway. No such escape is possible for Dmitri Karamazov, caught as he is in the humiliating "prosaics" of circumstance.[23] (The very setting of *The Brothers Karamazov* in a miserable small town produces a similarly constricting effect, with high drama reduced to local scandal.) Among the possibilities opened by the promotion of commoners to positions of importance in novels is the commoner enchanted with the delusion of not being an ordinary person at all. Such a commoner is Dmitri, believing as he does that he is at the mercy of fortune and misfortune like someone lost in the magic world of romance.

In a novel that immortalizes the theme of the flight from freedom, Dmitri not only enslaves himself to a purely imaginary need for money but is so oppressed by his own power to act that he dreams of having no such power at all. Even with 1,500 roubles around his neck he acts as though only someone else could solve his money troubles and he himself had no ability to restore that very sum to Katerina. Dmitri's hope that money, and with it redemption, "would somehow fly down to him by itself, from the sky no less" (367) is as quixotic as his hope that Samsonov of all people will be its supplier (or indeed that Katerina would allow Dmitri to buy her off in the first place, in effect selling her honor). The man who tells his interrogators, "I understand now that for men such as I a blow is needed, a blow of fate, to catch them as with a noose and bind them by an external force" (509) is not only oppressed by freedom but thinks of his fate as something that comes down from the sky. Such beliefs might make more sense if Dmitri were the hero of a Greek romance, exposed to the power of the extraordinary, the plaything of fortune and misfortune, one to whom events just happen.[24]

This sort of exposure to the force of events is dramatized by one of the commonplaces of the Greek romance: abduction. Suddenly brigands appear and you are taken. You are no more an agent in your own capture than you were in receiving identity at birth or losing your birth identity—your nobility—by misfortune. In *Daphnis and Chloe* the former is momentarily borne away by pirates, an episode included, it seems, for no other reason than to honor or parody the romance formula. Treating such formulas ironically in the tradition of Cervantes, Dostoevsky reveals Dmitri's image of himself as a special victim of fortune as one more quixotic delusion, and among his most sensational. Considering that Dmitri gets carried away by passion, it may be no wonder that he thinks of himself as a victim like those literally carried away in the Greek romance. Not being at one with himself, he knows otherwise, however, as does the reader.

For our own passions do not act on us like external events. When Dmitri declares that if Grushenka presents herself to his father, he may kill him or he may not, depending on the intensity of the moment, he talks as if he were buffeted by his own passions like a sailor in a squall.[25] Supporting the delusion that his own deeds somehow happen to him, such talk is itself dangerous. When, in the event, Dmitri strikes down not his father but the servant Grigory, the act is narrated as if he himself did not perform it.

> "Parricide!" the old man shouted for the whole neighborhood to hear, but that was all he had time to shout: suddenly he fell as if struck by a thunderbolt. Mitya jumped back down into the garden and bent over the stricken man. There was a brass pestle in Mitya's hand, and he threw it mechanically into the grass. (394)

It is almost as if the pestle came from the sky and performed the crime "by itself." If the heroes of the Greek romance are subjected to chance (or in the case of *Callirhoe,*

Fortune), with Dmitri it is purely a matter of chance whether or not he kills the drunken peasant from whom he hoped to get 3,000 roubles shortly before his encounter with Grigory. "On another occasion Mitya might have killed the fool in a rage, but now he himself became weak as a child" (379). In view of Dmitri's sense that his own actions somehow befall him, it seems poetically just that he should be *un*justly arrested for another's deed.

Once again it is Dmitri's quest for 3,000 roubles that brings out the folly of his belief that he is a plaything of circumstance like someone abducted or delivered—but in any case, removed from the realm of ordinary existence—in an ancient romance. Throughout this sequence Dmitri is possessed by the idea that his very fate rests in the hands of another—first the merchant Samsonov, then the drunken peasant to whom Samsonov refers him as a malicious joke, third the scatterbrained Madame Khokhlakov. "Oh, the irony of fate!" Dmitri exclaims upon finding the peasant "on whom my entire fate now depends" unconscious from drink (376–77). When he approaches Madame Khokhlakov, "at first things seemed to smile on him" (383); then his fortune turns. To the reader it becomes apparent that Dmitri is the victim not of fate or fortune or some persecuting force but his own folly and miscalculation, and finally his very belief that someone else has got to rescue him. Even before we discover that he is wearing 1,500 roubles next to the silver icon Madame Khokhlakov slips around his neck, we sense that Dmitri could hardly have chosen three unlikelier persons on this earth to hear his suit, that his dream of someone delivering him from his crisis is as vain as his dream of carrying Grushenka far away to begin another life, all debts cleared. When Dmitri puts it to old Samsonov that he (Samsonov) must "choose: me or the monster [that is, his father]" (371), we wonder how it is that Dmitri himself seems to have so little power of action that this misanthrope must be his savior. Dostoevsky allows Dmitri no possibility of a miraculous deliverance, no escape from the net of circumstance, no exemption from the sort of conditions binding equally on all of us. Nor is Dmitri at the mercy of fortune. On the contrary, like his belief that others are plotting against him (390), his notion that he is the plaything of events is both an abdication of his own freedom and a delusion worthy of a Quixote—the error, at once pathetic and ludicrous, of one whose head has been turned by romantic visions. Where Don Quixote bumps into stories about himself, Dmitri is undone by the stories that circulate about him, such as his having spent a full 3,000 roubles at one throw some weeks before the murder: a fiction authored and published by himself.

While the one who does and suffers these things is revealed as the great fool of *The Brothers Karamazov,* his higher yearnings and passionate delusions rouse in us a kind of love for this modern Quixote. In Prince Myshkin, the Idiot, Dostoevsky had indeed created a Quixote, but one too Christlike, as it happened, to call forth laughter and derision as well as pity, wonder, and love in the fully orchestrated manner of Dmitri Karamazov.[26] In Dmitri the contradictory potentials of Don Quixote are richly realized. Like that knight encountering rival versions of himself, in the courtroom Dmitri runs into errant accounts of his own exploits—accounts that all seem true to those who offer them, owing to the many-sidedness of his nature.

Dmitri's own deeds thus come back to haunt him, as they also contribute to the murder of his father in ways he does not and cannot understand at the time. But as I have said, neither can we understand at the time. So intricate is the web of circumstance in *The Brothers Karamazov* that only after the fact do we begin to understand just how Dmitri's actions contributed to the crime, and by then Dmitri is beginning to understand, too. Rather than allowing readers the privilege of higher knowledge, Dostoevsky constructs *The Brothers Karamazov* in such a way that it reminds us continually of what we do not know; and it intimates that incomplete knowledge, in the double form of a liability to error and a capacity for surprise, is a feature of our common humanity. Early in the novel, looking back on his military days, Dmitri tells Alyosha, "I didn't understand a thing then: not until I came here, brother, and even now until these very last present days, maybe even not until today, did I understand anything in all these financial squabbles between me and father" (111). The experience of incomprehension and belated understanding is also dealt to the reader of *The Brothers Karamazov*.

Inasmuch as the full consequences of his actions escape him, Dmitri's story confirms unforgettably the principle that action is risky, both because acts cannot be undone and because their effects pass from our control. This double burden of risk undertaken by one who acts is brought out with great clarity by Hannah Arendt in her discussion of the nature of action itself. It has long been known, she writes, that "he who acts never quite knows what he is doing, that he always becomes 'guilty' of consequences he never intended or even foresaw, [and] that no matter how disastrous and unexpected the consequences of his deed he can never undo it."[27] But if the meaning of an action "never discloses itself to the actor but only to the backward glance of the historian who himself does not act"[28]—which comes close to Tolstoy's doctrine that history can be understood only in retrospect—*The Brothers Karamazov* supplies no such historian, and it is left to us to determine, if we can, exactly how each brother's actions contribute to the Karamazov disaster. For just because of the part each brother plays by act or omission in the murder of their father, all of them stand morally responsible for the crime. Without the complicity of each, the act could not have been committed. In contrast to a "collective guilt" divided into ever smaller pieces as it is shared out among more and more, each of the brothers, then, whatever his "part" (and Dmitri's is large) bears a full measure of moral guilt. If Hamlet famously exceeds the part of the avenger that has been assigned him, the brothers bear a guilt that exceeds their part in the crime, if only because real guilt is not and cannot be fractional in nature. A jury today may find a defendant 42 percent liable for a plaintiff's injuries, but Dostoevsky does not think like that jury and does not subscribe to such Euclidean reckonings.

Then too, even if one who acts does not understand, the "historian" is in no position to look down on those who assume the risks of action. No one ever embraced those risks more fervently than Dmitri Karamazov. If the actor doesn't know what he is doing, then Dmitri must be the actor supreme. Dmitri in truth never knows what he is doing (which is what makes the prosecution's portrayal of him such a caricature). Even when he snatches up a pestle he could hardly say why. Like everything else he does, however, this deed of a moment proves irreversible and "fateful." As his acts pass out of his hands, Dmitri becomes guilty of a murder he did not commit; but as the quotation marks in which Arendt encloses the word "guilty" imply, you cannot be held guilty in a strict legal sense for doing you know not what. The guilt that descends on the actor as the price of his own temerity, the guilt that descends on Dmitri Karamazov for enabling a murder by his own sensational recklessness, can only be moral guilt. As Dmitri's case is heard in the courtroom, his actions are interpreted in the light of legal categories as ill-fitting as the clothes he was given to cover his nakedness under interrogation. Strangely, these categories too are affiliated with the tradition of romance.

In *Callirhoe,* all of Babylon buzzes with news of the trial of Mithridates on the charge of seduction. "During the thirty days men and women in Persia talked of nothing but this trial, and, to tell the truth, all Babylon became a courthouse" (247). The most sustained episode in *Callirhoe,* the trial scene itself has been judged "much superior in dramatic effect to anything one meets with elsewhere in the Greek romance," the peak moment of the genre.[29] All of Russia seems abuzz over the trial of Dmitri Karamazov. Throwing open the shutters of the Karamazov household, the event is a public spectacle charged with the thrill of revelation and heightened with displays of rhetorical art. (Recall Father Zosima: in a modern society of unequals men live for display.) The trial of Dmitri is a great drama; it is also a circus, a grievous mistake, and a theater of sophistry. As such, it reminds us that the truth passes unnoticed, as Tolstoy, Dickens, and George Eliot might agree.

Romance tends to divide characters into friend and foe, hero and villain, so that "every typical character in romance tends to have his moral opposite confronting him, like black and white pieces in a chess game."[30] It may be in the courtroom that the principle of formal opposition and contest is played out most vividly, as argument meets counterargument. As it happens, the Greek romance not only features legal trials but has certain links to the sophistic tradition that arose alongside the legal culture of ancient Athens and concerned itself with the construction of legal arguments, both pro and contra. By contrast, the clash of point and counterpoint in Dmitri's trial only illustrates the superficial character of the event as a public spectacle, for in a real exchange as Dostoevsky understands it, speakers do not stoop to a detailed refutation of the other's claims. "They never argue over *separate points,* but always over *whole points of view.*"[31] Every last point in the case against Dmitri is argued over.

The Greek romance is sometimes called sophistic, and the courtroom arguments in *The Brothers Karamazov* are certainly that. In his peroration, Dmitri's lawyer rises to a higher rhetorical level even as he discredits all that fails the test of rational analysis, for example, the superstition that even the worst father, even Fyodor Pavlovich Karamazov, deserves the love of his son. Using the incendiary language of rights, the lawyer contends that the son of such a man "has the right henceforth to look upon his father as a stranger and even as his enemy" (746). He proceeds to give a fanciful account of the crime (the kind of tale he himself elsewhere calls a romance) in which unfortunate things happen to Dmitri in the course of killing his father. Dmitri does not author events; they befall him. A pestle finds its way into his hand. At the sight of his father "a feeling of hatred took hold of him involuntarily" (746), under the dominion of which the act of murder took place, if in fact it took place at all. In narrating the event, the one thing the lawyer never quite says is that Dmitri Karamazov actually killed his father:

> But even then the prisoner did not kill—I assert it, I cry it aloud—no, he merely swung the pestle in disgusted indignation, not wishing to kill, not knowing that he would kill. Had it not been for that fatal pestle in his hand, he would perhaps only have beaten his father, and not killed him. He did not know as he ran away whether the old man he had struck down was killed or not. Such a murder is not a murder. (746–47)

The act here described—a murder that is not a murder, performed by a magic pestle—is sui generis, outside of existing categories. Before his arrest, Dmitri acts as if he himself were outside the limitations binding on an ordinary person.

From the lawyer's account, at any rate, Dmitri emerges as a victim of misfortune, a direct if distant descendant of the storm-tossed figures of romance. But if the meaning of an action reveals itself only in retrospect, still the lawyer claims too much knowledge for himself and leaves Dmitri with too little. However much Dmitri might like to imagine himself the victim of his passions and his star, even he denies that he acted involuntarily, unconsciously, as though in his sleep. Nor is his role in events a simple one. Like his dream of bearing Grushenka away with his own money, which reads both like an innocent if vain romantic fantasy and like the sort of enthralling delusion to which moderns surrender their own freedom according to Zosima, so the story of Dmitri's actions confounds the very categories of guilt and innocence decisive in romance.[32] Of course he is innocent of the murder for which he stands trial, and yet he very nearly fractures Grigory's skull, threatens in writing to do the same to his father, assaults others as well, provides cover for the actual murderer (however unwittingly), and in any case builds up such a mountain of evidence and seeming evidence against himself by his own actions that a reader, even knowing the truth of the matter, can hardly fault the jury for lacking the faith to move the mountain. Where a hero of the Greek romance, who really has been removed from the world of the ordinary, undergoes a series of adventures, Dmitri both authors and suffers his fate. The opposite confronting him in the chess game, like a nemesis, is himself.

A Victim of Circumstance?

In accordance with his aim of deflating human glory, Tolstoy makes the argument in *War and Peace* that an action assumes historical significance only insofar as it merges with other actions in a great fabric of coincidence. Coincidence serves to keep any one action from becoming too important. Only as they receive a kind of accidental support from the actions of others do our deeds become important to history. The murder of the father in *The Brothers Karamazov* really is a joint venture, and an action that none of the sons would probably have performed unassisted, but in this case we have to do not with world-historical events but the drama of a single household, and the role of coincidence is reduced accordingly. In this closely plotted tale coincidences—things that inexplicably, "fatefully," happen to occur together—are for the most part an illusion. The novel is designed, however, so that only in retrospect and upon reflection does their falsity become apparent. In real time, as it were, we do not and cannot know what's what. In the case of the almost simultaneous death of Father Zosima and old Karamazov, we can't be sure even on reflection that the conjunction of events is accidental. Perhaps if Alyosha had been less preoccupied with his dying elder, he would have been able to devote more of himself to preventing a catastrophe in his own household. Again, that Dmitri happened to drag Captain Snegiryov by the beard in the town square just as the schoolboys, including the captain's son, were coming onto the scene (203–4) may be coincidental; but even so, Dmitri is not the victim but if you will the perpetrator of the coincidence, and it is as an eventual consequence of his act of almost unfathomable cruelty that the captain's son, Ilyusha, dies.

Arrested shortly after shedding one man's blood for the murder of another, Dmitri finds himself trapped in what seems to him an evil web of coincidence. His entrapment is and is not a coincidence; mainly not. Exactly how Smerdyakov knew to batter Fyodor Pavlovich's skull with a blunt instrument just as Dmitri battered Grigory, no one can say, but that he used Dmitri as a decoy to deflect attention no one can doubt. Upon analysis, the murder of old Karamazov just after Dmitri's actions have presented Smerdyakov with the perfect cover is no more coincidental than the fact that the events of the novel take place immediately after the brothers happen to assemble for the first time. The elements of a dangerous mixture come together. While *The Brothers Karamazov* does contain its fraction of truly inexplicable coincidences to enrich the mix and add confusion and wonder, by and large the linkages in this work more closely resemble the taut logic of tragedy than the improbabilities of romance. Only in the mind of Dmitri (or the impressions of an amazed reader) are the events enmeshing him "a wonder, an absurdity, an impossibility" (458), as if they took place in what Dmitri calls "an Arabian tale" (116) and he had been specially targeted by the power of misfortune.

An ancient romance like *Callirhoe* or the *Ethiopian Story* turns upon the purest of coincidences: not just love but mutual love at first sight. In the latter work it happens that two persons who are each the epipsyche of the other find themselves in the same place at the same time. "At the moment of meeting" Theagenes and Chariclea "looked and loved, as though the soul of each at the first encounter recognized its fellow and leaped toward that which deserved to belong to it."[33] On this most perfect of coincidences is predicated all the subsequent action of the tale. In a thoroughly ironic rendering of the motif of the meeting of the eyes, Dmitri and Katerina are locked in love/hate from the moment of first sight.

> I saw her sizing me up; it was at the battery commander's, but I didn't go up to her then: I scorn your acquaintance, thought I. I went up to her a bit later on, also at a party; I began talking, she barely looked at me, pressed her contemptuous lips together. Well, thought I, just wait, I'll get my revenge! (111)

In the scene this leads into, a Dmitri possessed by "the kind of hatred that is only a hair's breadth from love, from the maddest love" (114) hands 5,000 roubles to Katerina without taking sexual advantage of her. Aftershocks of the encounter are felt throughout *The Brothers Karamazov*. What makes the encounter possible in the first place is the accident (which must seem to Dmitri a double godsend at the time) that money from his father has fallen into his hands at the very moment when Katerina's father is desperately in need of money. Truly a coincidence, but one with ironic qualifiers attached. It turns out that Dmitri's thousands come to him only after he signs away his rights to the remainder of his inheritance, another act that returns to haunt him. So too, while the money seems to come to Dmitri of its own accord, it enables him to toy with Katerina of *his* own accord and at his own risk and peril. In the courtroom it is Katerina who destroys Dmitri's last hope. Things seem to fall into place for Dmitri when, by good fortune, money puts Katerina in his power; later all the pieces of the case against him fall into place as well, and Fortune's child becomes misfortune's darling.

Dmitri's rescue of Katerina in the manner of a kind of irregular chivalric hero sets up what must be, next to the commission of the murder just as he flees from the scene, the purest non-coincidence of *The Brothers Karamazov*. A month before the action of the novel begins, Katerina, now rich and betrothed to Dmitri, entrusts him with 3,000 roubles to telegraph to Moscow—this "precisely at that fatal moment" (490) when he has become enchanted with Grushenka. Possibly more than any other single factor, it is the weight of 1,500 roubles of Katerina's money around his neck that drives Dmitri to distraction, to the point that he imagines himself singled out for suffering. While he does not know this at the time (119), there is nothing coincidental about Katerina's placing in his hands, at just this moment, a sum of money that will enable him to run off with Grushenka if such is his desire. Dmitri is being tempted. He is subject not to the whims of fate or the abstract power of coincidence, not to extraordinary forces that do not afflict his fellow human beings, but to the vengeful will of Katerina Ivanovna, a will roused by his own acts.

By the time Dmitri cries out in open court, "I intended to become an honest man ever after"—as though fairy-tale endings were possible in life—"precisely at the moment when fate cut me down" (661), his complaint of being a victim of circumstance has taken on a hollow, repetitive sound. (If Ivan were to complain that his father was killed "just at the moment" when he set off for Moscow to begin a new life, he would simply be advertising his own blindness. Only belatedly, however, do both Ivan and the reader unravel the connection between these two events.) Dmitri was struck down by fate after he struck Grigory down, and what drove him to his father's garden in the first place was his obsession with Grushenka, the object of his quixotic fantasy of running away to begin a new and honest life (always assuming his debt of honor to Katerina could be cleared for the sum of 3,000 roubles). Wrongly accused of murder, Dmitri is the victim of such a gross error that he does not always grasp that he is nevertheless responsible for his plight and that the evidence stacked against him measures his own recklessness. The same evidence makes for another ironic, or if you will Cervantesque, comment on romance. In the world of romance, tokens like Odysseus's scar and pin serve to establish identity. In the anti-romance of *The Brothers Karamazov,* the tokens are a pestle and blood-soaked clothing, and what they establish is the false case against Dmitri. That the only exculpatory evidence Dmitri can produce is a story about a rag nowhere to be found, a rag that no one but Alyosha and the reader believe in, a rag that would prove precisely nothing even *if* found, illustrates his desperate position.

Though Dmitri finds himself in the tragic bind of one who undergoes complete humiliation and suffers excessively even as he authors his own ruin, he is nevertheless not "the tragic hero" of *The Brothers Karamazov,* if only because all of this is also true of Ivan. With the public making Dmitri the great focal point of gossip and speculation, it is as if those given to the satisfaction of imaginary needs (as Zosima said) had turned the case into a drama for their own gratification; or as if those addicted to spectacle were entertaining themselves with the spectacle of Dmitri. Why is it that Dmitri fills the role of the central figure of the case so well? According to Bakhtin, a "Ptolemaic" perception of language lacks an appreciation of its "plenitude."[34] It is exactly Dmitri's richness as a character, his plenitude, that makes the different stories or romances circulating about him seem believable to those who credit them. At once reckless and in one "fatal" instance calculating, fanatically suspicious and yet astonishingly naive, innocent and guilty, the man is a cornucopia, distinguished more by the wealth of his traits than by any single trait. And much of that wealth derives from the great exemplar of the tragicomic, Don Quixote, also endowed with both nobility and folly, and also an object of notoriety within his own tale.

Denial of Superior Knowledge

When we finally meet the hero in book 5 of the *Odyssey,* he has already consulted Tiresias in the underworld and heard the prophecy of his own homecoming, but of this he gives no sign. Nor, when Calypso releases him, does he have the feeling that the prophet's prediction is at last coming to pass. Why is this? Not because Homer wants to keep us in uncertainty about the hero's chances or because the hero is withholding a secret from us, but simply because the narrative of the *Odyssey* hasn't reached Tiresias yet and so can't refer to his prediction, as it does not refer to any of Odysseus's adventures before his arrival on Calypso's island. When the *Odyssey* finally does come to Tiresias and the hero is told, in effect, that the survival of his crew depends on their leaving the cattle of Helios untouched, he suffers no agonies of suspense. If his crew is made of such poor stuff that their moral strength is uncertain as his is not, by the same token they are beneath a hero's concern. Suspense concerns the unknown, and in this case the unknown are Odysseus's mostly nameless sailing companions dismissed by the poet himself as fools for violating the sun god's decree. In the matter of Dmitri and his 1,500 roubles, everything is otherwise. Before we ourselves come to know of it, he does give signs of the money's existence, at one point even striking himself high on the chest, although we cannot possibly interpret these indications until after the fact. About Dmitri's money affairs Dostoevsky keeps us in the most acute uncertainty. The question is electrified with suspense, all the more because Dmitri keeps his secret from us until it is forced out of him in the course of events. It seems that in order for Dmitri to be the moral equal of his own author, he must have not only the power to speak but the right to remain silent.

Not from the narrator but from Dmitri himself, under the duress of interrogation, do we learn the story of his rag containing 1,500 roubles. Far from knowing more than Dmitri in this matter, Dmitri himself is the source—the only source—of our knowledge. So pronounced is the shift of storytelling responsibility to the persons of the drama in *The Brothers Karamazov* that it gives rise to the impression that these are beings like the author or the reader, outside the narrative itself. On this impression the argument of Bakhtin's remarkable study of Dostoevsky is raised. Dostoevsky's characters, argues Bakhtin, are the equals of their author, free agents "capable of standing alongside their creator, capable of not agreeing with him and even rebelling against him." Such a work as *The Brothers Karamazov* represents a "*great dialogue* in which characters and author . . . participate with equal rights."[35] That a

Dmitri Karamazov is an autonomous being with the power to oppose and surprise his own creator is a proposition that cannot really be demonstrated. You accept it or you don't. Clearly, however, we ourselves enjoy no superiority of knowledge over these characters, depending on them as we do for our information. As though Dostoevsky had revolutionized the device of direct speech that originates in Homer, our knowledge of events in *The Brothers Karamazov* derives very largely from the drama of dialogue. It is the predominance of direct speech in *The Brothers Karamazov* that underwrites our impression that its great characters have burst the frame of narrative. No longer simply placed in a story, they tell their own story. They are not spoken of, so much as they speak in their own right—and keep silence.

In the ironic sense that unauthorized Don Quixotes sprang into being owing to the success of the tales of his earlier exploits, Cervantes' hero as well took on an existence independent of his author. But assuming that Dostoevsky hoped the message of *The Brothers Karamazov* would root and sprout in Russia in accordance with the novel's epigraph—"Verily, verily I say unto you, Except a corn of wheat fall into the ground and die, it abideth alone: but if it die, it bringeth forth much fruit"—then he too thought books could come alive. If quixotism takes life for literature and literature for life, is there not already some trace of this noble malady in Dostoevsky as Bakhtin envisions him—one whose own inventions possessed the rights and privileges of living beings?

An author whose Quixote is fully real to him is himself a Quixote. But if there is something to Bakhtin's idea that Dostoevsky's characters stand equal to him, implying that he does not really possess knowledge superior to theirs in spite of being their creator, then still less does a reader know more than they. This means that for all Dmitri's quixotism, never can a reader survey his folly from a position of superior understanding, as we do continually with Don Quixote himself. Never do we share Don Quixote's mistakes of perception; but often in *The Brothers Karamazov* we see with Dmitri's eyes. In effect Dostoevsky completes what Bakhtin calls the Copernican revolution of modern prose by denying readers the privileged position of observation allowed them even in one of its greatest works.

By analogy, consider the difference between the handling of jealousy in *The Brothers Karamazov* and in *Othello.* (Jealous eyes after all see things, like Don Quixote.) In an essay on jealousy inserted into the section of the novel devoted to Dmitri's search for 3,000 roubles, Dostoevsky writes:

> Jealousy! "Othello is not jealous, he is trustful," Pushkin observed, and this one observation already testifies to the remarkable depth of our great poet's mind. Othello's soul is simply shattered and his whole world view clouded because *his ideal is destroyed.* Othello will not hide, spy, peep: he is trustful. On the contrary, he had to be led, prompted, roused with great effort to make him even think of betrayal. A truly jealous man is not like that. (380)

However revealing this may be as a reading of *Othello*, it does point toward a critical difference between the case of the famous Moor and that of ex-lieutenant Dmitri Karamazov. In Othello's case we, the readers or spectators, know for certain of Desdemona's innocence. Dramatic irony is worked to its highest pitch. Of Grushenka's intentions we have no such knowledge or assurance, nor can we possibly tell that she is playing with the fire of Dmitri's jealousy in order to distract herself from her own troubles, if that is really what she is up to.[36] On the night of the murder we do not even know her whereabouts until Dmitri discovers, too late, that she is miles away. Dmitri's agony is the reader's uncertainty. As for the famous insufficiency of the motives of Othello's tormentor and destroyer Iago, its immediate equivalent in *The Brothers Karamazov* would be the undermotivation of Smerdyakov (who like Iago resents his subordinate position and uses honesty as his pose, at once a villain and a mystery). But Grushenka's motives too, whatever they are, hardly account for the magnitude of her deeds—the detonation of an explosive conflict in the Karamazov household. For that matter, if Fyodor Pavlovich raped an idiot girl in order to impress his friends, as seems likely, the crime far exceeded the triviality of its own motivation. (Is this not what is meant by the "banality of evil" after all—that monstrous actions should arise inexplicably from commonplace motives?) Similarly, Dmitri's humiliation of Captain Snegiryov in the town square, while the captain's son kisses his very hand, is an act of such cruelty that no motive—certainly not the meager available motive of getting even with the captain for being involved somehow with his father—seems capable of "explaining" it. Unlike Iago, then, Smerdyakov is not alone in the drama of *The Brothers Karamazov* in being undermotivated.[37] Indeed, his undermotivation is but a variant of the "surplus of humanness" enjoyed by the major characters of the tale: just as Dmitri can't be reduced to a figure of dissipation or Grushenka to a reformed harlot, so Smerdyakov can't simply be identified as, say, a denied son envious of his brothers, as though this closed the matter. In *The Brothers Karamazov* Iago's lack of transparency becomes something like a general condition, which for the reader means a loss of certainty. As a close student of *Othello* remarks, we just don't know much about Iago.[38] At this point the contrast between Dostoevsky's procedure and that of Cervantes comes into focus.

Recall the famous "terrifying and never-before-imagined adventure of the windmills" early in *Don Quixote*. The episode begins as follows:

> Just then they came in sight of thirty or forty windmills that rise from that plain, and no sooner did Don Quixote see them than he said to his squire: "Fortune is guiding our affairs better than we ourselves could have wished. Do you see over yonder, friend Sancho, thirty or forty hulking giants?"[39]

The reader never has a chance to enter into Don Quixote's error of perception, that is, to identify the windmills as monstrous enemies. Before he speaks the shapes in the distance are defined to us as windmills. And so it is throughout *Don Quixote*. Never do we partake of Don Quixote's illusions or forego our advantage of perception, though Cervantes beautifully complicates things by making folly so nearly indistinguishable from nobility and by endowing Sancho Panza, who calls a windmill a windmill, with his own generous portion of folly. As Dmitri races from one unlikely candidate to another in a misguided and highly quixotic search for 1,500 roubles, we do not know the critical fact that this amount is all the time around his own neck. Not only are we allowed no advantage in knowledge, we know less than Dmitri at this moment. Not until later do we discover the existence of the 1,500—significantly, from his own lips and no one else's—and only at that point do we begin to understand his earlier frantic actions as a sign of the torment caused by that money, worn around his neck like an amulet of shame. If Dulcinea exists she is a coarse, ill-smelling peasant girl. Dmitri's election of Grushenka as his queen seems ludicrous, but who is to say that she doesn't possess the moral beauty he sees in her? The fact is that Dmitri in his folly and nobility infuses an uncertainty into *The Brothers Karamazov* that does not exist in a world where a thing is either a windmill or a giant.[40] From moment to moment in *The Brothers Karamazov,* even to the end, we never really know what Dmitri will do next, as though the author had loaded him with such an excess of potential that for everything he does there exists a kind of immediate possibility of him doing otherwise (which is also to say that Dmitri is like all of us, only more so). He can be imagined dreading to touch the cursed rag around his neck, tearing it off, dividing it in half, restoring the whole sum to Katerina in an attempt to quit his debt, reverting to Katerina, spending the whole sum in despair, and maybe even casting himself penniless at Grushenka's feet. Except perhaps for his beautiful discourses and spells of lucidity, such unpredictability has no equivalent in Don Quixote. In part because what Dmitri does do is no more probable than what he doesn't, the interrogators, prosecutor, and jury have great difficulty believing his story but no difficulty believing that he killed and robbed his father. (To the deluded prosecutor he seems a man of "resolution, cold-bloodedness, and calculation" [477]—the attributes of Odysseus.) We know better; but earlier in the novel, when he tells Alyosha that he might kill the old man and might not, we find ourselves as readers in the same position of uncertainty before the future as he himself is in.

If Dostoevsky confers on his characters, at least his great characters, rights equal to his own, certainly he also denies readers a position superior to those characters. Only after the fact do we learn of Grushenka's whereabouts on the night of the murder. We make the discovery when Dmitri does. (Indeed, not until the trial, that is, practically at the end of the novel, do we learn Grushenka's surname, Svetlov. We learn it when the narrator does.) Only after the fact do we learn that Dmitri actually had 1,500 roubles on his person as he raced around begging for money. Only after the murder do we ascertain how it was committed, and only then can we begin to piece together each brother's role in that complex event. The very nature of this polyphonic novel as "a work in which several consciousnesses meet as equals and engage in a dialogue that is in principle unfinalizable," that is, endlessly surprising[41]—this in itself seems to dictate that the reader of *The Brothers Karamazov* will possess no marked advantage of knowledge, no immunity to surprise or error, nothing comparable in degree or kind to the privilege of knowing possessed by some and not others in the *Odyssey.* Not until the members of the Karamazov family, minus Smerdyakov, assemble for a "dialogue" in an elder's cell do we discover what is going on in that household; and that state of affairs is so volatile and complicated that no one, not even the actors, can tell what will happen next. Only after the fact (a day later) do we learn what Father Zosima meant by kneeling before Dmitri in his cell, and then only darkly. After the scene in the cell when the cynical Rakitin comments that the Karamazov family "stinks" of crime (78), we have hardly heard of, and have not yet seen, Smerdyakov, whose name carries the epithet "Stinking," so that if Rakitin's choice of words constitutes foreshadowing, it is the kind of foreshadowing that reveals itself only in retrospect. All in all, it seems that Dostoevsky binds the reader by what Tolstoy calls "the rule forbidding us to eat of the fruit of the Tree of Knowledge" (*War and Peace* 1007), and he does so, I believe, to impress upon us the always incomplete nature of our knowledge—the correlate of the "unfinalized" nature of our being.

At a few points in the Shakespeare canon modern editors reassign a speech in the belief that it seems "out of character" for the original speaker. Commenting on this practice, Frank Kermode remarks that "the motive is not a good one, for it assumes that editors already know all they need to about the limits of the character."[42] Reading *The Brothers Karamazov,* we discover that we do not already know all we need to know, and even in retrospect can hardly tell what the "limits" of Dmitri's character may be.

Much Is Concealed

"Equality is only in man's spiritual dignity," says Zosima (316).[43] By the design of an author who so believes in the equality of souls that, arguably, he endows his heroes with a sort of equality to himself, a reader cannot really enter into those characters without giving up every pretense of superior knowledge. Within the world of *The Brothers Karamazov* itself there is no Tiresias, after all, who knows what lies ahead. Father Zosima bows down to Dmitri because he "seemed to see something terrible" (285) in Dmitri's face—a premonition nothing like Tiresias's road map of the future—and when Alyosha asks the elder to explain himself, he is checked in language that recalls the traditional injunction against thirsting for excessive knowledge: "Do not be curious" (285). (How different is the spirit of his warning from "The Tale of Ill-Advised Curiosity"—an extended fabliau—in *Don Quixote.*) Perhaps in Zosima's admonition lies some hint of the author's reasons for keeping the reader of *The Brothers Karamazov* always in the presence of the unknown. As moderns and especially as children of the Enlightenment, we pride ourselves highly on our knowledge. By now it is an article of secular faith that knowledge liberates, that you cannot really have too much of it, and that anything that impedes the quest for knowledge is a shackle on human progress. As a critic of modern rationalism Dostoevsky can't be expected to go along with such doctrines, and I believe that by divesting readers of *The Brothers Karamazov* of their proudest possession and dearest pretense—their knowledge—he imposes on us something like the awe before the unknown that Father Zosima enjoins on his young disciple. Says Father Zosima, "There is much in the strongest feelings and impulses of our nature that we cannot comprehend while on earth. . . . Much on earth is concealed from us" (320). Exactly who threw the stone that killed the boy Ilyusha, exactly who put the pillow under Dmitri's head following the ordeal of his interrogation is hidden from us. Certainly volume 2 of *The Brothers Karamazov* is hidden from us.

Each of the moderns considered in these pages, whatever his ideology, cautions against the pride of knowledge. To be told that

> in historic events the rule forbidding us to eat of the fruit of the Tree of Knowledge is specially applicable. Only unconscious action bears fruit, and he who plays a part in an historic event never understands its significance (*War and Peace* 1007)

is to be reminded of traditional prohibitions and to have the pride of knowledge mortified. Those who act, even act well, do not fully know what they do, while those who survey the past with belated knowledge pay for that knowledge with their own insignificance. In *Great Expectations,* the reader who does not know joins the company of Pip, ignorant that Biddy has married Joe; of Herbert, ignorant that Pip has established him in business; of Magwitch, ignorant of Miss Havisham; of Miss Havisham, ignorant that her ward is Magwitch's daughter. Ignorance unites, as though it belonged to our humanity itself. In *The Brothers Karamazov* people may be ignorant or they may just ignore.

Somehow Dmitri manages to ignore the dishonor he does to Katerina by relating the story of her humiliation to Grushenka. Somehow, too, he ignores the evidence that Grushenka's thoughts are not with his father but with her former lover, the Pole:

> Everything was clear as day: he knew about him, he knew everything perfectly well, knew it from Grushenka herself, knew that a month ago a letter had come from him. So for a month, for a whole month this affair had been going on in deep secret from him, up to the present arrival of this new man,

> and he had not even given him a thought! But how could he, how could he not give him a thought? Why had he simply forgotten about the officer, forgotten the moment he learned of him? (396)

Similarly, Ivan fails to discern Smerdyakov's ill intentions when he leaves for Moscow and the young Zosima failed to notice that the woman he was interested in was already betrothed. (The young Zosima had a quixotic streak of his own, challenging the woman's husband to a duel not so much because he loved her as because he was enamored of the romantic role he was playing. "Later I perceived and realized that I was perhaps not so greatly in love with her after all" [296].) Such critical lapses of attention—critical because they can alter the direction of a life—suggest that we have no option to abandon the quest to know and fall back on the comforts of "unconscious action." What we need to know, however, may lie in full view. Of his lady friend's betrothal, Father Zosima says, "Almost everyone knew, and I alone knew nothing" (296).[44] Nor is his blindness forever cured by this episode. Of Smerdyakov, the half-brother of his disciple and the ruin of the Karamazov household, Father Zosima appears completely unaware. The wisest person in the novel knows nothing of the most malevolent.

Immediately before affirming that "we must all serve each other" (289), Father Zosima's brother, the inspiration of his conversion, asks how it is that he failed to recognize such a simple principle before *his* conversion: "How is it that I did not know it, that I did not appreciate it before?" (288–89). Readers of *The Brothers Karamazov* ask themselves the same question. Like Zosima himself, they too "know nothing." In *Don Quixote* everyone but the hero, that enthusiast of delusion, can perceive things more or less as they are. In *The Brothers Karamazov* everyone from the sage Zosima to the very reader is liable to the power of error.

8

Reflections: Literature and Human Equality

As an example of a work of literature that, in contrast (say) to *The Brothers Karamazov,* does place superior knowledge in the reader's hands, consider the Knight's Tale, the inaugural tale of Chaucer's collection. Toward the end of the tale (the longest of all the *Canterbury Tales,* as though the Knight were exercising his pride of place in narrative form), some years after the freakish death of his cousin at the very moment of victory, Palamon is sent for by Theseus "unwist of hym what was the cause and why"—without knowing the reason. We, the readers of the tale, however, know that Theseus intends him to marry Emily for political reasons. This is one of many such discrepancies of knowledge in the Knight's Tale. If the heroes of the tale, the two noble kinsmen, weren't possessed of greatness and raised above the common level of humanity, the higher powers would take no interest in them; because they do take an interest in them, the two mortals become subject to those powers, and precisely as subjects are in the dark on certain things. Arcite does not know that Venus has granted Palamon's prayer; Palamon does not know that Mars has granted Arcite's prayer. But that is also to say that we ourselves do know. Neither of the knights knows, although we do, that Saturn resolves the conflict between Venus and Mars by the political stroke of awarding one knight victory and the other the lady. Only we, and the Knight, therefore, know the story behind the story of Arcite's death. Although Theseus at the end of the tale lectures Palamon and Emily about the governance of the universe, not even he has any idea of what took place on high. From the Knight's sense of his own eminence, both as the highest-ranking pilgrim and the first tale-teller, it seems to follow that his knowledge should extend into the heavens and should therefore exceed the knowledge available to the tale's own actors, noble as they are. The tale is told in the pride and pathos of superior knowledge. It is as though the Knight possessed complete knowledge because the heroic age itself is complete. The tale's first word, "Whilom," sets it in the remote past.

But the first word of the Miller's Tale, that victorious travesty of the Knight's

Tale, is also "whilom," and it is the turn from the Knight's to the Miller's Tale that sets the *Canterbury Tales* themselves in motion, activating the potential of an occasion that gives people from different social worlds the same opportunity to woo or offend others, to idealize or avenge themselves—in a word, to speak. Resemblances across social classes in Shakespeare are in the tradition of the play between the Knight's Tale and its comical sequel. By the same token, Shakespeare does not argue for the abstraction, human equality, any more than Chaucer does.

When Shakespeare gives Hippolyta no less a voice than her conqueror, when he makes Theseus (who seems to reflect his predecessor in the Knight's Tale) as confused in his own way as the mechanicals with their tragical mirth, when he reveals both the well-born Claudio and Pompey Bum as men that would live, the effect is not to expose the falsity of the social order in the manner of a Rousseau. In each case, it is the very reality of social distinctions that gives these resemblances their dramatic force. Social distinctions constitute the background against which they stand out. Perhaps Shakespeare's most startling image of the state of nature—"unaccommodated man" as "a poor, bare, fork'd animal" (*King Lear* 3.4.106–8)—takes its force from the fact that a king has now been reduced to this condition. A strain of carnival runs through *King Lear* and its complex fooling. And if the doublings just cited are in some sense carnivalesque, carnival itself was a temporary departure from the normal order and presupposed a return to that order, as indeed the holiday nature of the Canterbury pilgrimage presumes the background of a normal world where millers cannot throw words in the face of knights. It has been said that Falstaff is Carnival; but by the same token, "carnival ends, [and] social discipline is resumed."[1] "I know thee not, old man" (2 *Henry IV* 5.5.47). With their zeal for unmasking, the revolutionaries of France disapproved of carnival, but they might also have disapproved of its attachment to the very institutions it made the objects of blasphemy. Theatrically speaking, Shakespeare's plays are attached to the institutions they demystify, from kingship on down. His acceptance of class distinctions accounts in part for Tolstoy's relegation of Shakespeare to the same category to which he came to assign almost all of his own fiction, that of bad art. (Yet *War and Peace* contains its own *Midwinter Night's Dream*—the mummer episode where Nicholas Rostov, under "fairyland" [565] influence, falls in love with Sonya. As the fairy-haunted woods lie beyond the bounds of Athenian law, love between Nicholas and this poor relation is itself out of bounds from the viewpoint of the Countess Rostova, and she puts a stop to it. Carnival ended, social discipline is resumed.)

It is the very abstraction of the principle of equality that gives it such power to indict existing institutions. "We hold these truths to be self-evident." No such abstraction is espoused by Shakespeare. Of *Measure for Measure* it has been said that it "doesn't discuss any issues, solve any problems, expound any theories or illustrate any doctrines," despite showing the almighty Angelo as no better, and arguably worse, than one he condemns to death.[2] And this indifference to doctrine colors the Shakespearean portrayal of human equality generally. In one of its moods *Cymbeline* regards distinctions of high and low as constructions of human vanity, as when Imogen replies to Arviragus's question, "Are we not brothers?" with "So man and man should be. / But clay and clay differs in dignity, / Whose dust is both alike" (4.2.3–5). What are social distinctions in the face of death? Without recognizing it, however, Arviragus and Imogen really are "brothers" by blood, and in the end the play entertains no abstract ideal of human brotherhood but the mystery of noble blood, the blood that flows through Cymbeline's sons and inspires them to noble deeds even in the wilds of Wales.[3] Says Belarius, who abducted them as children,

> O worthiness of nature! breed of greatness!
> Cowards father cowards, and base things sire base:
> Nature hath meal and bran, contempt and grace. (4.2.25–27)

In order for there to be nobility there has to be baseness, and there must also be inequalities of knowledge, for the ironies, confoundings, and riddles implied in Jupiter's policy of "Whom best I love, I cross" (5.4.101) are not things to make themselves known to all equally or to all at once.

As characters of different rank mirror one another with surprising cross-effects, so, on another level, the comic *Midsummer Night's Dream* doubles the tragic *Romeo and Juliet.* Both dated to 1595–96, the one makes light of a situation that could have turned tragic and converts the Pyramus and Thisby story into an occasion of mirth, while the other re-creates Pyramus and Thisby in contemporary Italy. A comedy set in ancient Athens and a tragedy in the Italy of the present—this in itself seems a reversal of form, as does a comedy about a great hero and a tragedy about a pair of unknowns. When Dickens elevates a commoner to a tragic position, he realizes fictionally the criticism of unnatural distinctions. In the first number of his magazine *Household Words* Dickens announced his ideal of "bring[ing] the greater and lesser, to a degree, together," and this his fiction does by linking characters in different social conditions almost like members of a single extended family.[4] (In Dickens the gravedigger tells Hamlet, "I worked hard that you should be above work.") If the novelist who writes about persons unknown to the reader gains freedom of invention, Dickens seems to exult in his own freedom to the point of making superfluous displays of it. But bound up with modernity's affirmation of the freedom of the imagination are the erosion of hierarchy and valorization of equality, "and that in all sorts of dimensions, between social classes, races, ethnic and cultural groups, and the sexes."[5] So it is, perhaps, that even amid such signs of decadence as the contest for imaginary precedence in Miss Havisham's household and such evidences of corruption as the unequal justice dealt out to Abel Magwitch, *Great Expectations* brings to life a world where people are connected whether they know it or not. The regal Estella is the daughter of the criminal Magwitch. Not that Dickens makes political speeches. In *Little Dorrit* we get a taste of the rhetoric of equality from an impostor, Mrs. Merdle:

> "If we could only come to a Millennium, or something of that sort, I for one might have the pleasure of knowing a number of charming and talented persons from whom I am at present excluded. A more primitive state of society would be delicious to me. There used to be a poem when I learnt lessons, something about Lo the poor Indian whose something mind! If a few thousand persons moving in Society, could only go and be Indians, I would put my name down directly."[6]

Nor does Dickens codify the principle of equality like a Bentham. If Bentham believes in the greatest happiness of the greatest number, this in turn presupposes that everyone's happiness counts the same. ("Every man to count for one and no one to count for more than one.") Not because of its egalitarianism but its rigidity and unreality as a system Dickens took issue with this school of thought critical, as he himself was, of things established. For similar reasons, Tolstoy in *War and Peace* unfavorably portrays Speranski, an admirer of Bentham responsible for his translation into Russian. Both authors, it seems, view the construction of systems as an exercise in vanity even, or especially, when the system rests on so important a principle as equality. As if theories stood for the sort of self-deception burned out of Pip (and later Ivan Ilych) in the course of experience, both satirize theory-building as such.[7]

As cross-resemblances in Shakespeare suggest, it is possible to put class differences in question without expounding a theory or defending a doctrine of equality. Jane Austen's *Midsummer Night's Dream* is *Emma.* A romantic comedy of mischief and mistakes, *Emma* too features pairs of lovers who take time to find their proper places, and lightly parodies the conventions of romantic resolution. Both worlds—Shakespeare's Athens and Austen's Highbury—are stratified. But in one cardinal respect Jane Austen does not follow Shakespeare. Never in *A Midsummer Night's Dream* does the audience commit the same mistake as the mistake-makers in the play. In *Emma,* which is written somewhere between the first and the third person, the reader is constantly and deliberately drawn into the same misreadings as Emma herself, quite as though both parties were equally subject to delusion and faults of judgment, whatever their differences of condition. For both reader and heroine, the tale is a journey through a maze of misperception, and in Emma's case many such mistakes spring from a belief in her supremacy in the local world, the same sense of ruling without an equal that emboldens her to toy with other lives as though they were figurines. Without ever employing the rhetoric of equality, the author reveals the heroine as but another reader and reveals both the heroine and the actual reader as liable to delusion and surprise. In her best-loved novel, *Pride and Prejudice,* simply by playing down her own authority and allowing us to see through the eyes of an independent protagonist—by making us participants in error and discovery rather than receivers of knowledge—Jane Austen gives the page a kind of liberal tone all the more striking in an author whose sympathies do not seem to lie with the liberal side in the war of ideas. Darcy is "a gentleman; I am a gentleman's daughter; so far we are equal," says Elizabeth Bennet to Lady Catherine de Bourgh, but the liberalism of *Pride and Prejudice* may be more an illusion of its telling than the reflection of a political position.[8]

A work of literature may question class differences without espousing equality as a political thesis. Similarly differences of color. Following the *Ethiopian Story* backwards, we find that the originating event of the entire sequence is the Queen of Ethiopia's giving birth to a white daughter (Chariclea), an event so contrary to the expected course of things that she exposes the child, its story inscribed on a swathe, rather than face her husband's accusations. With black parents producing a white daughter, the implication that color doesn't matter follows inescapably, though never does Heliodorus insist on the point or even voice it. Similarly, the earlier novel *Callirhoe* establishes a kind of working equality between hero and heroine by dividing the tale between them, though in no sense does the author make a polemical issue of it or imply that the two have equal rights before the bar of reason. Whatever doctrines they may discuss, Shakespeare's romances dignify their heroines—Marina, Imogen, Perdita, Miranda—simply by giving them the power of enduring exile and adversity that once belonged to the incomparable Odysseus. No more than Chariton does Shakespeare orate in favor of women, and Mary Wollstonecraft, who does so orate, despises romance, but without the heightened importance of women in romance and the novel (beginning with the prominence of women in the *Odyssey*), the equality of women preached by Mary Wollstonecraft might not have taken hold of the imagination and caught on eventually as a political principle. Near the end of *War and Peace* we learn that the issue of women's rights leaves Natasha cold:

> There were then, as there are now, conversations and discussions about women's rights, the relations of husband and wife, and their freedom and rights, though these themes were not yet termed *questions* as they are now; but these topics were not merely uninteresting to Natasha, she positively did not understand them. (1238)

As Kitty and Levin come together in *Anna Karenina,* the conversation around them happens to concern the position of women.

> It would seem that what they were saying about the rights and education of women ought to have interested Kitty. How often she had thought of it . . .

> how often she had wondered what would happen to her if she did not get married, and how many times she had argued about it with her sister! But now it did not interest her in the least. (389–90)

Tolstoy himself rejoiced to see Mill's essay on *The Subjection of Women* attacked in print. But whatever his hostility to women's rights in the abstract, *War and Peace* seems to one well-informed scholar "dominated by the female principle."[9] Napoleon, the deposer of kings, among the most charismatic figures in history, appears an absurd mannequin next to Natasha, who when we meet her is playing with a doll. Natasha it is who, during the abandonment of Moscow, orders the servants to make over the Rostov carts to the wounded. Says her father in tears, "The eggs are teaching the hen" (923)—an expression Platon Karataev might appreciate. The admirable Karataev himself uses the intonations of "old Russian peasant women" (1035), and in restoring the captive Pierre to life serves as "a very distinct mother surrogate."[10] As to Kitty and Levin, he doesn't know what to do for his dying brother, but she does. "Many great masculine minds, whose thoughts about it [Levin] had read, had pondered death and yet did not know a hundredth part of what his wife and Agafya Mikhailovna [his servant] knew about it" (496). So much for the great men.

Neither Tolstoy nor any other author discussed here espouses a program of equality that would meet today's standards and be approved by the arbiters of political taste. In a recent article on possible sources for *Great Expectations* in the author's notebooks and other writings, a scholar remarks on "Dickens's racism," his "spleen against minorities," his "acquiescence in what was to be called The White Man's Burden," "his distaste for The Races Not So Blest As We," his partiality for "reasonably sane non-Catholic Continental caucasians," and "his bigotry against people whose marginal lifestyle repelled, perhaps even frightened him"—none of which enter importantly into *Great Expectations* itself.[11] Analogous charges could be brought against Tolstoy and Dostoevsky. To me it seems that to prosecute these authors, in the name of equality, for their failure to come up to our own standards of enlightenment is to claim a false superiority—a privilege of the kind denied the reader of their fiction. The false note audible in the ridicule of Dickens's "distaste for The Races Not So Blest As We" is precisely the note of disdain for one not so enlightened as we.

Each according to its own principles, *Great Expectations, War and Peace,* and *The Brothers Karamazov* deny the reader superior knowledge—the sort of knowledge we receive in the *Odyssey* when we learn, over the hero's head, that the order has been given for his release from Calypso's island. Readers of *Great Expectations* know only what Pip knew at any given moment. Readers of *The Brothers Karamazov* soon learn that they actually know less than the principals about their own history. No doubt some would consider the denial of privileged knowledge a poor substitute for the destruction of privilege as such, but on the other hand, those who embark on a program of destruction with a sense of absolute knowledge—of being in possession of some power that exposes hidden motives, dispels illusion, and reveals the direction of history itself—are unlikely to prove friendly even to equality.

Nor of course does equality cure all evils. In Tocqueville's reflections on *The Old Regime and the French Revolution*—a work that entered into Tolstoy's thinking around the time of the composition of *War and Peace*—the point is made that equality is consistent with tyranny; that is, the two may coexist.[12] Equality represents not the supreme good but one good among others, and potentially in conflict with those others. Nevertheless, the ideal of equality possesses a simplicity that sets it apart and endows it with special attractions. "In its simplest form," writes Isaiah Berlin, "the ideal of complete social equality embodies the wish that everything and everybody should be as similar as possible to everything and everybody else." Again, "In its extreme form egalitarianism requires the minimisation of all differences between men, the obliteration of the maximum number of distinctions, the greatest possible degree of assimilation and uniformity to a single pattern."[13] In reality, Berlin maintains, the claims of equality must be weighed against others no less important. Made an absolute, reduced to its "extreme" form, transformed into a mandate for "obliteration," equality becomes a threat to anything deemed not to comply with its dictates. There is something in Berlin's language of reduction to the last simplicity, of obliteration, that suggests a graveyard. As we learn in the first paragraph of *Great Expectations,* the grave of Pip's five dead brothers has five identical stone markers.

The fanatical pursuit of equality leads to death. The Khmer Rouge of Cambodia "took seriously Mao's famous adage: 'It is on a blank page that the most beautiful poems are written.' The aim was to get rid of everything that would not normally be found in the house of a poor peasant."[14] As the murder of much of the population of Cambodia demonstrates, this program of elimination extended beyond belongings and furnishings. Wishing not only that everything should resemble everything else as much as possible, but that everyone should resemble everyone, the Khmer Rouge turned the pursuit of equality into a work of annihilation. Mao's figure of the clean page, envisioning human beings as blanks they can never be (and implicitly condemning all who bear the traces of the past, that is, everyone), presents the ideal of equality at its most nihilistic. Equality means the elimination of all existing qualities so that the same "poem" can be imprinted on all the resulting blank slates. Somehow it is hard to imagine Mao undertaking to write a beautiful novel, rather than a poem, on all those slates.[15] Neither is it possible to imagine a work of literature with indistinguishable characters. Committed though he is to the "absolute equality" of souls, Dickens does not erase differences but rejoices in them, does not subject all things to a single pattern but caricatures those who are themselves pattern-bound, does not offer us one thing but a satiric plenitude. Set in an industrial town "inhabited by people equally like one another, who all went in and out at the same hours, with the same sound upon the same pavements, to do the same work, and to whom every day was the same as yesterday and tomorrow," Dickens's *Hard Times* protests all this sameness.[16] Not the equality of blank pages but the equality of moral subjects interests Dickens.

Not only may a work of literature speak to us of human equality without espousing a doctrine or program thereof, but a doctrinal belief in equality may rule out literature. In the name of the equality of souls Tolstoy eventually cast literature into the fire. As the story is told in his *Confession*, Tolstoy's spiritual impasse broke with the realization that his very way of life was at fault. Isolated from the peasants who made his existence possible and who alone lived well, he naturally lost touch with truth. Henceforward he must not just remember the peasants: he must love them. And as if to demonstrate that in spite of everything the poets have said love *can* be forced, Tolstoy claims to have succeeded:

> And of such people, understanding the meaning of life and able to live and to die, I saw not two or three, or tens, but hundreds, thousands, and millions. . . . And I learnt to love these people. The more I came to know their life, the life of those who are living and of others who are dead of whom I read and heard, the more I loved them and the easier it became for me to live.[17]

In the image of Tolstoy immolating his intellect and undergoing the ceremonies of Orthodoxy to make himself one with the people, there is something of Claudius forcing himself to kneel. "Bow, stubborn knees." Whether Tolstoy was really able to love the peasants categorically I cannot tell, though even if he was it would bring the act no closer to the normal range of human nature. This much seems clear. If the kind of coercion Tolstoy used to humble his intellect and his pride were harnessed politically, the results would be fatal to liberty—possibly a despotism like the Grand Inquisitor's. To some Tolstoy's very prose seems inhuman. There really is something inhuman about his comparison of people returning to the ruins of Moscow to a mass of ants. In a rejected draft of an early section of *War and Peace* Tolstoy proclaims his scorn of "merchants, coachmen, seminarists, convicts, and peasants," who from the height of his pride appear equally petty and one-dimensional.[18] Later, his contempt was turned against art and its consumers, but contempt it remained. And firing the later Tolstoy's indictment of art is something very like the will to get rid of everything not found in the house of a peasant. The Khmer Rouge emptied the city of Phnom Penh, driving its inhabitants into the countryside: Tolstoy makes the city a synonym for corruption and identifies the man of unperverted tastes as "a labouring man, not a city-dweller."[19] We might say of a work of art like "The Death of Ivan Ilych" that it keeps Tolstoy's hatreds from becoming the absolutes they are in his polemic against art in the name of equality. Still, those hatreds are strong. Dickens's characters, Tolstoy once wrote, are "the friends of all mankind" because of the love shown them by Dickens himself.[20] Many of Tolstoy's characters are treated with sovereign contempt. A political regime that wrung confessions out of its subjects as moral and physical suffering wring from Ivan Ilych an understanding of his errors would be the enemy of humanity.

So strong are the Rousseauian principles driving "The Death of Ivan Ilych" that they threaten to overpower this tale of a man of no originality or depth, a man seemingly of wood, who nevertheless proves capable of moral life. Ivan Ilych breaks through his own limits. Yet characters no worse than he stand before us defined absolutely, as though the total of their capacities were already known and it came to nothing. The literary cousin of Pierre Bezukhov's first wife, Praskovya Fedorovna exemplifies insincerity and corruption as Rousseau understands these evils. Especially odious is the love of show expressed in her social brilliance as a girl, her insistence on a celebrity physician, her fondness for the theater itself (an institution excoriated by Rousseau), and above all her theatrical displays of grief. Her very life an affectation of distinction, Praskovya Fedorovna is thus the human image of false distinctions in an unequal society, and of her Tolstoy seems to say—in spite of his own art—that we can expect no change and no awakening, that she contains within herself no possibility of being other than as she is, inasmuch as her existence is infected to its roots with fraud. Strangely, a sort of doctrinal hatred of inequality rules out a world where people partake equally of human possibility. But a world where an Ivan Ilych achieves tragic stature is such a world already.

If equal things cannot be distinguished from one another, then, oddly, the most perfect equality belongs to those who share the condition of being "unnoticed, unremarked, and undocumented," for the simple reason that they cannot be distinguished at all.[21] Tolstoy does believe that the truth resides with those invisible to history (as he comes to assert that great art is anonymous). But by the same token, simply to portray someone on the page is to break the spell of invisibility—to set that person off from others. In one critical respect literature is more honest about human equality than the language of political argument. Equal we may be before the law, but we are so only by virtue of an act of abstraction that strips away whatever traits we have. Quantities are equal—not qualities. In itself, the word "e-quality" points to a removal or deprivation of qualities, and it seems fitting, if also ironic, that equality should be a favored theme of political discourses whose note is sheer abstraction. Equality is the political equivalent of zero, a potent invention of the human mind.[22]

Discussing envy, Joseph Epstein cites a dystopian novel in which all citizens are given the same face through plastic surgery, lest anyone look better than anyone else.[23] Literature, of course, abounds with portrayals of the human face, and precisely because it portrays qualities and not the absence of qualities—and even Tolstoy, for all his concern with the fallacies of notice, certainly cannot help noticing and documenting—it necessarily reminds us of everything lost in the thin air of abstraction, everything that might otherwise be left out of account. In the world of literature things tend not to be identical. Although Palamon and Arcite, the noble kinsmen of the Knight's Tale, seem identical, one prays to Venus and the other to Mars, and on this difference the tale depends. Hermia and Helena of *A Midsummer Night's Dream* may once have been like a double cherry, but one is now short, dark, and spirited, the other tall, fair, and pathetic. "Human beings are not like sheep; and even sheep are not undistinguishably alike," says Mill.[24] A principle dramatically enforced in Dickens. Even if Dickens had never written *Hard Times* we would know from his way of practically overburdening characters with singularity that he will have nothing to do with the reduction of persons to statistical units. In *The Brothers Karamazov* it is the Grand Inquisitor who speaks of human beings by the million as ants driven by an identical desire to unite themselves in a single mass, a vision still more abhorrent than a herd of human sheep. Pierre's guards "saw in him only No. 17 of the captured Russians" (1025). In Tolstoy's "God Sees the Truth, But Waits," the innocent merchant loses the purely generic character he possesses in Platon Karataev's telling of the tale, acquires a name, undergoes a radical deprivation of knowledge, and longs to avenge himself on the actual murderer for whose crime he has been punished, but when given a golden opportunity to do so, refuses. A parable becomes a virtual drama of moral complexity. In "The Death of Ivan Ilych," even as he tells us of the hero's lack of distinguishing features, Tolstoy makes him a man and deplores by implication his practice of "exclud[ing] everything fresh and vital" (139) from the cases before him. Any transformation of persons into identical quantities, statistical units, legal fictions, or for that matter representatives of classes and categories will necessarily leave out something fresh and vital.

If Shakespeare keeps us from believing in "the singularity of Lear's fate," Ivan Ilych seems deprived of singularity altogether.[25] A nullity, he becomes a man. But upon examination, it is clear that even he is not denied all distinguishing qualities. True, his Petersburg house has "all the things people of a certain class have in order to resemble other people of that class" (138), and his little parties "resemble all other parties" (140). But as though literature abhorred a vacuum, Ivan Ilych acquires a certain character even before his illness. He somehow overdoes things. Not only does he apply the new Code of 1864, he is "one of the first men" to do so (132). Not only does he have the ability to separate professional from personal considerations, he has it "in the highest degree" (139). Like some Chaucerian type—say the Man of Law—superlative of his kind, Ivan Ilych through such details becomes an individual. His life as a whole is pronounced not simply ordinary, but "most ordinary" (129), a kind of latent paradox. The man is "so interested" in decorating his new house "that he often did things himself, rearranging the furniture, or rehanging the curtains" (136), and in so doing suffers his fatal bruise. One who was less of an overdoer would have left the hanging of the curtains to the tradesman. To the obsessed decorator, antiques are not just "comme il faut" but "particularly *comme il faut*" (137); and as the narrator of Tolstoy's *Youth* reports, the difference between those who can be considered "comme il faut" and those who cannot is that only the former can be deemed equals.[26]

With his overeagerness, his way of "completely" excluding his personal opinions in a legal matter (132), his marriage to a "thoroughly" eligible young woman (133), all amounting to a "most ordinary" life, Ivan Ilych overfulfills the role of the average man of his class. Even this apparent nobody possesses what Bakhtin names the "surplus of humanness" that distinguishes the novelistic hero. For such a hero, writes Bakhtin, no single role exists

> that would be able to incarnate once and forever all of his human possibilities and needs, no form in which he could exhaust himself down to the last word like the epic or tragic hero; no form that he could fill to the very brim, and yet at the same time not splash over the brim.[27]

In Western literature, arguably the first character endowed with such an excess of potential is Odysseus. Displayed not only as a warrior but a spy, a captive, an adventurer, a beggar, a father, husband, and son, Odysseus is filled with human possibilities that the role of "a hero of the Trojan War" cannot begin to encompass. With his remarkable inwardness and his possession of a private as well as public existence, Odysseus altogether exceeds other heroic figures of the *Iliad,* who show a kind of archaic simplicity by contrast. To suit the times, we are told, Ivan Ilych made himself a new man. In literature, Odysseus is the first new man.

In Ivan Ilych the descent of "the hero" to a mere protagonist is complete. But this descent, too, begins with Odysseus. The *Iliad* has no protagonist, though many military heroes; and I think it significant that Odysseus vanishes from those books of the *Iliad* dominated by the purely heroic figures, Hector, Patroclus, and Achilles. As the protagonist of the *Odyssey,* that is, as a *literary* hero, Odysseus is placed in settings such as a cannibal's cave where warrior values do not apply and the great ones of the *Iliad* cannot even be imagined. According to Bakhtin, the novelistic hero can never be reduced to any given role (as we cannot reduce Dmitri Karamazov to a military officer, a rake, or anything else), but in the case of Odysseus a unique ability to assume diverse roles as events dictate qualifies him to be the protagonist of an extended tale in the first place. Where others are distinguished by some heroic quality, Odysseus is distinguished by many-sidedness itself—the very character necessary in the "hero" of a tale of many trials. Who else among the warriors of the *Iliad* has a nature various enough to sustain the multiplicity of the *Odyssey*'s adventures? For that matter, who else would consent to wear the rags of a beggar? But it is by doing such things that Odysseus proves himself a worthy protagonist—that is, somebody whose story is worth telling. At its origin, the institution of the literary hero implies a certain diminution of the heroic. Polyphemus was forewarned that one named Odysseus would blind him; but he expected somebody heroic, not "a little man, niddering, feeble" (9.515), albeit cunning. At various points of the *Odyssey* Odysseus suffers hunger, is overcome by sleep, yields to sexual desire. Godlike by title, he is nevertheless all too human. Achilles, the nominal hero of the *Iliad,* chooses heroic death over long life; Odysseus, the survivor, is promised a "sleek old age" (11.136). He too is a man that would live.

The century of Hitler, Stalin, and Mao cannot be said to have borne out Tolstoy's dismissal of the history-making Leader as a delusion, though by the same token, it would have been better for the world if Tolstoy had been right.[28] Within a half century of the appearance of *War and Peace* the heroic language of warfare ("steed" for "horse") was falsified by poison gas, the machine gun, and slaughter on a scale unimaginable before the fact.[29] With his disbelief in the heroic and his vision of war as carnage, Tolstoy would well have understood the recoil against heroic illusions brought about by the First World War. By now, traditional "kings and battles" history is disfavored in the universities, overshadowed by the study of more ordinary people and events—"social history." Had he not despised experts of all kinds, Tolstoy might have approved of this trend, too; after all, he ridicules the myth of the great man who makes history, portrays the best of the Russian generals now weeping and now sleeping, and marks as the turning point of the war an event that was not even a battle—the burning of Moscow. But as this may suggest, even though our culture prides itself fiercely on its superiority to the past and its emancipation from traditional illusions, suspicion of the heroic is itself traditional by this point; and if much of the work of devaluation had not already been done—that is, if belief in the heroic were really intact—today's practitioners of social history might not be able to go about their work with such assurance. The dragon has already been slain. Even Tolstoy's attitude toward the heroic has behind it the Enlightenment emphasis on ordinary motives and common experience. Civil society as it came to be understood in the eighteenth century "had little need for heroics"; the ethos of common sense on which it was founded "challeng[ed] older prescriptions for bravery and daring."[30] Commenting implicitly on kings-and-battles history, Samuel Johnson remarked that the sort of account that "never descend[s] below the consultation of senates, the motions of armies, and the scheme of conspirators" does not much interest the common reader. He goes on to say, "I have often thought that there has rarely passed a life of which a judicious and faithful narrative would not be useful," a principle observed by each of our novelists in one way or another.[31] No believer in human equality as a political ideal, Johnson nevertheless does believe that almost every life is a story worth telling.

In turn, this revaluation of the ordinary follows upon "the affirmation of ordinary life" that began a century and more before.[32] "To know / That which before us lies in daily life / Is the prime wisdom," states Milton.[33] But instead of tracing our suspicion of the heroic back into the past by increments, we might look all the way back to the *Odyssey*, where this study began, for if Johnson distinguishes grand histories "which never descend below the consultation of senates [and] the motions of armies" from those narratives of private life we would call novels, Homer charters this very distinction in moving from the field of war in the *Iliad* to the exploration of private life in the original novel, the *Odyssey*. The first departure from kings-and-battles history toward history of another sort takes place in the *Odyssey*. From the *Odyssey* a sharp-eyed historian like M. I. Finley can construct a detailed picture of a social world.[34] Moreover, if Odysseus is indeed godlike, the god he most resembles is a woman—his patron Athena. In using Poseidon's absence to plead her case with Zeus, Athena herself exercises a kind of Odyssean cunning, just as the hero's skill in deceit rivals hers. "You and I both know / sharp practice," she tells him (13.296–97). Among the heroes of the Greek expedition to Troy, Odysseus is notable for the *less* heroic quality of resourcefulness—a capacity that uniquely fits him for the role of adventurer. Who else but Odysseus can be imagined spying on the Trojans in the guise of a beggar, the same disguise he uses in Ithaca? So it is that even as he records Odysseus's exploits, Homer makes him the first hero in a purely literary sense, the first protagonist, in our literature. Calypso is shown in her power and her weakness. We might say that Odysseus is a hero in both the strong and weak sense of the word. Even while narrative interest in the *Odyssey* is restricted to the noble, even while some in the poem have more power or knowledge than others, the portrayal of a less heroic hero in the person of Odysseus marks a revolution in itself, and opens up possibilities that poets, novelists, and historians are still filling in.

Notes

Introduction

1. Northrop Frye, *Anatomy of Criticism* (New York: Atheneum, 1967), 33–34.

2. Erich Auerbach, *Mimesis: The Representation of Reality in Western Literature*, trans. Willard Trask (Princeton: Princeton University Press, 1953), 4.

3. Auerbach, *Mimesis*, 21.

4. In the case of the blinding of Polyphemus, which the hero achieves by his own wits and without divine assistance, it turns out that the deed was predicted "of old" (*Odyssey* 9.507). Even here, surprise is precluded.

5. Jenny Strauss Clay, "The Whip and Will of Zeus," *Literary Imagination* 1 (1999): 40–60.

6. M. M. Bakhtin, *The Dialogic Imagination*, trans. Caryl Emerson and Michael Holquist (Austin: University of Texas Press, 1981), 366–67.

7. The *Odyssey* has one pursuer of delayed revenge, *Great Expectations* two—their plots dependent on one another.

8. Gary Saul Morson, *Hidden in Plain View: Narrative and Creative Potentials in "War and Peace"* (Stanford: Stanford University Press, 1987), 58.

9. Leo Tolstoy, *What Is Art?* trans. Richard Pevear and Larissa Volokhonsky (Harmondsworth, Eng.: Penguin, 1995), 9.

10. By the same token, when Anna Pavlovna Scherer is described on the first page of *War and Peace* as "well-known," the word bears the full force of Tolstoyan irony.

11. Upon Dostoevsky's death in 1881, Tolstoy did write, however, "How I should like to be able to say all I feel about Dostoyevsky. I never saw the man, never had any direct contact with him, and suddenly, at his disappearance, I realized that he was the closest of all to me, the most precious and essential. . . . I always thought of him as a friend, and was convinced that one day we would meet. . . . And all of a sudden, during dinner . . . I read of his death. It was as though one of my supporting pillars had suddenly buckled. I had a moment of panic, then I realized how precious he was to me and I began to cry. I am still crying." Cited in Henri Troyat, *Tolstoy*, trans. Nancy Amphous (Garden City: Doubleday, 1967), 419. As he set out on his last journey, Tolstoy asked for the second volume of *The Brothers Karamazov*, as though completing his duty to or his reckoning with his rival at last.

12. Cited in Lionel Trilling, *Sincerity and Authenticity* (Cambridge, Mass.: Harvard University Press, 1972), 117.

13. The best discussion of this is the last chapter of Robert Louis Jackson's

Dialogues with Dostoevsky: The Overwhelming Questions (Stanford: Stanford University Press, 1993).

14. Bakhtin, *Dialogic Imagination*, 37.

15. *The Rambler* no. 4. In this paper Johnson ridicules the conventional improbabilities of romance. In different ways, *Great Expectations*, *The Brothers Karamazov*, and "The Death of Ivan Ilych" could all be classed as anti-romances.

16. Ben Edwin Perry, *The Ancient Romances: A Literary-Historical Account of Their Origins* (Berkeley: University of California Press, 1967), 35–36.

17. Frank Kermode, *Shakespeare's Language* (New York: Farrar, Straus and Giroux, 2000), 271–72. In *What Is Art?* Tolstoy regards such concealments as a depraved innovation and a perversion of art; see p. 90.

18. Andrew S. Cairncross, introduction to *The Third Part of King Henry VI*, by William Shakespeare, Arden edition, ed. Andrew S. Cairncross (London: Routledge, 1964), lvii, lix.

19. Compare George Eliot, *Daniel Deronda* (New York: Modern Library, 2002), 202: "Of a truth, Knowledge is power, but it is a power reined in by scruple, having a conscience of what must be and what may be; whereas Ignorance is a blind giant."

20. Ian Watt, *The Rise of the Novel: Studies in Defoe, Richardson and Fielding* (Berkeley: University of California Press, 1957), 16.

21. John Locke, *An Essay Concerning Human Understanding* (New York: Meridian, 1974), 341.

22. Thomas Hardy, *The Trumpet-Major* (Harmondsworth, Eng.: Penguin, 1986), 200, 358. In Hardy's reworking of the David-Saul story in *The Mayor of Casterbridge*, the David figure, Donald Farfrae, is thin and minor compared to the Saul figure, Henchard. It has been said of the biblical stories of David and Saul that they "interlock antithetically on the theme of knowledge. Saul, from first to last, is a man deprived of the knowledge he desperately seeks," while David, at least at first, "seems peculiarly favored with knowledge." See Robert Alter, *The David Story* (New York: Norton, 1999), xix–xx.

23. Eliot, *Daniel Deronda*, 625.

24. Henry James, *What Maisie Knew* (Harmondsworth, Eng.: Penguin, 1985), 175.

25. Norman Maclean, *A River Runs Through It and Other Stories* (Chicago: University of Chicago Press, 2001), 103.

26. Iris Murdoch, *The Sea, the Sea* (Harmondsworth, Eng.: Penguin, 2001), 302.

27. Bakhtin, *Dialogic Imagination*, 32.

28. Isaiah Berlin, "The Hedgehog and the Fox," in *The Proper Study of Mankind* (New York: Farrar, Straus and Giroux, 1998).

29. Morson, *Hidden in Plain View*, 120.

30. George Eliot, *Middlemarch* (Boston: Houghton Mifflin, 1956), 613.

31. Bakhtin, *Dialogic Imagination*, 55.

32. Ian Watt, *Myths of Modern Individualism: Faust, Don Quixote, Don Juan, Robinson Crusoe* (Cambridge, Eng.: Cambridge University Press, 1997), 70.

33. Cited in Mikhail Bakhtin, *Problems of Dostoevsky's Poetics,* trans. Caryl Emerson (Minneapolis: University of Minnesota Press, 1984), 128.

34. Jenny Strauss Clay, *The Wrath of Athena: Gods and Men in the Odyssey* (Princeton: Princeton University Press, 1983), 56.

35. Auerbach, *Mimesis,* 521.

36. Jerome Meckier, *Dickens's "Great Expectations": Misnar's Pavilion versus Cinderella* (Lexington: University of Kentucky Press, 2002), 40.

37. Robert Garis, *The Dickens Theatre* (Oxford: Clarendon, 1965).

38. Isaiah Berlin, *Concepts and Categories: Philosophical Essays* (Harmondsworth, Eng.: Penguin, 1981), 81.

Chapter 1

1. Morson, *Hidden in Plain View,* 183.

2. Among the serving women of Odysseus's household, only Eurycleia knows that Telemachus has sailed to Pylos (2.412). When Penelope later discovers, from the herald Medon, that Telemachus has done so and that the suitors have now laid an ambush for him, she still does not know that Eurycleia alone knew the secret. The suitors meanwhile suppose that Penelope "is consenting to marriage / with one of us, not knowing how the murder of her son is appointed" (4.770–71). "Thus," Homer adds immediately, weaving his own complex tapestry of irony, "one of them would speak, not knowing what was appointed" (4.772).

3. H. D. F. Kitto, "The *Odyssey:* The Exclusion of Surprise" in *Homer's "The Odyssey": Modern Critical Interpretations,* ed. Harold Bloom (New York: Chelsea House, 1988), 13.

4. In canto 10 of the *Inferno,* the father of Guido Cavalcanti asks for news of his son. The damned have no knowledge of the present, a deprivation that marks the misery of their condition.

Chapter 2

1. Compare *Odyssey* 23.296.

2. Indeed, Callirhoe's prayer to Aphrodite that her child be considered the son of Dionysius (143) is granted, while her accusation that the goddess permitted the murder of Chaereas (187–89) is false.

3. Ernst Cassirer, *The Myth of the State* (New Haven: Yale University Press, 1946), 103.

Chapter 3

1. Compare 2 *Henry IV* 2.2.52–55: "What wouldst thou think of me if I should weep?" asks the Prince. Says Poins, "I would think thee a most princely hypocrite."

2. B. P. Reardon, "Theme, Structure, and Narrative in Chariton," *Yale Classical Studies* 27 (1982): 11.

3. When we first meet Chariclea in the *Ethiopian Story*, she has a quiver slung over her shoulder; later we learn that the many bodies of men slain by arrows are her work.

4. In *A Midsummer Night's Dream*, for example, all that happens behind the back of the characters is made known to the audience.

5. Discussed in Jerome Buckley, *Season of Youth: The Bildungsroman from Dickens to Golding* (Cambridge, Mass.: Harvard University Press, 1974), 29.

Chapter 4

1. Perry, *Ancient Romances*, 48–49.

2. John J. Winkler, "The Mendacity of Kalasiris and the Narrative Strategy of Heliodoros' *Aithiopika*," *Yale Classical Studies* 27 (1982): 93–158.

3. Additionally, at the novel's crisis "the mother and father [of Estella], unknown to one another, were dwelling within so many miles, furlongs, yards if you like, of one another" (*Great Expectations* 51.420).

4. Significantly in this connection, "Provis," suggesting "provide" and thus "foresee," is the false name taken by the returned Magwitch.

5. Edgar Johnson, afterword to *David Copperfield*, by Charles Dickens (New York: Signet, 1962), 873.

6. Cited in Joseph Frank, *Dostoevsky: The Mantle of the Prophet, 1871–1881* (Princeton: Princeton University Press, 2002), 111. On the difference between real time and retrospect, see Sherwin Nuland, *The New Republic*, September 13 and 20, 2004, 38: "Looking back with unbridled condemnation on the beginnings of racial hygiene does not enlighten today's thoughtful man or woman in regard to how he or she might have responded at the time."

7. As reported by Dickens's friend and biographer John Forster; cited in Donald Fanger, *Dostoevsky and Romantic Realism* (Cambridge, Mass.: Harvard University Press, 1965), 92.

8. John Rawls, *A Theory of Justice* (Cambridge, Mass.: Harvard University Press, 1971), 18–19.

9. Winkler, "Mendacity of Kalasiris," 95.

10. By keeping the narrative "solution" from the reading audience for months on end, serialization is well adapted to the conveyance of imperfect knowledge.

11. Jean-Jacques Rousseau, *A Discourse on Inequality,* trans. Maurice Cranston (Harmondsworth, Eng.: Penguin, 1984), 119.

12. John Stuart Mill, *On Liberty* (New York: Norton, 1975), 45–46.

13. "It is thus that we each find our profit at the expense of our fellows; and one man's loss is nearly always the good fortune of another" (Rousseau, *Discourse on Inequality,* note I, p. 148).

14. Jean Starobinski, *Jean-Jacques Rousseau: Transparency and Obstruction,* trans. Arthur Goldhammer (Chicago: University of Chicago Press, 1988).

15. Garis, *Dickens Theatre,* 97.

16. Perry, *Ancient Romances,* 45.

17. Heliodorus, *Ethiopian Story,* trans. Sir Walter Lamb (Rutland, Vt.: Everyman, 1997), 70.

18. "You are part of my existence, part of myself," Pip says (*Great Expectations* 44.368).

19. Hans Aarsleff, *From Locke to Saussure: Essays on the Study of Language and Intellectual History* (Minneapolis: University of Minnesota Press, 1982), 27.

20. William Wordsworth, preface to the *Lyrical Ballads,* in *The Great Critics,* ed. James Harry Smith and Edd Winfield Parks (New York: Norton, 1951), 506.

21. Bakhtin, *Dialogic Imagination,* 37. This observation appears in an essay investigating the difference between the still-evolving genre of the novel and the finished world of epic, only novels being capable of moving toward an unknown outcome. Presumably Bakhtin would agree with the judgment that the *Odyssey* lacks suspense, as in fact he notes the complete irrelevance to the *Iliad* of questions like "How does the war end? Who wins? What will happen to Achilles?" In *Great Expectations* the already closed tale of Pip's youth is delivered exactly like a tale moving toward an unknown destination. If the question of how the Trojan War ends is of no interest because everyone already knows how it ends, Pip is a complete unknown whose tale is also fraught with the unknown.

22. Jean-Jacques Rousseau, *The Confessions,* trans. J. M. Cohen (Harmondsworth, Eng.: Penguin, 1953), 232.

23. Bakhtin, *Dialogic Imagination,* 107.

24. Henry Fielding, *Joseph Andrews* (Harmondsworth, Eng.: Penguin, 1985), 315.

25. Discovered not to be brother and sister as they feared, Joseph and Fanny are free to marry; Pip and Estella, adopted son and natural daughter of a criminal both sinned against and sinning, are estranged by a force as strong as that binding the other two. Where Fielding diversifies the romance plot with a satiric medley of materials, Dickens seems to apply a satiric corrective to romance as such.

26. Bernard Schilling, *The Rain of Years: "Great Expectations" and the World of Dickens* (Rochester: University of Rochester Press, 2001), 94.

27. "I loved [Estella] against reason, against promise, against peace, against hope, against happiness" (*Great Expectations* 29.234), in fine, against himself.

28. Bakhtin, *Problems of Dostoevsky's Poetics*, 73.

29. Exceptions are the Ghost in *Hamlet* and Agamemnon in the *Odyssey*.

30. Anny Sadrin, *Parentage and Inheritance in the Novels of Charles Dickens* (Cambridge, Eng.: Cambridge University Press, 1994), reads *Great Expectations* as a novel haunted by parricide. What might the author say of *The Brothers Karamazov*?

31. Clay, "Whip and Will of Zeus," 40–60.

32. See Phillip V. Allingham, "Shadows of 'Things That Have Been and Will Be' in *Great Expectations*," *ELN* 41 (2004): 55.

33. Northrop Frye, *The Secular Scripture: A Study of the Structure of Romance* (Cambridge, Mass.: Harvard University Press, 1976), 66, 71.

34. On Dickens's ironization of the Homeric simile, see Bakhtin, *Dialogic Imagination*, 305–6.

35. On *Great Expectations* as tragicomedy, see Meckier, *Dickens's "Great Expectations,"* chap. 1.

36. Adam Smith, *Lectures on Rhetoric and Belles Lettres* (Indianapolis: Liberty Classics, 1985), 124: "Kings and Nobles are what make the best characters in a Tragedy. The misfortunes of the great as they happen less frequently affect us more. There is in humane Nature a Servility which inclines us to adore our Superiors and an inhumanity which disposes us to contempt and trample under foot our inferiors. We are too much accustomed to the misfortunes of people below or equal to be greatly affected by them." Elsewhere Smith observes that "in ease of body and peace of mind, all the different ranks of life are nearly upon a level, and the beggar, who suns himself by the side of the highway, possesses that security which kings are fighting for" (*Theory of Moral Sentiments* [Indianapolis: Liberty Classics, 1982], 185). Smith's sometimes-dinner companion Dr. Johnson observed characteristically in an *Idler* paper on sleep that "there is reason to suspect that the distinctions of mankind have more shew than value, when it is found that all agree to be weary alike of pleasures and of cares, that the powerful and the weak, the celebrated and the obscure, join in one common wish, and implore from Nature's hand the nectar of oblivion" (*The Idler* no. 32, November 25, 1758).

37. Denis Donoghue, *The Practice of Reading* (New Haven: Yale University Press, 1998), 182. On some of the bonds between Swift and Dickens, see Stewart Justman, *The Springs of Liberty: The Satiric Tradition and Freedom of Speech* (Evanston, Ill.: Northwestern University Press, 1999).

38. Jonathan Swift, *Writings* (New York: Norton, 1973), 178.

39. The tragic element appears in *Little Dorrit* in the form of strong echoes of *King Lear*, the title character being an unmistakable Cordelia.

40. Frye, *Anatomy of Criticism*, 212.

41. Odysseus begins the slaughter of the suitors at the banquet table. Miss Havisham imagines the suitors for her wealth feasting on *her*, laid out on the banquet table (88). This is surely a bizarre way of disappointing their great expectations.

42. Rousseau, *Discourse on Inequality,* 119. In the state of nature, Rousseau believed, people do not experience the desire for revenge. See note O, p. 168.

43. Edward Shils, *Tradition* (Chicago: University of Chicago Press, 1981), 291.

44. Perry, *Ancient Romances,* 29.

45. Arguably, it is the satiric energy of *Ulysses* that makes it, in Northrop Frye's words, a "complete prose epic." A work that is all at once "novel, romance, confession, and anatomy" (*Anatomy of Criticism* 314) does not really belong to any given genre.

46. Bakhtin, *Dialogic Imagination,* 55.

47. Ibid.

48. Morson, *Hidden in Plain View,* 83.

49. Letter written by Tolstoy in 1904 to one James Ley.

Chapter 5

1. Leo Braudy, *The Frenzy of Renown: Fame and Its History* (New York: Oxford University Press, 1986), 400.

2. Morson, *Hidden in Plain View,* 183.

3. Morson, *Hidden in Plain View,* for example, 184.

4. Maxim Gorky, *Reminiscences of Leo Nikolaevich Tolstoy,* trans. S. S. Koteliansky and Leonard Woolf (New York: B. W. Huebsch, 1920), 53.

5. Northrop Frye, *On Shakespeare* (New Haven: Yale University Press, 1986), 62.

6. Hannah Arendt, *Men in Dark Times* (New York: Harcourt Brace Jovanovich, 1968), 166.

7. Gary Saul Morson, *Narrative and Freedom: The Shadows of Time* (New Haven: Yale University Press, 1994), 169.

8. Nor does *Anna Karenina* advance toward a preconceived conclusion. In attaching to *Anna Karenina* an epilogue concerned with the Russo-Turkish War, which had not even begun until the serialization of the novel was almost complete, Tolstoy weaves the quality of the unpredictable into the composition of the work itself.

9. Tolstoy comes close to Mandeville in his contention that during the French occupation of Moscow, most Russians "paid no attention to the general progress of events but were guided only by their private interests, and they were the very people whose activities at that period were most useful" (*War and Peace* 1007).

10. Morson, *Hidden in Plain View,* 120.

11. Tolstoy claims that this rule applies "specially" but not solely to historical events.

12. Cited in Isaiah Berlin, *Russian Thinkers* (Harmondsworth, Eng.: Penguin, 1978), 245.

13. Berlin, *Proper Study of Mankind,* 449.

14. Cited in John Bayley, *Tolstoy and the Novel* (Chicago: University of Chicago Press, 1988), 64.

15. Bakhtin, *Dialogic Imagination,* 164.

16. Perry, *Ancient Romances,* 137.

17. Tolstoy, *What Is Art?* 9.

18. Recall the warm portrayal of a tutor, a serving woman, and a holy idiot in Tolstoy's early *Childhood,* a work alive with a kind of Sternean sentiment.

19. Joan Landes, *Women and the Public Sphere in the Age of the French Revolution* (Ithaca: Cornell University Press, 1988), 71.

20. Landes, *Women and the Public Sphere,* 24.

21. Jean-Jacques Rousseau, *Emile,* trans. Allan Bloom (New York: Basic, 1979), 268.

22. Cited in Starobinski, *Jean-Jacques Rousseau,* 76.

23. Cited and discussed in Boris Eikhenbaum, *Tolstoi in the Seventies,* trans. Albert Kaspin (Ann Arbor: Ardis, 1982), 31.

24. Starobinski, *Jean-Jacques Rousseau,* 141.

25. Jean Starobinski, "Rousseau and Revolution," trans. Arthur Goldhammer, *New York Review of Books,* April 25, 2002, 60.

26. Rousseau's *Discourse on Inequality,* it has been said, terminates in the conclusion that virtue is possible only for "courageous minds prepared to withdraw from society." Surely this is how Tolstoy, a man of courage who lived on his own land, imagined himself. See Starobinski, *Jean-Jacques Rousseau,* 302.

27. Rousseau, *Discourse on Inequality,* 123.

28. Introduction to Rousseau, *Discourse on Inequality,* 39.

29. Rousseau, *Emile,* 37.

30. Rousseau, *Discourse on Inequality,* 136.

31. Ibid., 119.

Chapter 6

An earlier version of this chapter appeared in my *Seeds of Mortality* (Chicago: Ivan R. Dee, 2003).

1. Rousseau, *Discourse on Inequality,* 136.

2. Berlin, *Russian Thinkers,* 247.

3. Aristotle, *Poetics,* trans. Malcolm Heath (Harmondsworth, Eng.: Penguin, 1996), 9.

4. George Steiner, *The Death of Tragedy* (New Haven: Yale University Press, 1996), 243. On the influx of tragedy into realism, see also Auerbach, *Mimesis,* 481: "Since French classicism and absolutism, not only had the treatment of everyday reality become much more limited and decorous, but in addition the attitude taken

toward it renounced the tragic and problematic as it were in principle. . . . A subject from practical reality could be treated comically, satirically, or didactically and moralistically; certain subjects from definite and limited realms of contemporary everyday life attained to an intermediate style, the pathetic; but beyond that they might not go."

5. The analogy of such friendship in *Great Expectations* would be the Pockets' angling for Miss Havisham's favor in the hope of reward at the time of her death.

6. Morson, *Narrative and Freedom.*

7. Lionel Trilling, *The Opposing Self* (New York: Viking, 1955), 163.

8. Keeping as a matter of principle on a level with everyday experience (as classical tragedy emphatically does not), Tolstoy adheres strictly to the realism that modern fiction calls for, according to Dr. Johnson. "The works of fiction with which the present generation seems more particularly delighted are such as exhibit life in its true state, diversified only by accidents that daily happen in the world. . . . [The province of this kind of writing] is to bring about natural events by easy means, and to keep up curiosity without the help of wonder: it is therefore precluded from the machines and expedients of the heroic romance" (*The Rambler* no. 4). A slip on a stepladder is in the strictest sense the sort of accident that happens every day.

9. Vronsky too is "caught unawares" by Anna's pregnancy (*Anna Karenina* 350).

10. Aristotle, *Poetics,* 21.

11. The principle of the peripeteia, described by Frank Kermode as "a falsification of expectation, so that the end comes as expected, but not in the manner expected," is also observed in "The Death of Ivan Ilych," where the hero dies as expected, but only after achieving an insight no one would have foreseen. Such twists are too common in the world of literature to be considered an Aristotelian device. See Frank Kermode, *The Sense of an Ending: Studies in the Theory of Fiction* (Oxford: Oxford University Press, 1967), 53.

12. As a rule, literature is much more interested in courtship than in marriage; pursuit than attainment. *A Midsummer Night's Dream* ends with a cluster of marriages, *The Tempest* with Ferdinand and Miranda soon to be married, almost as if the spirit of romance had no interest in the couples beyond the altar. If the English novel is a race to the altar—a race strewn with complications, like a steeplechase—what race holds our interest beyond its own finish? Dostoevsky, averse to finality and fascinated with indeterminate states, makes Katerina not the wife of Dmitri Karamazov but his "betrothed," a status with enough uncertainty in it to heighten the drama of *The Brothers Karamazov.* Pip for his part is not even "betrothed" to Estella, but deludes himself into believing she has somehow been promised to him. In literature's disproportionate interest in the lead-up to marriage, and certainly in its portrayal of the married themselves so often as ridiculous objects, there is an implication that the end we seek in courtship crumbles to dust once in our hands. We wake up from romance and find ourselves in a satire. So it is in "The Death of Ivan Ilych."

13. Mill, *On Liberty*, 95.

14. Lord Byron, *Don Juan*, 1.26.

15. Byron, *Don Juan*, 1.29.

16. Steiner, *Death of Tragedy*, 247.

17. "They sat down at the table—she on a sofa and Peter Ivanovich on a low pouffe, the springs of which yielded spasmodically under his weight. Praskovya Fedorovna had been on the point of warning him to take another seat, but felt that such a warning was out of keeping with her present condition and so she changed her mind. . . . On her way to the sofa the lace of the widow's black shawl caught on the carved edge of the table. Peter Ivanovich rose to detach it, and the springs of the pouffe, relieved of his weight, rose also and gave him a push. The widow began detaching the shawl herself, and Peter Ivanovich again sat down, suppressing the rebellious springs of the pouffe under him. But the widow had not quite freed herself and Peter Ivanovich got up again, and again the pouffe rebelled and even creaked" ("Death of Ivan Ilych" 126–27). A shawl catching is another of those accidents that happen every day. For that matter, the reaction of a spring is not so different from Ivan Ilych's countermovement when he slips on the ladder.

18. Perry, *Ancient Romances*, 77.

19. *The Rambler* no. 4. In the same paper, authors are reminded of the risks they take in abandoning traditional plot artifices and following nature. Such performances have "little indulgence, and therefore more difficulty. They are engaged in portraits of which everyone knows the original, and can therefore detect any deviation from exactness of resemblance. Other writings are safe . . . but these are in danger from every common reader; as the slipper ill executed was censured by a shoemaker who happened to stop in his way at the Venus of Apelles." In keeping strictly within the circuit of ordinary experience, Tolstoy does not so much test his skill as a draftsman as keep faith with the ordinary folk, the shoemakers, represented in the tale by the admirable Gerasim.

20. A few lines later Tolstoy refers in so many words to "his point of view" ("Death of Ivan Ilych," 142).

21. On lawyers and doctors, see for example the satire on both in Jonson's *Volpone* and in bk. 1, chap. 13 of Fielding's *Joseph Andrews*. Among the Houyhnhnms "was neither physician to destroy my body, nor lawyer to ruin my fortune" (Swift, *Gulliver's Travels*, pt. 2, chap. 10).

22. In Ivan Karamazov, who kept himself legally blameless in the murder of his father, innocence itself is a kind of aggravation of guilt. The principle of Ivan Ilych's case is the same even if there is no blood on his hands.

23. Compare Dr. Johnson in *The Rambler* no. 158: "As the design of tragedy is to instruct by moving the passions, it must always have a hero, a personage apparently and incontestably superior to the rest, upon whom attention may be fixed, and the anxiety suspended."

24. Steiner, *Death of Tragedy,* 243.

25. Sarah Bernhardt actually did appear in St. Petersburg in 1881–82. See Roger Shattuck, *Candor and Perversion: Literature, Education, and the Arts* (New York: Norton, 1999), 166–67.

26. See Rogers Brubaker, *The Limits of Rationality: An Essay on the Social and Moral Thought of Max Weber* (London: George Allen and Unwin, 1984), 3.

27. Frye, *Anatomy of Criticism,* 208.

28. Bakhtin, *Problems of Dostoevsky's Poetics,* 59.

29. Somewhat analogously, in rewriting the story of David and Saul in *The Mayor of Casterbridge,* Hardy makes the Saul figure, Henchard, the center of interest, and reduces the David figure, Farfrae, to a kind of secondary character.

30. On the decentering of classical tragedy in Euripides, see William Arrowsmith, "Euripides and the Dramaturgy of Crisis," *Literary Imagination* 1 (1999): 201–26.

31. Like Kolya Krasotkin of *The Brothers Karamazov,* Vasya is thus a child who is no longer a child.

32. Berlin, *Proper Study of Mankind,* 468.

33. Starobinksi, *Jean-Jacques Rousseau,* 76.

34. Rousseau, *Confessions,* 218.

35. Ibid., 572.

36. Morson, *Narrative and Freedom,* 172.

37. Ibid.

38. "When he began to speak, the author blessed what he had meant to curse" (Leo Tolstoy, "An Afterword to Chekhov's Story 'The Darling,'" in *The Portable Tolstoy,* ed. John Bayley, trans. Aylmer and Louise Maude [Harmondsworth, Eng.: Penguin, 1978], 883).

39. Bakhtin, *Dialogic Imagination,* 37.

40. Donna Irwin, "Did Dostoevsky or Tolstoy Believe in Miracles?" in *A New Word on "The Brothers Karamazov,"* ed. Robert Louis Jackson (Evanston, Ill.: Northwestern University Press, 2004), 129.

41. Rousseau, *Emile,* 268.

Chapter 7

1. Bakhtin, *Dialogic Imagination,* 37.

2. Fielding, *Joseph Andrews,* 25. As Fielding says on his title page, the novel was "Written in Imitation of the Manner of Cervantes, Author of *Don Quixote.*"

3. On the surplus of narrative possibilities, see Morson, *Narrative and Freedom.*

4. Even the theme of sexual rivalry between father and son, fraught as it is with tragic potential, recalls Greek New Comedy. The figures of the soldier and the cook—Smerdyakov's trade—are also ingredients of New Comedy.

5. On the dual nature of jealousy, see E. A. J. Honigmann, introduction to *Othello*, by William Shakespeare, Arden edition (Walton-on-Thames, Eng.: Thomas Nelson & Sons, 1997), 76–77: "Even if Othello were not an older and almost doting husband, jealousy—especially causeless jealousy—was thought ridiculous in itself, a folly deserving laughter, as the bystanders tell us in *The Winter's Tale* (2.1.198; 2.3.128). We do not laugh at either Leontes or Othello, yet the dramatist, a master of emotional chiaroscuro, knew that the conventions of comedy can tone in with tragedy."

6. Auerbach, *Mimesis*, 137.

7. Fielding, *Joseph Andrews*, 86.

8. The portrayal of the downtrodden Captain Snegiryov nevertheless contains a strong indictment of the class system; see 242–43.

9. At least this is Bakhtin's position in *Problems of Dostoevsky's Poetics*. In *The Dialogic Imagination* Dostoevsky is one among many.

10. Bakhtin makes the "rights" argument throughout the early chapters of *Problems of Dostoevsky's Poetics*. According to Bakhtin, the polyphonic author knows no more than his own characters—he renounces the "authorial surplus" (72). Dickens moots the question of authorial surplus by making Pip the "author" of *Great Expectations* and giving him, in that capacity, greater knowledge than he originally had. According to Bakhtin, "Only in the form of a confessional self-utterance, Dostoevsky maintained, could the final word about a person be given, a word truly adequate to him" (55–56). *Great Expectations* constitutes a confessional utterance.

11. Cited in Frank, *Dostoevsky: The Mantle of the Prophet*, 546.

12. Bakhtin, *Problems of Dostoevsky's Poetics*, 58. It has been said that our humanity itself "entails not having complete insight into the motives and intentions of other people and even into our own," that "knowledge forbidden to us [lies] in the very midst of our existence" (Roger Shattuck, *Forbidden Knowledge* [New York: Harcourt Brace, 1996], 314).

13. Morson, *Hidden in Plain View*.

14. Cited and discussed in Eikhenbaum, *Tolstoi in the Seventies*, 138.

15. Joseph Frank, *Dostoevsky: The Seeds of Revolt, 1821–1849* (Princeton: Princeton University Press, 1976), 168.

16. Fyodor Dostoevsky, *A Writer's Diary, vol. 1, 1873–1876*, trans. Kenneth Lantz (Evanston, Ill.: Northwestern University Press, 1993), 411.

17. Robert Louis Jackson, "Alyosha's Speech at the Stone: 'The Whole Picture,'" in *New Word on "The Brothers Karamazov,"* 249–50.

18. *The Rambler* no. 4.

19. Erasmus, *The Praise of Folly*, trans. Robert M. Adams (New York: Norton, 1989), 48. Speaking of bewilderment and uncertainty, Folly also says, "That's what it is to be a man" (32).

20. Watt, *Myths of Modern Individualism,* 70.

21. "Mitya was also struck by the face of Kuzma Kuzmich, which had become extremely swollen recently: his lower lip, which had always been thick, now looked like a kind of drooping pancake" (*Brothers Karamazov* 369).

22. In the *Odyssey,* the original romance, the hero returns to a palace debauched by the suitors. In *The Brothers Karamazov* the sons return to a house debauched by their father.

23. On "prosaics" see Gary Saul Morson and Caryl Emerson, *Mikhail Bakhtin: Creation of a Prosaics* (Stanford: Stanford University Press, 1990).

24. Compare Bakhtin's discussion of the Greek romance in *The Dialogic Imagination,* 86–110.

25. "I don't know, I don't know . . . Maybe I won't kill him, and maybe I will. I'm afraid that at that moment his face will suddenly become hateful to me" (*Brothers Karamazov* 122).

26. Watt, *Myths of Modern Individualism,* 224–26.

27. Hannah Arendt, *The Human Condition* (Chicago: University of Chicago Press, 1958), 233.

28. Arendt, *Human Condition,* 233.

29. Perry, *Ancient Romances,* 133.

30. Frye, *Anatomy of Criticism,* 195.

31. Bakhtin, *Problems of Dostoevsky's Poetics,* 96.

32. If history, in Tolstoy's judgment, eludes the interpretive grid the historians seek to impose on it (Morson, *Narrative and Freedom,* 157), the story of Dmitri eludes the official procedures used to establish guilt and innocence. The truth seems to flow right through these proceedings without being caught by them, like water running through a net.

33. Heliodorus, *Ethiopian Story,* 70.

34. Bakhtin, *Dialogic Imagination,* 366.

35. Bakhtin, *Problems of Dostoevsky's Poetics,* 6, 71. Compare Iris Murdoch, *Existentialists and Mystics: Writings on Philosophy and Literature* (Harmondsworth, Eng.: Penguin, 1997), 254: "Here, I think, we naturally envisage a relation between the author and his character as if the character could turn around and say to the author, 'You have been unfair to me.'"

36. Not once on Calypso's island or on the way to Ithaca is Odysseus shown consumed with jealousy and suspicion over the suitors. Such is the difference between the romance of the *Odyssey* and the anti-romance, *The Brothers Karamazov.*

37. From the viewpoint of his interrogators, the rag around Dmitri's neck, if it existed, cannot account for the torments he attributes to it—an ironic instance of insufficient motivation.

38. See Honigmann, *Othello,* 31. When, in the first scene of the play, Iago

claims that Othello snubbed those who pled for his promotion, we cannot tell if this ever took place, and when, in the last scene, he is asked why he caused such ruin, he refuses to answer.

39. Miguel de Cervantes, *Don Quixote,* trans. Walter Starkie (New York: New American Library, 1964), 98.

40. On Dostoevsky's transcendence of Cervantes, see chapter 11 ("The Ridiculous Man—Beyond Don Quixote") in Robert Louis Jackson, *The Art of Dostoevsky: Deliriums and Nocturnes* (Princeton: Princeton University Press, 1981).

41. Morson and Emerson, *Bakhtin: Creation of a Prosaics,* 238–39.

42. Kermode, *Shakespeare's Language,* 178n.

43. Spiritual equality is to be set against "socialist" equality as defined later in the novel by young Kolya Krasotkin. Socialism, says Kolya, repeating formulas, is "when everyone is equal, everyone has property in common, there are no marriages, and each one has whatever religion and laws he likes, and all the rest" (527). When Alyosha greets him as an equal (538), Kolya responds with the human warmth missing from these words.

44. Compare the words of Father Zosima's brother: "We are all in paradise, but we do not want to know it" (*Brothers Karamazov* 288).

Chapter 8

1. Kermode, *Shakespeare's Language,* 49.

2. Frye, *On Shakespeare,* 153.

3. Compare the analysis in Robert M. Adams, *Shakespeare: The Four Romances* (New York: Norton, 1989), 107–8, of Perdita's declaration that the sun shines on the court and the cottage alike.

4. Cited in Fanger, *Dostoevsky and Romantic Realism,* 72.

5. Charles Taylor, *Sources of the Self: The Making of the Modern Identity* (Cambridge, Mass.: Harvard University Press, 1989), 395.

6. Charles Dickens, *Little Dorrit* (Harmondsworth, Eng.: Penguin, 1967), 289.

7. According to the final solution to the human problem devised by Shigalov in Dostoevsky's *Devils,* "one-tenth [of humanity] will receive personal freedom and unlimited power over the other nine-tenths. The latter must forfeit their individuality and become as it were a herd; through boundless obedience, they will attain, by a series of rebirths, a state of primeval innocence," which is to say that nine-tenths of humanity will be subjected to equality in the brute sense of having their qualities, all that distinguishes one from another, erased (*Devils,* trans. Michael R. Katz [Oxford: Oxford University Press, 1992], 427–28).

8. Jane Austen, *Pride and Prejudice* (New York: Norton, 1966), 245.

9. Bayley, *Tolstoy and the Novel,* 104. *Anna Karenina* suggests that the difference

between Stiva Oblonsky and Anna (brother and sister) is "that he is a man, with all the immense advantages of a man of his place, class, and epoch, and she is a woman, with all the attendant pitfalls and handicaps that surrounded a woman in her position" (John Bayley, *Leo Tolstoy* [Plymouth, Eng.: Northcote House, 1997], 32).

10. Robert Louis Jackson, "The Second Birth of Pierre Bezukhov," in *Modern Critical Interpretations of Leo Tolstoy's "War and Peace,"* ed. Harold Bloom (New York: Chelsea House, 1988), 57.

11. Edgar Rosenberg, "Towards *Great Expectations:* From Notebook to Novel," *Q/W/E/R/T/Y* 9 (1999): 73–74, 77.

12. Alexis de Tocqueville, *The Old Regime and the French Revolution,* trans. Stuart Gilbert (New York: Doubleday, 1955), xiv. On Tolstoy and this work, see Kathryn B. Feuer, *Tolstoy and the Genesis of "War and Peace"* (Ithaca: Cornell University Press, 1996), chap. 9.

13. Berlin, *Concepts and Categories,* 90, 102.

14. Stéphane Courtois and others, *The Black Book of Communism* (Cambridge, Mass.: Harvard University Press, 1999), 620.

15. *The Brothers Karamazov* is so filled with the evidence of the past—the very thing to be eradicated, according to Mao—that it takes a great effort of literary excavation by Bakhtin to unearth its ancient sources.

16. Charles Dickens, *Hard Times* (Harmondsworth, Eng.: Penguin, 1969), 65.

17. Leo Tolstoy, *A Confession,* in *Portable Tolstoy,* 710.

18. Cited in Feuer, *Tolstoy and the Genesis of "War and Peace,"* 146.

19. Tolstoy, *What Is Art?* 115.

20. Cited by Angus Calder in his introduction to *Great Expectations,* by Charles Dickens (Harmondsworth, Eng.: Penguin, 1985), 11.

21. Morson, *Hidden in Plain View,* 144.

22. We can well imagine that a community dedicated to equality, such as an Israeli kibbutz of the 1960s, would get into arguments over points of theory and practice, for the simple reason that whatever distinguishes one person from another potentially threatens a regime of sameness.

23. Joseph Epstein, *Envy* (New York Public Library, Oxford University Press, 2003), xxiv.

24. Mill, *On Liberty,* 64.

25. George Steiner, *Tolstoy or Dostoevsky: An Essay in the Old Criticism* (New Haven: Yale University Press, 1996), 96.

26. See chapter 31 of *Youth.*

27. Bakhtin, *Dialogic Imagination,* 37.

28. Another leader who mattered, Churchill did well what the good general does, according to Tolstoy: raise the morale of the troops.

29. Paul Fussell, *The Great War and Modern Memory* (Oxford: Oxford University Press, 1975).

30. Marvin Becker, *The Emergence of Civil Society in the Eighteenth Century* (Bloomington: Indiana University Press, 1994), 6.

31. *The Rambler* no. 60.

32. Taylor, *Sources of the Self.*

33. John Milton, *Paradise Lost,* 8.192–94. These lines are also cited by Ian Watt in a discussion of the Puritan belief in an eternal scheme in which "all souls had equal chances" (Watt, *Rise of the Novel,* 77).

34. M. I. Finley, *The World of Odysseus* (Harmondsworth, Eng.: Penguin, 1985).

Editions Cited

All works listed are cited by page number in text and notes unless otherwise indicated here.

Chariton. *Callirhoe.* Translated by G. P. Goold. Cambridge, Mass.: Harvard University Press, 1995.

Dickens, Charles. *Great Expectations.* San Francisco: Rinehart, 1948. (Cited by chapter and page numbers.)

Dostoevsky, Fyodor. *The Brothers Karamazov.* Translated by Richard Pevear and Larissa Volokhonsky. San Francisco: North Point, 1990.

Homer. *The Iliad.* Translated by Richmond Lattimore. Chicago: University of Chicago Press, 1961. (Cited by book and line numbers.)

———. *The Odyssey.* Translated by Richmond Lattimore. New York: HarperCollins, 1991. (Cited by book and line numbers.)

Tolstoy, Leo. *Anna Karenina.* Translated by Richard Pevear and Larissa Volokhonsky. Harmondsworth, Eng.: Penguin, 2000.

———. "The Death of Ivan Ilych." In *Tolstoy's Short Fiction,* edited and translated by Michael R. Katz. New York: Norton, 1991.

———. *War and Peace.* Translated by Louise and Aylmer Maude. Oxford: Oxford University Press, 1991.

Index

About the Author

Stewart Justman is a professor in the liberal studies program at the University of Montana. He is the author of *Fool's Paradise: The Unreal World of Pop Psychology* and *Seeds of Mortality: The Public and Private Worlds of Cancer,* which won the 2004 PEN Award for the Art of the Essay. Two other books, *The Springs of Liberty: The Satiric Tradition and Freedom of Speech* and *The Psychological Mystique,* were previously published by Northwestern University Press.